PUBLIC CHOICES AND POLICY CHANGE

PUBLIC CHOICES
AND POLICY CHANGE

The Political Economy of Reform
in Developing Countries

MERILEE S. GRINDLE
AND JOHN W. THOMAS

THE JOHNS HOPKINS UNIVERSITY PRESS
BALTIMORE AND LONDON

The Johns Hopkins University Press
701 West 40th Street
Baltimore, Maryland 21211
The Johns Hopkins Press Ltd., London

The paper in this book meets the minimum requirements
of American National Standard for
Information Sciences—Permanence of Paper
for Printed Library Materials,
ANSI Z39.48–1984.

Library of Congress Cataloging-in-Publication Data

Grindle, Merilee S.
Public choices and policy change : the political economy of reform
in developing countries / Merilee S. Grindle and John W. Thomas.
p.   cm.
Includes bibliographical references and index.
ISBN 0-8018-4155-0 (alk. paper).—ISBN 0-8018-4156-9
(pbk. alk. paper)
1. Developing countries—Economic policy—Decision making.
2. Policy sciences. I. Thomas, John W., 1933–   . II. Title.
HC59.7.G7495   1991   338.9′009172′4—dc20   90-19212   CIP

Significant portions of the following article appear throughout this book: Merilee S.
Grindle and John W. Thomas, "Policy Makers, Policy Choices, and Policy Outcomes:
The Political Economy of Reform in Developing Countries," *Policy Sciences* 22 (1989):
213–48. *Policy Sciences* is published by Kluwer Academic Publishers. A previous
version of Chapter 6 has also been published: John W. Thomas and Merilee S. Grindle,
"After the Decision: Implementing Policy Reforms in Developing Countries," *World Development* 18, no. 8 (1990): 1163–81. *World Development* is published by Pergamon
Journals, Ltd., Oxford, U.K. We are grateful to both publishers for permission to reprint
these materials.

To those who shaped our views of the world

June D. Serrill   Mary S. Thomas
Douglas E. Serrill John W. Thomas
Steven H. Grindle

And to those who heightened our concern about its future

Stefanie and Alexandra Grindle
Stephen, Patricia, and Gwen Thomas

Contents

Tables and Figures

Tables

Figures

Preface

By the 1980s, the primacy of policy as the basis for encouraging and sustaining economic growth and social welfare had come to be widely accepted among those concerned about promoting development. What was not understood, however, was the process by which such policies could replace those in existence. In fact, because policy changes often impinge on the interests of important groups in society or the self-interests of the public officials who must adopt them, many development analysts have been pessimistic about the possibilities for policy reform. They often have had little hope of change because of the belief that societal groups and public officials are wedded to extracting "economic rents" from established policies.

Moreover, when it comes to considering how to introduce and sustain improved policies, analysts who look to the literature in political economy and political science find few insights into the process of policy choice. In fact, most academic analyses are much better at explaining why policy change would not occur than in assessing conditions under which it will. Practitioners, on the other hand, often have considerable understanding of reform in particular countries but few generalized concepts that can be broadly applied across a range of countries. And their perspectives are rarely sought by those who generate frameworks for understanding political and economic relationships in developing countries. But despite a pessimistic perspective on the possibilities for reform, and despite the lack of analytic tools for understanding the process of change, major policy and institutional innovations were widely introduced in developing countries in the 1980s. This book is about how changes such as these occur.

Having had unique opportunities to see the process of policy making and implementation from inside several developing country governments and having had the opportunity to work closely with a number of policy makers and managers who were actively seeking to bring about important changes, we believed that the process could be better understood and that the basis for making a set of broad generalizations about the political economy of reform existed. Intuitively, we also held a more positive view of the opportunities for change and the range of concerns of the public officials who must adopt and implement new policies than many other analysts. Our experiences as advisers and researchers suggested that the officials whom we had observed often made decisions within a significant range of opportunity, or "policy space." We believed that these officials were not simply creatures of the societies or classes from which they came, nor were they always motivated by narrowly defined self-interest, nor were they merely agents who represented the interests of the organizations in which they worked. Was it possible to go beyond such understandings to account for the roles of public officials in the process of policy and institutional change and to assess the ways in which they shape and influence that process?

Over the years, our organization, the Harvard Institute for International Development (HIID), offered us and many of our colleagues opportunities to work within developing country governments as policy advisers; we believe this experience has given us unique perspectives from which to assess this question. HIID and the John F. Kennedy School of Government, in which we teach, emphasize the importance of direct involvement in public affairs and make it possible for their faculty members to spend periods of time working inside public organizations and government. Such experiences provided us with significant opportunities to gather insights into and information about the process of policy making and implementation from the vantage point of those who work within government in developing countries. The research on which this book is based, then, spans our professional experiences in development advising, policy-related research, and teaching.

The first step in generating the framework that forms the central focus of this book was taken in 1986, when we asked several of our colleagues who had worked in particularly interesting situations of policy reform to present their experiences in a workshop to explore policy reform in developing countries. The workshop sessions proved suggestive, so we followed them up by developing each presentation into a case in policy or institutional reform, based on additional interviewing and documentary research. We assessed these cases in an effort to begin building a set of generalizations and hypotheses about the process. Initial presentations of what was eventually to become our analytic framework laid bare additional questions that needed to be explored. We were also aware that our cases relied overmuch on the perspectives of expatriate advisers. We needed to develop additional cases based on the experiences of policy makers and managers in their own countries.

The Edward S. Mason Program in Public Policy and Management provided us with an opportunity to explore unanswered questions and broaden the base of our cases. Each year, this program brings fifty or more midcareer officials from developing countries to the Kennedy School to study public policy and management. Before coming to Harvard, the Mason Fellows have had extensive experience in public affairs in their own countries. In 1988, we decided to offer a six-week course for a selected group of Mason Fellows and a small number of other international students with similar experiences. The purpose of the course was to present and refine our framework and to apply it to a case of policy or institutional change in which these midcareer officials had been involved prior to coming to Harvard. From our perspective, this was a successful enterprise because it allowed us further opportunities to modify our framework and to assess our basic assumptions; we were gratified to hear that the students found it helpful to think systematically and retrospectively about the policy-making and -implementing experiences they had been involved in.

The course also provided us with several fully developed new cases, written and presented by officials who had been personally involved in reform efforts, that form a significant part of this book. We were encouraged to repeat the course, in modified form, in the summer of 1989, with a different and larger group of Mason Fellows and with the support of the World Bank's Economic Development Institute. The cases generated through the second course are not used in this book, since they were completed after the current effort was largely written. Nevertheless, these additional cases helped confirm our expectation that the framework we generated would prove useful to practitioners in enabling them to think systematically about the process of reform and about strategies to pursue changes in policies and institutions in their countries.

The third major opportunity to refine and test our framework was provided by HIID. In October of 1988, the institute held a conference in Marrakech, Morocco, on the topic of economic policy reform in order to reflect on the extensive experience of its staff in working with developing country governments on a variety of policy and institutional changes. While many of the papers presented at the conference focused on the technical analysis of economic policy alternatives, we circulated in advance a paper describing our framework and asked that participants address political as well as economic variables in their papers. The conference therefore provided a further opportunity to broaden our information base and to test our approach against a wider range of experiences. Fourteen cases that provided information on the political economy of reforms occurring in the 1980s were used to test our framework more systematically. This work constitutes Chapter 7 of the book.

Clearly, then, this book grows out of our unique opportunities to gain access to a range of perspectives and information through our professional activities and institutional affiliations. We believe these experiences have given us the chance to see and analyze the process of policy reform from different perspectives and to arrive at conclusions that are distinct from those that prevail in much of the literature of political economy and political science.

Out of this experience comes a view of the prospects for change that is guardedly optimistic. It asserts that public officials make a critical difference in the introduction, scope, and pursuit of policy reform. It further asserts that to understand the complex motivations and activities of these officials as the pursuit of self-interest, class interest, or organizational interest is greatly to misunderstand their role. People do change policy, and they do it from motivations and perspectives that are imbued with personal and professional values and that frequently include serious concern for the public interest and public welfare of their societies. Decisions made in the pursuit of reform may not turn out well and may not in fact serve the public interest, but the factors that influence policy making and implementation provide ongoing opportunities for correction and change in the future.

Acknowledgments

The contributions of many are at the heart of this book. We are very aware that it could not have been initiated or completed without their assistance.

In undertaking this project, we recognized the unique opportunity we had as faculty members at both the Harvard Institute for International Development and Harvard's John F. Kennedy School of Government. Over the years, we and our HIID colleagues have had unique opportunities to be involved in policy changes in governments in our role as policy advisers. As faculty members in the Kennedy School, we have had the good fortune to have many midcareer officials from developing countries in our classes.

Many of the cases on which this book is based are the work of our colleagues at the Harvard Institute for International Development. Richard Cash, David Cole, Richard Hook, Richard Mallon, Michael Roemer, Joseph Stern, and Peter Timmer, as well as Stephan Haggard of the Department of Government at Harvard University, shared case histories and professional experiences with generosity and deep insights. We are grateful for the time and interest they put into our project, particularly in its early days.

Other cases that form the core of our analysis were provided to us by our students at the John F. Kennedy School of Government at Harvard University. Shyam Bajpai, Raymond Broize, Ncedo Mlamla, Evelyne Rodriguez-Ortega, Valerie Veira, and Yiwei Wang, all midcareer officials, worked diligently to share their policy-making and -implementing experiences with us and with one another during a course we organized in the fall of 1988. We found this work to be extremely valuable and are indebted to these former students for their participation in the course. The doctoral thesis of Eduardo Doryan-Garrón, a friend and former student, is the source of another case we have used. We owe him our thanks and appreciation also.

More recently, Chinmay Basu, Yashawant Bhave, René Castro-Salazar, Kamari Zaman Juhari, Fanny Law Fan, How-Sheng Lee, Angelo Reyes, Mauricio Sanz de Santamaría, Yeon-Sung Shin, Tee How Tan, Peter Whitehall, and Mekki Zouaoui, all Mason Fellows at the Kennedy School, shared their experiences with us, helped us to refine our ideas, and encouraged us to believe that our work could prove useful to policy makers and managers in developing countries.

Rich material from papers prepared by John D. Balling, Richard Barichello, David C. Cole, William Cummings, Frank Flatters, Anne-Marie Foltz and William J. Foltz, Yamil Kouri, Marc Lindenberg, Richard Mallon, Malcolm McPherson, Steven Radelet, Michael Roemer, Steve Schall, Donald S. Shepard, Joseph Stern, Peter Timmer, Phillip A. Wellons, and Betty Slade Yaser is also incorporated into this book. We would like to thank these colleagues for their willingness to consider political economy issues at an HIID conference held in Marrakech, Morocco, in 1988 and for continuing to discuss and analyze their cases with us.

At HIID, Dwight Perkins was generous in providing us with the time and institutional support to work on this book. Michael Roemer has also proved a highly valued colleague for his ongoing interest, questions, and suggestions.

Colleagues at other institutions discussed the project with us and sometimes asked uncomfortable questions that encouraged us to define, rethink, specify, and improve our work. Among those we value for this assistance are Judith Tendler of MIT, Robert Paarlberg of Wellesley College, Peter Knight and Arturo Israel of the World Bank, Stephan Haggard of Harvard University, Joan Nelson of the Overseas Development Council, John Sheahan and Brian Levy of Williams College, and Tony Killick of the Overseas Development Institute.

Special thanks are due to Wally Falcon and Ann Peck, who invited John Thomas to spend three months of 1988 at the Food Research Institute of Stanford University to work on the manuscript. They and their colleagues provided an ideal environment in which to think and work.

We owe a very special note to Stephen J. Reifenberg, a colleague and friend at HIID, who read, assessed, and added to this book in both substantive and intangible ways. He is the principal analyst and author of Chapter 7, a chapter that owes much to his diligence and intelligence. His insights and suggestions, as well as his supportive spirit, have done much to sharpen our ideas and analysis. We hope that collaboration has been as positive for him as it has been for us.

Michael Harrington was instrumental in keeping drafts of the book manuscript up-to-date and protected against a variety of computer mishaps. At the Johns Hopkins University Press, Henry Tom, executive editor, was supportive and effectively managed the mysterious business of publishing a book.

Steven, Alexandra, and Stefanie Grindle and Gwen, Trisha, and Stephen Thomas were sources of support, motivation, and perspective. We wish to thank them for helping shape this book. Sometimes they contributed with laughter and diversions. Often they contributed through thoughts and perspectives that are deeply present in this book.

PUBLIC CHOICES AND
POLICY CHANGE

CHAPTER 1

Introduction:

Explaining Choice
and Change

The 1980s will be remembered as a decade in which fundamental changes in public policies were introduced around the world. In the Soviet Union, the policy of *perestroika* challenged the hegemony of a huge and centralized bureaucratic apparatus and sought to achieve greater efficiency and dynamism in the economy. In Eastern Europe, countries that had maintained rigidly controlled economies for decades moved rapidly toward more open systems in the wake of profound political movements. Even in China, Mao's successors worked for much of this period to decentralize powerful and rigid bureaucratic hierarchies and to introduce competitive markets into the state-controlled economy, although some of those policies were reversed in the wake of the popular uprising in 1989. In Great Britain and the United States, conservative leaders extolled the virtues of individual initiative and competitive markets and sought to redefine the responsibility of government for economic and social welfare. These changes were unexpected in the degree to which they were directed at undoing decades of prior policy, during which state bureaucracies had been consistently enlarged and when extensive regulation of the economy had been taken on as a normal function of government.

These efforts to alter historical trends dominated headlines during the decade, but changes of equal significance occurred throughout much of the developing world as well. Although less visible, these events nevertheless signaled fundamental changes in national development strategies, in the historical role of the state, in public ideologies about how development is best achieved, and in the intended beneficiaries of public policies. The changes could be compared to those introduced in the 1930s and 1940s in Latin America, in the post–World War II period in Asia, and in the 1960s in Africa. In those times, national leaders, supported by international donors, assigned extensive responsibilities to their governments for guiding economic development and bringing advances in conditions of social welfare to their populations.

The 1980s brought a redefinition of these long-accepted goals and of the strategies considered appropriate for achieving them. In these new visions of how to achieve development, the state was no longer to be the principal force for achieving economic growth and welfare. Such a change was significant for many developing countries because it implied a shift of power away from central governments to the market and to more local levels of government. Reform recommendations of the 1980s were broadly congruent in part because of the ascendance of neoclassical economic perspectives that challenged earlier Keynesian approaches. The neoclassical critique of prior development efforts was strongly supported by large international donor agencies, which, during the decade, focused their influence on changing policy in many countries.

While much of the analysis of the issues confronting developing countries has centered on the intractability of the problems and the obstacles to resolving them, in fact, the policy changes that occurred in the 1980s were more widespread and fundamental than generally acknowledged. Despite substantial economic and political barriers to introducing new policies, changes in macroeconomic and sectoral policies were made and organizational reforms were adopted in country after country during the decade. How can such changes in important economic policies and institutions be accounted for? This question lies at the heart of our book. In attempting to answer it, we center our analysis on the role of decision makers and policy managers, the choices they make, and the factors that influence those choices.

What we seek to explain is complex. We believe that decision makers are not simply forced by events, interest group pressures, or external agencies to make particular choices; generally they have a significant range of options in the management of public problems—including at times the option of not addressing them. Moreover, solutions to any given set of policy problems are not obvious because the impact of policy cannot always be known in advance, because the logic of economics and the logic of politics frequently do not coincide, and because real costs are imposed on specific groups in society when policies and institutions are altered. All policy choices thus involve uncertainty and risk. If these assertions are valid, and if policy elites are relevant to defining the content of public policy—i.e., if they are not simply forced to act in predetermined ways or have no choice but to accept certain courses of action—then the dilemmas and choices they confront are critical to understanding policy change.[1]

The dilemmas and choices are real. Consider, for example, the situation faced by many policy elites in developing countries in the 1980s. Confronted by advisers, international agencies, development specialists, and others advocating a package of policy and institutional changes, they also had to consider the costs of altering existing practice. In this assessment, they were confronted with the fact that the ranks of opposition to change were filled with the beneficiaries of the status quo: economic elites supported by existing policies; ethnic, regional, and religious groups favored in allocative decision making; bureaucrats and bureaucratic agencies wielding regulatory power; political elites sustained through patronage and clientele networks; military organizations accustomed to spending generous budgets with few questions asked.

Moreover, decision makers, even those convinced of the need for economic policy changes, could not escape considering the political wisdom of adopting and pursuing them: in the name of efficiency and development, many changes of the 1980s implied a significant decentralization of decision making, a shrinking of the size of the public sector, and an important shift in the strongly interventionist role of the state in the economy. For decision makers schooled in the importance of state building, practiced in the methods of centralizing power in order to survive politically, familiar with the use of the public sector for patronage and regulation, and imbued with development doctrines emphasizing planning and control, the logic of many proposed reforms was not always politically or philosophically obvious. Under conditions such as these, explaining change takes on added importance.

We have found little theory to guide us in understanding the political economy of policy reform. Although techniques of policy analysis to generate recommendations for economic and organizational reforms are well developed, the process by which such changes are adopted and sustained is much less well understood. In the literature that spans political science, political economy, and policy science, a large number of questions about processes of change remain unanswered, particularly about how agenda setting, decision making, and implementation occur. Thus, there is little theory to explain how issues of reform come to the attention of government decision makers or how reform of policies and institutional arrangements becomes part of their agenda. Even less is known about how policy elites weigh the often urgent and well-articulated advice they receive about policy and institutional changes, their own intellectual and political views about such changes, and economic and political pressure to alter policies, against equally pressing concerns about the impact of their decisions on existing political and bureaucratic relationships. The factors that affect whether policies will be pursued, altered, reversed, or sustained after they have been decided upon are also generally left unexplained because implementation and sustainability are often considered to be matters of effective administration, not political processes.

Our interest in the process of policy and institutional change has led us to investigate policy decision making and implementation within government. We are concerned centrally with the issue of reform, defined here as deliberate efforts on the part of government to redress perceived errors in prior and existing policy and institutional arrangements.[2] We take instances of reform as our unit of analysis and the interrelated processes of agenda setting, policy making, and implementation as a critical arena for understanding the factors that can account for how, why, and when policy and institutional changes occur. The focus of analysis is what occurs within the state and what occurs at the overlapping boundaries of state and society, in those events in which policy elites confront or are affected by pressures for change or stasis that originate in domestic and international environments.[3] Our intent in this book is to propose an analytic framework that takes decision makers and decision making seriously in accounting for reform but that does not isolate them from influences that originate outside the state.

In our analysis of reform situations, we generate a series of observations relevant to politics and policy in developing countries. First, we take issue with much of the literature in political science and political economy because it does not systematically address the role of decision makers and managers in the policy process and fails to provide useful explanations of how and when change occurs. In fact, much current theory would not be able to explain the changes that occurred in the 1980s because it is narrowly focused on the analysis of obstacles to change and is more able to explain why things are the way they are than to predict how or when they change.

Moreover, much current theorizing about development policy making begins with an assumption of narrowly defined self-interest as the basis of all political action, an assumption that leads to pessimistic conclusions about the potential for change and the ability of policy elites and citizens to conceptualize and act upon some broader vision of the public interest. If policy makers and public managers are conceptualized as "rent-seekers," motivated only by the desire to remain in power—a widely accepted view—little can be expected of them in terms of leadership or the management of change. If all political action is assumed to emanate from a desire to capture the state for personal benefit—a view similarly widespread—then there is little basis for anticipating reasoned dialogue about the content of public policy. Other perspectives limit possibilities for change to incremental adjustments in current practice, failing to account for major reversals or alterations in policy or the possibility that factors such as leadership, values, and technical analysis can help chart new courses in public policy.

In contrast, we find that policy elites often articulate goals for their societies and for the activities of the state and strategize about how change can be introduced. They are generally aware of the societal pressures and interests, historical contexts, and bureaucratic capacity that limit the options available to them, and they often seek to maneuver within these constraints and to craft policy solutions that will be politically and bureaucratically acceptable but that will also encapsulate serious efforts to address public problems. The cases of policy change—and their success or failure—that we consider in Korea, Costa Rica, the Philippines, Ghana, India, Argentina, and Colombia, for example, cannot be explained without reference to the leadership and strategic management of policy makers and managers.

We believe that the perceptions and behavior of policy elites need to be explained systematically, as do the constraints on their actions. To accomplish this, a systematic understanding of the values, experiences, and perceptions of policy elites and the historical, political, and institutional context within which they operate is essential to understanding specific instances of reform. These factors, combined with elites' perceptions of the circumstances under which a reform becomes an active part of the policy agenda, have a critical influence on what happens to a reform initiative.

Second, we show how factors unique to a particular policy initiative affect the dynamics and process of decision making among policy elites, although they do not necessarily determine the outcome of that process. Accordingly, we assess the circumstances that surround how a reform measure gets on the policy agenda and is deliberated within government. In particular, whether a reform initiative is considered under conditions of perceived crisis, such as our case of devaluation in Ghana, or under conditions that can be termed "politics as usual," such as our case of planning in Colombia, is critical in understanding the stakes involved in reform, the type of public official involved in decision making, the degree of change introduced, and the timing of decision making.

If, for example, elites perceive a crisis and the reform as a response to that crisis, then there is likely to be strong pressure for reform, and the stakes for the government are likely to be high. As a result, the issue will command the attention of senior policy makers. Their decisions are likely to be more radical or innovative than when a crisis does not exist, and action will often come quite quickly. If there is no perception of crisis, the stakes for government are lower (although they may be relatively high for the individual proponents of reform), the issue is usually dealt with by middle-level decision makers, and change tends to be more incremental.

Third, our analysis of reform situations indicates that decision makers apply a series of criteria to the changes they consider, discuss, debate, and plan. They weigh decisions in response to their understanding of the technical aspects of the policy area under consideration, the probable impact of their choices on bureaucratic interactions, the meaning of change for political stability and political support, and the role that international actors have assumed in the reform process. Which of these criteria is most important in specific decision-making contexts is frequently determined by the circumstances that surround the particular policy initiative. In crisis-ridden reforms, for example, concern about national welfare, political stability, and broad coalitions of political support tends to dominate their deliberations. This was clearly the case in our discussions of development policy changes in Korea and Costa Rica. In politics-as-usual reforms, on the other hand, concern about bureaucratic and narrow clientelistic relationships is much more apparent. We find much evidence of this dynamic in our cases of decentralization in Kenya, primary health care in Mali, and planning in Argentina.

A fourth aspect of the framework indicates that the characteristics of particular reforms determine the type of conflict and opposition that surround their implementation. In fact, characteristics of a policy have a powerful influence on whether it will be implemented as intended or whether the outcome will be significantly different. The distribution of the costs and benefits of a policy or institutional change, its technical complexity, its administrative intensity, the extent to which it involves active participation of bureaucrats or beneficiaries, and its short- or long-term impact determine reaction to the initiative, how that reaction is likely to be manifested, and the resources policy makers and policy managers require if the change is to be pursued successfully. Implementation becomes a filter that often alters intended policy. Thus, anticipating where reaction to new policy initiatives is likely to occur—in a public or political arena, or in a bureaucratic arena—and who the principal figures in such a reaction are likely to be, is critical to successful implementation. Such analytic capacity has the value of enabling the analyst to determine whether a policy reform is actually feasible. The frequency of serious adverse reactions to reform initiatives in the past and the number of failures that have occurred suggest that such an analytic capacity has been inadequate. Policy managers in our case of public water supply in India appeared to understand such issues; those responsible for primary health care in Mali apparently did not.

At the most general level, we find that decision makers play important roles in shaping policy and institutional outcomes and that the process through which issues get on reform agendas, through which they are deliberated within government, and through which they are pursued and sustained is critical to understanding how, why, and when change occurs. The actions of individuals and interactions of officials do not, of course, provide fully convincing explanations of reform initiatives. The historical contexts, coalitions, conflicts, opposition and support, constraints, and opportunities that surround important public issues are vital ingredients in explaining issue formation, policy making, and implementation. Such societal factors are clearly important, but we do not believe that, by themselves, they explain the actions of governments.

Reform implies authoritative choices about development that can only be fully understood by giving due attention to the perceptions, motivations, values, skills, and opportunities of the decision makers and to the impact that characteristics of the decision-making process have on the choices that are made. For us, then, societal pressures and constraints and historical, cultural, and international contexts are essential variables in reform initiatives because they shape the perceptions, options, and actions of those who make authoritative decisions or because they affect the consequences of those decisions. We propose a framework that acknowledges room for choice—and calculation and miscalculation—in the design and pursuit of public policy in developing countries and that indicates the factors that influence these choices.

Policy Elites and Reform Initiatives

These perspectives on the political economy of reform reflect our experience as researchers and policy advisers who have had the opportunity to observe policy makers and policy managers in action in developing countries. Moreover, colleagues, graduate students, officials, and former officials with similar experiences inside government have helped substantiate our observations about the important impact of policy elites in the reform process.

First, our experience has consistently been that the options available to policy elites are not fully determined by the interests of social classes, organized groups, international actors, or international economic conditions, or by the hold of history or culture on policy choices. These factors clearly determine the outer boundaries of choice; but, regardless of the issue, decision makers appear to have room for maneuver and capacity to influence the content, timing, and sequence of reform initiatives. This room for maneuver and influence defines a "policy space" for any given issue, a space that is determined by the ability of a regime and its political leadership to introduce and pursue a reform measure without precipitating a regime or leadership change or major upheaval and violence in the society, or without being forced to abandon the initiative. Within issue areas, a policy space consists of the range of options that could be introduced without major adverse consequences for policy makers, the regime, or the reform itself. The space may be narrow or wide, depending on the ability of decision makers to utilize information, the impact of the change on existing bureaucratic relationships, the nature of regime stability and opposition, and relationships with international actors. The boundaries of policy space can be enlarged or constricted by the actions of policy elites and their skill in utilizing the technical, economic, political, and bureaucratic resources available to them. The boundaries of policy space will also differ by issue area because distinct issues impose differential costs and benefits on societal groups that have differential capacities to promote and defend their interests.

Second, within their perceptions of what constitutes the available space for any given issue, policy elites play important roles in defining the content of policy. Our experience has confirmed that decision makers generally have articulate and logical explanations for the problems they seek to solve. Thus, for any given problem they confront, they are likely to have or develop a coherent explanation of its causes and a set of ideas about how best to respond to it. These understandings and perceptions of cause-and-effect relationships (for example, that rural poverty is caused by technological backwardness, or alternatively, by exploitative relationships with rural elites) are important in terms of the measures adopted to deal with particular problems—introduction of new technology as opposed to agrarian reform, for example. Thus, an important ingredient in reform initiatives is how decision makers define a problem and what they perceive to be viable solutions. Moreover, intellectual constructs about cause-and-effect relationships can be understood independently of the social class background or economic interests of the societal groups from which the decision makers come, thus refuting some of the more deterministic theories of elite behavior. Neither can such constructs always be defined away as the result of bureaucratic politics or organizational interests, as some scholars assert. Instead, they may be the result of prior experience in the problem or policy area, professional expertise in a particular discipline, personal values, ideology, or study, debate, and discussion among a group of individuals concerned with similar issues.[4]

Third, we have observed that decision makers can alter their ideas about appropriate solutions to particular problems and thus enlarge or alter the range of options considered as solutions. The cases considered in this book as well as the rich policy and management experience among colleagues, officials, and others in developing countries attest to the potential for learning and reflection among decision makers. Again, their views cannot be fully understood as rent-seeking or as a result of class background or bureaucratic maneuvering, but instead reflect the existence of a problem-solving orientation among many officials. The fact that policy elites can change their ideas about what constitutes a problem and how it should be resolved suggests again the potential of such officials to influence the content of reform initiatives.

Fourth, we have seen many situations in which decision makers have taken active and formative roles in shaping changes to make them politically and bureaucratically acceptable. In these cases, policy elites appeared to have had considerable capacity to think strategically about managing opposition, taking advantage of opportune moments, and putting together supportive coalitions for reform. They often had detailed knowledge of power relationships and bureaucratic interactions that could help or hinder efforts at reform. Thus, frequently they not only had preferred solutions to major policy and institutional problems, they also had the capacity for generating strategies to encourage the adoption and pursuit of preferred solutions. In many cases, this involved careful and politically sensitive crafting of the content, timing, and sequence of reform, as well as efforts to mobilize support and manage opposition.

Finally, our experience suggests that change, even significant reform, is not abnormal or unusual. In fact, within most governments, change is normal and continuous, with large numbers of officials occupied daily in study, discussion, and debate about how to improve, alter, and even dismantle existing policy and practice. At times, this activity is in response to societal and international pressures, but at other times it is best understood as a response of public officials attempting to achieve certain goals more effectively. Thus, in many countries, change is more or less continuously on the agendas of government decision makers. Even in cases of significant reform, change can be embedded within the normal course of politics and policy making, rather than emerging only through political or economic cataclysm. Exploring the opportunities for reform that occur under such conditions provides greater insight into the motivations of decision makers and the impact on them of broader bureaucratic and political contexts.

Choice and change are central dependent variables in this study. We have tried to account for the choices that are made about development policies and institutional arrangements by characterizing influences on decision makers within government, and we have tried to assess how changes in existing policies and institutions come about in a variety of circumstances. Thus far, little research has focused on developing approaches to the analysis of these issues, so our framework and conclusions focus specifically on them. We hope the study will stimulate greater interest in and concern about the ways in which choices and changes are made within the state.

The Cases and the Organization of the Study

This book is based on case studies reported from inside government decision-making processes. At times, getting inside government may appear to be an insuperable obstacle, particularly in developing countries where policy making is often closed to public scrutiny or widespread participation by interested citizens. A book that deals centrally with the strategic political motivations of policy makers, for example, simply asserts that these motivations center on the imperative to retain office. Getting inside the state is abandoned as infeasible. "Given that the regime [in Brazil] was a dictatorship, we cannot hope to determine the preferences of its leaders by direct observation of decision making, by analysis of documents, or by interviews with participants. We can only infer preferences from policy outputs. Thus, the fundamental question of this strategy was inductive: Given the policy evidence, what strategy (or strategies) might the regime have been pursuing?" (Ames 1987:219). We have tried to overcome this problem by basing our accounts on materials primarily presented by participants in reform initiatives.

We have selected twelve instances of reform initiatives from a variety of developing countries to which we had access through such participants. These cases span the range of macroeconomic change, sectoral initiatives, and organizational innovation.[5] By focusing on a variety of such changes, we have chosen to try to learn more about the process of reform generally than about the specifics of any particular policy area or type of reform—structural adjustment, agrarian reform, or decentralization, for example. The cases come from major regions of the developing world, with four cases each from experiences in Latin America, Africa, and Asia. Thus, we have again sought to develop general insights into the process of change rather than to develop great depth in understanding the uniqueness of any particular countries or regions of the world.

The cases also represent a variety of regime types because we are concerned about processes of change that may transcend the influence of regime. In fact, regime type as a variable was not a prominent factor in many of our cases, although it frequently influenced the motivations of decision makers. In focusing on issues of policy choice and change, on the ways in which authoritative decisions are made and pursued, we are not attempting to explain broader issues of political and social change in developing countries. Thus, this is not a book on the politics of developing countries, although we anchor our analysis within a broader contextual appreciation of the nature of political and economic relationships in the Third World and between industrialized and developing countries.[6] Finally, our cases are not limited to the reforms of the 1980s but record experiences that occurred as long ago as the early 1960s. In this, we have tried to go beyond the particularly intense difficulties of the 1980s to consider changes that occurred under a broader range of circumstances. Table 1.1 summarizes the case topics, the country experience they are based on, and the major sources of information we have used to construct the cases.

As indicated, our cases represent efforts in making significant changes in macroeconomic and sectoral policies and in altering organizational contexts for development. In each case, we have tried to tap the experiences of participants in the reform process because they often have unique insights and access to information about the pressures, considerations, and influences on those responsible for authoritative decision making. In each of our cases, we asked: (1) How did the issue of reform get on the agenda of government decision making? (2) What decision criteria—political, bureaucratic, technical, ideological—were important in promoting or inhibiting the process of change? and (3) What factors led to the sustainability or abandonment of reform initiatives? Across a range of cases, countries, political regimes, and historical time periods, we have tried to identify similarities and differences that in turn form the basis of our analysis.

The framework we develop is based on our analysis of these cases, and we believe that each is generally consistent with the overall analysis. We use the cases throughout most of the chapters only to illustrate more general aspects of the framework. Thus, the cases serve to demonstrate the meaning and logic of a series of hypotheses that, together, form the framework. In themselves, the cases do not prove the merits of our analysis, they only suggest its applicability. In Chapter 7, however, we do attempt to use a set of additional cases to test our hypotheses systematically.

These forays inside government decision making and our research, which focused on the experiences of participants in reform initiatives in developing countries, have left us dissatisfied when we turn to the literature that informs political science, political economy, and policy science. In Chapter 2, we consider the major frameworks of analysis—ranging from class analytic models to public choice theory and bureau-

TABLE 1.1
Cases in Policy and Institutional Reform

Policy Type	Country	Year(s)	Source(s)
MACROECONOMIC POLICY			
Devaluation	Ghana	1971	Policy advisers; Published and unpublished papers
Structural adjustment	Korea	1960–66	Policy adviser; Published and unpublished papers
Development strategy	Costa Rica	1948–81 1982–88	Senior policy maker; Supporting documentation in Ph.D. thesis
SECTORAL POLICY			
Agrarian reform	Philippines	1986–88	Policy adviser; Supporting documentation; Published and unpublished papers
Primary health care	Mali	1975–79	Policy adviser; Published papers
Rice pricing	Indonesia	1972–73; 1986	Policy adviser; Published and unpublished papers
Public water supply	India	1980–88	Senior policy implementer
Export manufacturing	Jamaica	1982–88	Senior policy implementer
ORGANIZATIONAL CHANGE			
Decentralization	Kenya	1976–78	Policy adviser
Planning	Colombia	1966	Policy adviser
Planning agency	Argentina	1962	Policy adviser
Reorganization of ministry	Kenya	1978–79	Policy adviser

cratic politics approaches—and find that, although often rich in insight, they do not provide convincing explanations of our observations and experience. This is so largely because many theoretical discussions (for example, Marxist and pluralist approaches) do not treat decision makers and decision making seriously. If they do, they do not view the intersection of state and society as a critical arena in explaining policy and organizational change (for example, bureaucratic politics and organizational process approaches). In the case of much public choice theory, the activities of policy makers and public managers are reduced to simplistic notions of rent-seeking that explain little about the complex nature of political decision making. Our approach, which builds on state-centered theories about policy choice, goes beyond current theory because it also builds on the unique experiences and insights of participants in reform efforts, considers the contextual factors that surround the consideration of particular policy or institutional issues, analyzes the criteria policy elites apply in making decisions about change, and assesses the role of policy characteristics in facilitating or inhibiting change. In each of these aspects, the model focuses on the links between what occurs within the state and what occurs at the intersection of state and society.

Implicit in this framework is an assumption that although each experience in policy and institutional change and each national context is in many ways unique, policy elites face similar dilemmas in the choices they make and share similar concerns. Moreover, within the significant diversity that exists among developing countries, broad historical, economic, and political conditions set a common context within which decisions must be made and carried out. In Chapter 3, the commonalities of historical, economic, and political conditions are developed in order to describe the general context of government decision making and implementation in developing countries. In particular, we describe the structural and ideological factors that tend to increase the importance of policy elites in decision making and implementation. Their perceptions and preferences take on added weight because of general characteristics of underdevelopment, legacies of statist approaches to development, and the ambiguities resulting from incompletely organized political societies. At the same time, characteristics of the policy-making environment mean that decision makers and implementers act in a context of great uncertainty, risk, and vulnerability. As a consequence, their concerns frequently go far beyond the substance of any particular policy problem to embrace issues of power and control over often conflict-ridden societies. Chapter 3 also provides a description of those who tend to be involved in making decisions within this context and the societal groups that attempt to influence them.

The general context of the policy process in developing countries forms a backdrop for the circumstances that place particular issues on the agenda for government decision making. Chapter 4 moves from the broader context of political and economic conditions in developing countries to the circumstances that surround the consideration of particular policy or institutional reforms. Characteristically, many reforms emerge and are considered in which policy elites believe that a crisis exists and that they must "do something" about the situation or they will face grave consequences. But frequently, also, reform issues emerge under conditions that can be described as "politics as usual," in which change is considered desirable but the consequences of not acting are not considered threatening to the decision makers or the regime. Our cases indicate that circumstances of crisis or politics as usual surrounding the emergence of a particular issue alter the dynamics of decision making by raising or lowering the political stakes for policy elites, altering the identity and hierarchical level of decision makers, and influencing the timing of reform. The cases of devaluation in Ghana and planning reform in Colombia provide good examples of the distinct dynamics of agenda setting and decision making that obtain under conditions of perceived crisis and politics as usual. Powerful as these circumstances appear to be in influencing the process of agenda setting and decision making, however, they do not determine the content of the decisions made. This chapter suggests that policy elites retain considerable scope for determining the specific content of policy and institutional changes, even under crisis-ridden conditions.

If policy elites retain some autonomy to shape policy outcomes, what factors appear to influence their decisions? This is the question considered in Chapter 5. In our cases, we find decision makers considering options available to them in terms of their appreciation of the technical—usually economic—aspects of the issues involved; the way in which changes will affect micropolitical relationships within the bureaucracy and between groups in government and their clienteles; the more general or macropolitical impact reform measures will have on overall political stability and the support bases of the regime in power; and the roles of pressure, support, or opposition that are assumed by international actors such as aid agencies or foreign governments. But these criteria appear not to be of equal importance, shifting in importance depending on the circumstances that surround the issue. Crisis-ridden reforms, for example, are likely to be assessed first and foremost in terms of their expected macropolitical impact. Politics-as-usual reforms, in contrast, are considered primarily in terms of how they will affect micropolitical relationships within the bureaucracy or with narrow clienteles. Thus, we find a systematic relationship between how issues get on a decision agenda and the way policy and institutional changes are assessed by policy elites.

That is, differential processes of agenda setting result in the adoption of different decision criteria by decision makers. Policy changes in South Korea and Costa Rica are indicative of the concerns that policy elites bring to the issues they confront.

Contextual factors loom large in the process of agenda setting and decision making when reform initiatives emerge and are considered. In contrast, the characteristics of particular policies or institutional changes appear to be the most critical factors determining the outcome of implementation efforts, as we argue in Chapter 6. The outcome of implementation efforts is highly variable, as cases from Indonesia, Ghana, Jamaica, and India suggest, and these outcomes are affected by the arena in which response to implementation largely takes place. Reforms with particular characteristics, for example, are likely to elicit highly visible and immediate public reactions, in which the stakes for government are high. Other types of reforms will be carried out or subverted largely within a bureaucratic arena where the potential for failure is great but the stakes for government are relatively low. Those who advocate particular policy or institutional changes can assess their characteristics in terms of the distribution of costs and benefits, the technical and administrative content, the degree to which they incorporate participation, and the immediacy of their impact in order to assess the kind of political and administrative resources needed to encourage effective implementation and sustainability. Thus, a central theme of this book, that policy elites have room for maneuver in pursuing reform initiatives, appears to be valid for implementation efforts also.

The hypotheses generated through the analysis of twelve cases are suggestive. Nevertheless, given the range of countries, time periods, and policy issues, they can be refined by further study. Cases of reform initiatives that provide insight into government decision making are relatively rare. In recent years, however, interest in such studies has heightened, and scholars and practitioners have been stimulated to consider how and when reform initiatives emerge and are pursued. We have identified fourteen cases of reform experiences from the 1980s and use them in Chapter 7 to "test" the hypotheses and framework suggested in the previous chapters. In general, we find that the nature of the reforms of the 1980s differed from most of our cases in terms of what they required of states, decision makers, and citizens, and in terms of the kinds of policies introduced and implemented. In particular, these reforms meant that governments had to abandon development strategies and undo political decision-making structures that had become well institutionalized in prior decades. Moreover, they were more often in the position of having to impose costs on their populations rather than to distribute benefits. Despite significant changes in the content of reform measures in the 1980s, however, the reform process we have identified remained largely the same. Policy elites continued to play centrally important roles in defining policy changes and in managing their introduction and pursuit. Circumstances of crisis and noncrisis and their relationship to the salience of various decision criteria continued to loom large in understanding reforms during this era. The dynamics of implementation continued to be influenced by reform characteristics. The analysis of these fourteen additional cases, while suggesting some modifications, generally affirms the utility of our framework in identifying important aspects of the political economy of reform decision making.

If, as our cases and framework suggest, policy elites play vital roles in shaping the timing, content, and viability of reform initiatives, then there is not only room for maneuver in such situations, there is also room for analysis and astute leadership. This is the theme addressed in Chapter 8 as we attempt to draw policy-relevant generalizations from our study. We review the framework that is developed in the book and indicate how it can be useful in identifying possibilities for maneuvering within variables of context, circumstance, and policy characteristics. In this way, we reflect on means of assessing what is alterable and what is not through the actions of those interested in introducing and sustaining policy and organizational change. The framework can become a starting point in developing strategies and principles of action for reformers.

We realize that the issue of reform is itself problematic. Those promoting particular policy and organizational changes consider that they are attempting to bring about reform, a change that will lead to a more desirable outcome than current practice permits. However, policies do not always achieve the goals intended by their proponents; and, even if they do, they may bring with them unintended and unwelcome consequences. Moreover, a more desirable outcome for one may be a less desirable outcome for another; reform is inherently conflictual because it imposes costs on some and provides benefits in terms of favorable policy on others. The ambiguous nature of reform was particularly evident in the difficult economic conditions of the 1980s, in which the widely advocated reforms incorporated in stabilization and structural adjustment had detrimental consequences for the most vulnerable groups in developing countries (Cornia, Jolly, and Stewart 1987). Whether a specific change is a reform or not may often depend on one's point of view and the consequences of change for individual or group welfare.

Thus, although our principal concern is about policy, we have not reviewed the range of policy options for addressing specific problems nor assessed or judged the appropriateness of any specific policy choice to resolve particular issues. Neither do we generate recommendations for how particular macroeconomic, sectoral, or institutional problems ought to be resolved. Instead, our intent is to provide a framework for understanding policy decision making and implementation in developing countries without passing judgment on the merits of particular reform initiatives. Viewed in the context of the literature, this is a book that is optimistic about change and about leadership. The evidence accumulated in the study decidedly supports the view that public officials and political leaders matter, that they are not simply creatures of organizations or societies, and that they can provide new directions in public policy. Furthermore, the book suggests that the prospects for successful reform and change can be improved. The systematic analysis of a reform initiative can generate insight into strategies for improving the prospects for implementing and sustaining such an initiative.

The book is addressed to analysts who, like us, wish to understand the process of change and to build toward a more realistic theory of policy change than currently exists in the literature. It is equally addressed to those in government or outside, in academic or more applied pursuits, who consider themselves to be reformers, or perhaps conscientious public officials, interested in promoting changes in policies and institutions in the expectation that they will lead to improvement in the economic, social, cultural, or political conditions in developing countries.

CHAPTER 2

Linking Theory
and Practice

Every day, governments make authoritative decisions that allocate public resources, define relationships between state and society, regulate interactions among citizens and institutions, and act on behalf of the nation in international contexts. In the Third World, where social needs are great, economic development frequently elusive, and the role of the state often extensive, these decisions take on added importance in terms of the costs and benefits they can impose on whole societies and on particular groups within them. Demonstrably, policy has a profound impact on the social, political, and economic destinies of millions of people in the Third World.

Indeed, because of a widely shared belief that policy is important to the societies of the developing world, significant resources in government, academic institutions, consulting firms, international financial institutions, and public interest organizations are annually invested in research and analysis to identify "good" policies, to avoid "bad" policies, and to promote "the public interest." However these policy characteristics are defined, investments in policy-oriented studies of development almost inevitably result in proposals to change existing policy or to introduce new policy where none existed. Despite such recommendations, policy research generally begs the important question of how such changes are to be brought about.

In Chapter 1, we presented a series of propositions drawn from the extensive experience of participants in policy-making situations in developing countries. These propositions, summarized below, reflect perspectives widely shared among such individuals. Stated generally, they may appear self-evident. Nevertheless, they stand in direct contradiction to major bodies of theory about the sources and dynamics of public policy.

- Decision makers are not fully constrained by the interests of social classes, organized societal interests, international actors, or international economic conditions, but have space for defining the content, timing, and sequencing of reform initiatives.
- Decision makers often have articulate and logical explanations of the problems they seek to resolve based on their experience, study, personal values, ideology, institutional affiliation, or professional training.
- Decision makers may alter their perspectives on what constitute preferred or viable policy options in response to experience, study, values, ideology, institutional affiliation, and professional training.
- Decision makers often take active and formative roles in shaping reforms to make them politically acceptable to divergent interests in society or in government.
- Bringing about changes in public policies and institutions is a normal and ongoing aspect of government and a normal and ongoing function of many officials.

According to these propositions, policy elites—those formally charged with making authoritative decisions in government—have considerable scope to identify problems, articulate goals, define solutions, and think strategically about their implementation. Do theories exist that help us explain why, how, and when these officials are important actors in the initiation and pursuit of policy change? Are there theories that would allow us to focus on them and explain their perceptions, activities, and institutional contexts, without isolating them from the broader historical, societal, and international factors that inevitably shape and constrain their behavior?

Identifying a theoretical perspective that encourages analysis of these issues is not easily done. Much theory that purports to explain the origin, content, and pursuit of public policy denies the existence or potential for the relative autonomy of policy elites or severely restricts its occurrence to special sets of circumstances. From these society-centered perspectives, the causes of decisions made to adopt, pursue, and change public policies lie in understanding relationships of power and competition among individuals, groups, or classes in society or in international extensions of class-based or interest-based societies. In contrast, other theoretical perspectives suggest that policy elites are virtually unconstrained by societal interests. In these state-centered approaches, the perceptions and inter-actions of policy elites and the broad orientations of the state more gen-erally account for policy choices and their subsequent pursuit.[1] Both sets of approaches tend to focus on obstacles to change and present arguments for why change does not occur or occurs only rarely.

The differences between society-centered and state-centered perspec-tives are not trivial. They present competing visions of where initiatives for stasis and change come from. For analysts, they indicate important distinctions among independent and dependent variables that underlie political theory. These are relevant distinctions for practitioners as well. . Promoters of reform who adopt a society-centered explanation of policy, for example, would be well advised to concentrate efforts on mobilizing interest group activities or attempting to create coalitions and alliances of classes and interests to influence authoritative decision making by government. If, on the other hand, a state-centered explanation of policy is adopted, reformers might better concentrate efforts on influencing the perceptions of decision makers about the goals and content of policy, and on identifying those within government who will benefit from new policy and mobilizing their support. As suggested below, theoretical is-sues rarely considered in policy-oriented research need to be addressed when analysts consider why, how, and when policy is changed.

Society-centered Explanations of Policy Choice

Explanations that emphasize the centrality of social class and interest group formations to policy choice dominate current research in political science and political economy. In class analytic, pluralist, and public choice formulations, the activities of states and policy elites are under-stood to be dependent variables. Thus, choices of policy and the behavior of policy elites can be predicted on the basis of an effective analysis of class and group formations in society or their extensions in international contexts. As discussed below, the values, perceptions, behavior, and in-stitutional contexts of public officials are therefore much less important than the values, perceptions, behavior, and historical or international contexts of social classes and interest groups.

Class Analytic Approaches

Marxist analyses locate the source of policy—and of policy change—in relationships of power and domination among social classes.[2] Depen-dency analyses, which have been widely adopted to explain the political economy of development, begin with relationships of domination and subordination that emerge through an international context of capitalist development and subsequently incorporate class relationships within a society (see, e.g., Amin 1977; dos Santos 1970; Cardoso and Faletto 1979). In both cases, economic relationships define the nature of conflict. Thus, political interaction derives from economic conflict, and politics is a significant manifestation of class conflict.

The primary function of the state in Marxist formulations is to ensure the legal, institutional, and ideological hegemony of the dominant class or class alliance over subordinate classes. Under normal conditions, the state is an instrument of domination that reflects the structure of class relationships, in its simplest form acting as an "organization of the possessing class for its protection against the non-possessing class" (Engels 1968:291). In classical Marxism, the repressive character of the state is preeminent, and the purpose of policy is to advance and protect the interests of exploiting classes over those of the exploited (Tucker 1969). In consequence, policy elites are best understood as tools of the dominant class to accomplish this end. In this view, policy elites have no autonomy, and policy change is explained by changes in the composition of the dominant class or dominant class alliance.

In the tradition of class analysis, however, this simple formulation proved inadequate in accounting for instances in which the state appears to assume some independence from dominant class interests, when it pursues policies that constrain or even impair the interests of these classes, when it initiates reforms that benefit subordinate classes, or when it acts to incorporate new groups into the political and economic system. Early on, Marxist scholars were challenged to account for such seeming anomalies and to consider the possibility of state autonomy. Engels (1968:290), for example, sought to account for such situations by arguing that at particular historical moments, no class may be dominant, allowing the enduring apparatus of the state to acquire some independence and ability to establish and pursue policies, even those that have a detrimental impact on the possessing classes.

More recently, a significant school of neo-Marxist thought has accorded considerably more importance to the state.[3] From this perspective, the state is instrumental for capitalism as a system and thus acts periodically to ensure the persistence of the system, even if the interests of specific fractions of the capitalist class or the class as a whole are constrained by such actions (see esp. Poulantzas 1973). This instrumentalist view provides the state with a structurally determined role in safeguarding the long-term interests of a capitalist economy. Given this role, neo-Marxist analysis takes state policy more seriously because of its capacity to rescue the capitalist order in moments of crisis. Similarly, policy elites can be treated as actors whose objectives go beyond the interests of specific classes to the survival of the capitalist order, nationally and internationally.

Despite the added possibility for autonomous action that neo-Marxists allow for the state, the approach remains essentially society-centered; autonomy is possible only when dominant classes are profoundly at odds with each other and unable to establish a ruling coalition, or when the interests of the capitalist economy as a whole are threatened (Skocpol 1985:5). The emergence of this relative autonomy of the state is thus an infrequent occurrence, corresponding to moments of significantly heightened class conflict or profound economic crisis. Reformist initiatives are adopted in order to resolve these crises of political legitimacy or economic disorder. To explain policy change or an increase in the initiating and directing role of the state, then, research and analysis would focus on shifting relationships among social classes or changes in relations of production that introduce new structures of conflict into society or an international order. Policy makers may vary in their ideas about how reform objectives are best achieved, but conflicts within the state over policy issues are little more than reflections of class conflicts within the society. For Marxists, neo-Marxists, and *dependistas,* then, the process through which decisions are made is not a useful focus of inquiry; what is important are the social class formations that give rise to policy initiatives and the differential impact of policy on particular classes in society (see, e.g., Stallings 1978).

Class analytic approaches usefully point to the linkage between societal power and public policy. As explanations of policy choice, however, they are at odds with our propositions suggesting the range of occasions on which policy elites initiate policy, the extent to which their perspectives shape the content of policy, the degree to which public officials actively promote change, the extent to which policy change is continuously on the agenda of decision makers and policy planners, and the evidence that at times decision makers prevaricate and even change their minds about appropriate policy responses to particular problems. Class analytic models correctly note that policy makers are constrained by economic structures and their political manifestations, but they define away the issue of choice in policy making, other than to assert that at specific historical moments, policy elites have relatively more independence to determine policy content than at other moments, when their actions are severely if not totally constrained by the class basis of political authority.

PLURALIST APPROACHES

In pluralist approaches to political analysis, public policy results from conflict, bargaining, and coalition formation among a potentially large number of societal groups organized to protect or advance particular interests common to their members.[4] These interests are usually economic, but groups also form around shared concerns for neighborhood, ethnicity, religion, values, region, and other issues. For pluralists, political society is composed of large numbers of such groups that compete and coalesce around the promotion of common policy goals. The state forms part of the political arena in which such groups conflict, negotiate, bargain, form coalitions, and generally do battle over policy output, but the initiative for policy is generated by society and is structured by the ways in which groups are organized around particular interests and the resources available to them for achieving their goals.

In *Federalist* paper number 51, James Madison explicitly advocated large numbers of competing interests as a safeguard for democratic society as a whole. In defending the idea of a federal republic, he states that "the society itself will be broken into so many parts and classes of citizens, that the rights of individuals or of the minority will be in little danger from interested combinations of the majority" (Hamilton, Madison, and Jay 1961:324). In the pluralist tradition, the fragmentation of society into competing groups is a political analogy to the competitive marketplace in classical economics; like the economic efficiency derived through an open and competitive market, the public interest is thought to be best served when policy emerges out of competition among large numbers of political interests.

For some pluralists, the state is a more or less neutral arena for conflicting and competing interests to shape policy output, and no groups are systematically discriminated against in their access to policy makers (Truman 1951; Dahl 1961, 1971). State institutions and procedural rules do little more than channel this competition into appropriate conflict resolution systems. For others, the resources of groups and their access to political institutions have an effect on whose interests are effectively promoted and which groups have a greater or lesser capacity to influence the output of policy (McConnell 1966; Lowi 1969). In either case, the role of the state is to act as arbitrator among competing interests; public officials may register preferences and at times seek to negotiate compromises among divergent interests, but their principal role is to respond to the pressures placed upon them by organized groups in society. The relative autonomy of the state, taken seriously in some class analytic models, is not an issue for pluralists (Nordlinger 1987). Not only is the initiative for policy linked to the mobilization of interests in society, but the source of policy change must also be sought in changes in the coalitions of interest groups or in their relative power in bargaining, negotiating, marshaling votes, and otherwise influencing the policy makers.

Pluralist perspectives on how, why, and when policy choices are made do not provide useful explanations for the five propositions presented earlier. Although they would admit that change in public policies is normal and continuous, pluralists place extensive constraints on the roles of policy elites in the initiation, formulation, and implementation of change. For pluralists, the activities of public officials and their commitment to policy change are always determined by the particular way in which societal interests are organized and articulated. This perspective may be particularly difficult to apply in the case of many developing countries, where votes and lobby activities may not be useful "currencies" for interpreting societal preferences, and where much policy may never be discussed outside the halls of government. In such countries, a model of policy change that takes the activities of organized interests in society as unique independent variables may be misleading. In fact, in many developing countries, interest groups may not be sufficiently well organized to put effective pressure on policy elites or may not have guaranteed access to them.[5] To the extent that this is true, a pluralist explanation would probably account for a relatively small proportion of instances of policy reform in the Third World.

PUBLIC CHOICE APPROACHES

In current scholarship, public choice theory has expanded and altered the theoretical implications of pluralist approaches. Like pluralist perspectives, public choice theory assumes that political society is composed of self-interested individuals who coalesce into organized interests. Interest groups, which tend to form around relatively narrow issues of special importance to their members, are created by individuals seeking specific self-interested goals. Individuals join with other self-seeking individuals to acquire access to public resources (see esp. Olson 1965). Formed into groups, they use money, expertise, political connections, votes, and other resources to extract benefits, or rents, from government through lobbying activities, through elections and other direct forms of political involvement, or through the imposition of rewards and sanctions on public officials (Colander 1984; Srinivasan 1985:43). So pervasive is such activity in some contexts that the term *rent-seeking societies* has come to characterize whole political systems and is a term widely adopted by neoclassical political economists (Krueger 1974).

Complementing the interest of groups in capturing favored status in the distribution of resources in society are elected public officials who are fundamentally concerned with remaining in power (Ames 1987; Anderson and Hayami 1986; Alt and Chrystal 1983). In order to do so, they consciously seek to provide benefits to a range of interests they believe will help them retain office; they systematically favor certain interests over others; and they maximize their returns from the allocations of public expenditures, goods, services, and state regulation as a way of attracting and rewarding supporters (Anderson and Hayami 1986; Bates 1981). In short, elected public officials follow a "strategic calculus" as they seek to use public resources to stay in power; the resources of the state become "a weapon for survival" (Ames 1987:1, 212–13; see also Bennett and DiLorenzo 1984).[6] Nonelected officials also respond to the pushing and hauling of interest groups because they can derive rents from providing favored access to public goods, services, and regulations (Colander 1984; Brock and Magee 1984; Krueger 1974; Wellisz and Findlay 1984; Bhagwati 1978). Politics, then, is the sum total of individuals seeking special advantage through public policy and individual officials seeking to benefit from public office through reelection and rents.

In public choice theory, the politically rational goals of private interests and public officials generally lead to ends that are economically irrational. Over time, policy elites may come under increasing pressure to extract and then "spend" public resources to maintain the political support of economically powerful actors. In one influential perspective applied to developing country politics, policy makers become trapped in a cycle of flagging support, declining legitimacy, and increased expenditures, but are unable to alter policies because of the political power of the beneficiaries of the status quo (Bates 1981).[7] The process generates increasing economic inefficiencies; in developing countries, this negative dynamic is thought to culminate in extensive political instability, widespread corruption, and successive regime changes. Politics, for those who adopt this perspective, is a negative factor in the search for appropriate public policy.

Public choice theory has been widely adopted by neoclassical economists because it offers a coherent and relatively parsimonious explanation for seemingly nonrational decision making by governments. Political society, like the marketplace, is composed of self-interested individuals who form coalitions and compete to acquire benefits from government. In the marketplace, however, competition and self-interest are expected to generate efficiency in the allocation of resources. In the political arena, self-interested behavior generates negative outcomes for society—a state that is captured by narrow interests, policies that are distorted in economically irrational ways by self-seeking groups, and public officials whose actions are always suspect (see esp. Bates 1981; Brock and Magee 1984; Colander 1984:6; Olson 1982; Srinivasan 1985; Krueger 1974). The approach thus makes it possible to respond to questions such as that posed by Robert Bates (1981:3), "Why should reasonable men adopt public policies that have harmful consequences for the societies they govern?" The solution to this problem of the state and the capacity of policy to distort resource allocation is to limit closely the activities permitted to fall under the regulatory power of the state (Buchanan 1980; Colander 1984:5).[8] Thus, while the public choice approach shares basic assumptions with pluralist theory, its assessment of politics stands in considerable opposition to the pluralist assumption that wise policy results from fragmented interest articulation in the political arena.[9]

Public choice theory goes beyond the pluralist view that the state is a neutral arbitrator or referee in conflicts over policy; it provides an explanation for the willingness of public officials to respond to the pressures and imprecations of lobby groups and other types of special interests. It also provides an explanation for policy choices that are detrimental to society as a whole over both the shorter and the longer term and offers a way of understanding the constraints on policy change that develop over time. In contrast, the approach is much less able to explain how policy changes or how policy itself can lead to broadly beneficial outcomes.[10] At best, the theory explains why "the public interest" is not often achieved. There is, then, little room in this perspective for public officials who adhere to particular ideologies, whose professional training provides them with independent judgment in the analysis of policy issues, or who may adopt goals that transcend the interests of any particular group or coalition of groups (Adler 1987; Orren 1988:15). Instead, policy elites are creatures of vested societal interests, however much they seek to work these to their individual rent-seeking advantage, and their actions—devoid of ideological or technical content—can be explained by motivations to maximize political support.[11]

By focusing on the power of vested interests, the public choice approach demonstrates the barriers to reform that are created by preexisting policies and by the political relationships that they engender. This is an important accomplishment, but the model suffers in not being able to explain how, why, or when reform occurs. Instead, it explains existing public policy as the result of an inevitable rationality of rent-seeking. Given this explanation of why things are the way they are, it is hard to understand how changes can occur, except perhaps through catastrophic events or the appearance of wise statesmen or technocrats who, for unexplained reasons, exhibit behavior that is politically irrational. In a discussion of the issue of reform, for example, Srinivasan (1985:58) concludes that "it would appear that leaders in developing countries are becoming increasingly aware of the negative economic and political consequences of rent-creating intervention in the economy," a conclusion that cannot be derived from a theory grounded in the assumption of self-seeking behavior on the part of individuals. Finally, although it indicates the importance of the power-seeking motivations of decision makers, public choice analysis tells us little about how their motivations are developed or altered over time.

State-centered Models of Policy Choice

While political science and political economy have emphasized society-centered approaches to explaining policy choices, the policy science literature has been more explicitly focused on the analysis of decision making within the organizational context of the state. As such, it takes as a principal unit of analysis the decision maker or the organization responsible for decisional outcomes. Not surprisingly, much of this literature credits the decision maker with considerably more capacity for choice and substantially more complex motives for making those choices than is the case with the society-centered approaches. Similarly, constraints emanating from societal contexts are considerably less powerful in explaining what policy makers can and cannot do. Rational actor, bureaucratic politics, and state interests models of policy choice accept the possibility that policy elites can develop new understandings of social and economic problems, that the state can assume new responsibilities for guiding or regulating society, and that the state can increase or diminish its capacity to do so. These interpretations often emphasize the interactions of bureaucratic and executive officials for understanding how policy initiatives emerge and change. State-centered explanations indicate that policy change is best understood by focusing first on the perceptions and interactions of decision makers and others in particular organizational contexts in government. When such perspectives consider the influence of societal interests, they generally do so by treating lobbying, pressure group politics, public opinion, and voting as intervening variables that affect the policy responses of public officials. Thus, they differ significantly from society-centered explanations in terms of where they expect the initiative for change to emerge.

RATIONAL ACTOR MODELS

Much discussion of policy decision making has revolved around the question of the extent to which policy makers can be considered rational actors who accumulate information, assess alternative courses of action, and choose among them on the basis of the potential to achieve the decision makers' preferences (see, for discussions, Allison 1971; Frohock 1979; Killick 1976; March 1978; Robinson and Majak 1967). Initially, rational actor models were derived from classical economic theory, in which an actor is presumed to be able to assess all possible alternatives on the basis of full information, and then to establish priorities among them in terms of an optimal way to reach a stated goal or preference.

Much of decision-making theory has involved subsequent modification of the perfectly rational actor model by introducing concepts such as "bounded rationality," "satisficing," and "incrementalism" (Kinder and Weiss 1978; March 1978). These revisionist perspectives generally argue that because of the complexity of perfectly rational choice and its costs in terms of time and attention, decision makers (whether individuals or organizations) do not usually attempt to achieve optimal solutions to problems but only to find ones that satisfy their basic criteria for an acceptable alternative or ones that meet satisfactory standards (March and Simon 1958:140–41). Moreover, individuals and organizations operate on the basis of "bounded rationality," a concept suggesting that information collection is costly and always incomplete; organizations develop means of dealing with recurrent problems in ways that obviate the need to assess separately each issue that requires a decision (March and Simon 1958:169–71). Decisions conform to "bounded rationality" because of the stable, structured way in which individuals and organizations attempt to simplify decision-making processes. In subsequent formulations, the concept of incrementalism was introduced, asserting that decision makers, when confronted with the need to change policy, attempt to reduce uncertainty, conflict, and complexity by making incremental or marginal changes over time (Braybrooke and Lindblom 1963). According to the model, the more uncertainty exists in a given decision situation, the more will incremental strategies be adopted.

Rational actor models, especially the modification of the pure theory of rational choice, establish a set of assumptions about the conditions under which decisions are made, and they focus on the options and strategies available to policy makers. Clearly, then, these models underscore the importance of the perspectives of decision makers in determining choices, as our propositions also suggest. While rational actor models tend to focus on the individual in the decision-making process or on organizations acting as rational individuals, they are also useful in exploring how organizational contexts simplify the decision process, minimize the amount of conflict engendered through policy change, and constrain the choices available (Frohock 1979:59). The models have been particularly useful in developing concepts such as "satisficing" and "incrementalism" that point to the emergence of similar decision strategies in a wide variety of circumstances. These concepts provide perspectives on the process through which decisions are reached and make it possible to view discrete decisions as part of an overall decision-making system with characteristics that can be described and that shape decisional outcomes (Frohock 1979; Killick 1976).

Indeed, it makes little sense to reject the notion of some sort of rationality underlying most decision-making processes. In particular, the incremental and satisficing models can be useful in explaining why far-reaching reform measures are not adopted more frequently. However, they are less useful in explaining the conditions under which initiatives for fundamental change—innovation, not incrementalism—are likely to be adopted (Bunce 1981). Rational actor models also restrict the rationality of decision makers to their organizational contexts and suggest that politics takes place within the confines of bureaucratic organizations. They provide little insight into how societal interests, historical experiences, ideologies, values, alliances, and other factors penetrate the world of the decision makers and shape or even determine decisional outcomes.

BUREAUCRATIC POLITICS APPROACH

Decision makers are also the focus of analysis in the bureaucratic politics approach to explaining policy outcomes. In this model, state policy is the result of competing activities among bureaucratic entities and actors constrained by their organizational roles and capacities (Allison 1971; Halperin 1974). Executive and bureaucratic "players" compete over preferred solutions to particular policy problems and use the resources available to them through their positions—hierarchy, control over information, access to key decision makers, for example—to achieve their goals. Their views on what policy should prevail are shaped by their positions within government; that is, the issue position of each player is defined by the bureaucratic position he or she occupies, such that "where you stand depends on where you sit" (Allison 1971:176). Goals usually involve "winning" agreement on the player's preferred policy but can also involve enhancing the player's position in government, gaining greater power, or acquiring more resources for the player's organizational unit. Winning can, of course, lead to the achievement of all these goals, but losing can threaten even greater losses, including those of power, access, and budgetary resources. For this reason, players are encouraged to negotiate and compromise with one another in order to minimize the impact of losing.

The autonomy of decision makers in shaping and pursuing policy is potentially very great in the bureaucratic politics approach, for it is constrained only by the power and bargaining skills of other bureaucratic actors and by their own hierarchical position of power, their political skill, and the bureaucratic and personal resources available to them. The approach provides a set of propositions that is useful for investigating and understanding intragovernmental bargaining, conflict, and decision making and that allows analysis to focus on the activities of the decision maker, an aspect of policy largely ignored in society-centered explanations. Any particular policy decision could be understood by assessing the stakes, resources, and skills of each participant in a decision-making process. The model indicates that change in policy results from the potential for variable outcomes in bargaining, negotiation, and conflict among the actors involved. From this perspective, policy clearly originates in the bureaucratic and policy-making apparatus, not in societal relationships of power and domination.

The bureaucratic politics model provides insights into the black box of government decision making that cannot be assessed using other models. It provides propositions that are useful for understanding conflict and negotiation within the state and that indicate the extent to which policy is the result of intense political processes and power relationships within government. As indicated previously, in developing countries, the role of the state is often extensive; the bureaucratic politics approach is a particularly important means of gaining insight into the process of decision making in large and complex states. Nevertheless, there are serious limitations inherent in the model. It was developed to help explain foreign policy decision making, an issue area largely dominated by executive decision makers; it is less well suited to explaining policy outcomes in which the issues involve extensive or prolonged societal conflict or those in which there is considerable pulling and hauling between executive and legislative entities. Thus, the model provides little insight into the ways societal pressures, historical contexts, and constitutional processes shape and influence policy outcomes. Indeed, societal actors appear only in the guise of resources to be used by bureaucratic players in their efforts to influence policy, as pawns to be used in bureaucratic "games." Finally, the approach provides little analytic capacity to deal with issues such as professional biases and alliances or consensus on technical analyses that cut across bureaucratic boundaries.

State Interests Approach

In a state interests approach, a broader perspective on the role and influence of government decision makers is adopted as a way of accounting for instances in which the state appears to have some autonomy in defining the nature of public problems and developing solutions to them. In contrast to the class and interest group models, states are analytically separable from society and considered to have "interests" that they pursue or attempt to pursue. Among the interests of the state, for example, are the achievement and maintenance of its own hegemony vis-à-vis societal actors, the maintenance of social peace, the pursuit of national development as defined by policy elites representing particular regimes, and the particular interests of regime incumbents in retaining power (Krasner 1978; Nordlinger 1987:36; Stepan 1978; Skocpol 1985:15; Trimberger 1978). At any particular moment, these state interests may or may not correspond to the interests of particular classes or groups in society. Thus, the objectives of state action may lead to policies that favor particular societal groups, but this does not necessarily imply that these groups imposed their preferences on the policy elites. The decision makers may have arrived at these policy options independently or in fact have been pressured by societal interests to adopt particular policies. It is clear, then, that from this perspective it is not possible to infer who initiates policy or who controls the state from who benefits from policy outputs. At other times, in pursuit of its own interests, the state may adopt policies that are not beneficial, and may even be detrimental, to the interests of powerful societal groups. The capacity to do so successfully depends on the strength and autonomy of the state, factors that are recognized to vary across time and regimes (Migdal 1987, 1988; Skocpol 1985). This means that the state is considerably more than an arena for societal conflict or an instrument of domination employed by the dominant class or class alliance. It is potentially a powerful actor in its own right. Thus, policy elites are not considered to be fully constrained by societal interests, and they have the capacity to generate explanations for various public problems and to develop strategies for dealing with them. In specific cases, they reflect not only the interests of the state but also those of the regime they serve.

In one influential exploration of state interests, Bennett and Sharpe (1985:44) explain how states acquire definable interests.

(1) Initial orientations are set down at its founding, particularly in establishing its social foundations. (2) These initial orientations are elaborated and altered as the state confronts new problems and devises strategies and builds capacities for dealing with them, although the institutionalization of the initial orientations constrains what is seen as a problem and what as an appropriate solution. (3) Major changes in state personnel bring new orientations or reformulations of old ones.

Bennett and Sharpe consider that "embedded orientations" of the state are "institutionalized in the ministries and agencies of the state—in their habitual ways of diagnosing and remedying problems and in their organization of staff responsibilities and resources" (43). In this way, states and the agencies that act for the state are credited with the potential for considerable autonomy. Empirically, the degree of autonomy is determined by historically and structurally derived relationships between the state and powerful interests in society and the international context (42). The state and, by extension, policy elites strive for autonomy to make and pursue policy choices but do not necessarily achieve it. Change in policy is accounted for by changing circumstances that encourage new definitions of problems and solutions to them, by efforts to achieve overarching state interests that may require new initiatives when prior policies have given rise to unintended consequences, or through conditions that alter the relative autonomy of the state (Grindle 1986a:17–19).

In the state interests approach, policy or institutional reform comes about because of the interaction of policy makers attempting to generate responses to public problems and the constraints placed upon them by political, economic, and social conditions and by the legacy of past policy. It is an important model for indicating the activism of political leaders and policy makers in determining policy outcomes and in focusing attention on how national development goals are shaped. It is useful in the context of the Third World, where the state often takes the lead in defining and directing society toward certain goals. Through the notion of embedded orientations, it is possible to explain the historical tendencies of particular states to pursue consistent courses of action in attempting to resolve problems for society. The state interests model demonstrates how policy elites play active roles in adopting theories of development, attempting to put together supportive coalitions, legislating reforms, and creating new bureaucratic entities. At the same time, in much of the scholarly research done to date, state interest analysis has remained almost as distant from actual decision-making situations as the class analytic and pluralist frameworks. Similarly, although the actions of policy makers can be understood from a state interests approach, the model does not provide a convincing explanation of how policy elites acquire particular preferences.

Policy Elites and Their Contexts

Our initial propositions do not easily fit within the major explanations of policy reviewed here. Society-centered approaches grant little initiative, leadership, or problem-solving capacity to policy elites, focusing instead on the activities and motivations of societal groups in accounting for the content of policy and the source of policy change and continuity. In these perspectives, policy elites mechanistically reflect societal preferences and collude with societal groups to circumvent or exploit the public interest, or, at best, broker agreements among groups. In contrast, our propositions suggest that policy elites often initiate reforms by placing issues on the agenda of government decision making. In so doing, they may shape the debate over such issues and use technical or professional expertise to influence discussions inside and outside government. Moreover, policy elites may shape reform strategies by influencing the timing and content of proposals so they are made more politically acceptable. The propositions suggest that policy elites can provide initiative, orientation, leadership, ideology, expertise, and political sensitivity to major issues of reform. None of these contributions is easily predicted from society-centered approaches to understanding public policy.

If society-centered approaches give insufficient recognition to those who work within government, some state-centered approaches tend to reduce policy decision making to a set of interactions among policy elites who are little encumbered by societal pressures, historical context, or the legacies of prior policies. Their activities correspond to rational choices or to bureaucratic games in which the stakes are personal, organizational, and positional. In contrast, our observations indicate that policy elites are always at least partially constrained by political, economic, and historical contexts. Moreover, while the stakes in decision-making situations frequently involve the power of individual policy elites, bureaucratic organizations, and the state more generally, decision makers are also influenced by ideological predispositions, their professional expertise and training, and their memories of similar prior policy situations. Thus, policy elites are individually and collectively embedded within particular historical, political, and social circumstances that shape their perceptions and actions with regard to policy choices.

In our view, specific policy choices are the result of activities that take place largely within the state and that are significantly shaped by policy elites who bring a variety of perceptions, commitments, and resources to bear on the content of reform initiatives, but who are also clearly influenced by the actual or perceived power of societal groups and interests that have a stake in reform outcomes. Our model of the policy process begins with two sets of factors. One set focuses on background characteristics of policy elites; the other emphasizes the constraints and opportunities created by the broader contexts within which they seek to accomplish their goals. These sets of factors are largely responsible for shaping the perceptions of policy elites about the urgency of reform, for signaling the "correct" solution to given policy problems, and for indicating which among a variety of "decisional criteria" will be most salient to them in selecting among policy options.

The framework, then, focuses first on a series of general factors that set the stage for particular reform initiatives. For an adequate explanation, it is important to know what policy elites bring with them—their personal attributes and goals, their ideological predispositions, their professional expertise and training, their memories of similar policy situations, their position and power resources, and their political and institutional commitments and loyalties. It is equally essential to know how contextual factors—societal pressures and interests, historical and international contexts, the bureaucratic capacity of the government, and the policy environment—shape their motivations, opportunities for reform, and perceptions of goals to be achieved. The model then shifts to the more specific conditions surrounding particular reform initiatives—circumstances of crisis or noncrisis, decision criteria, and policy characteristics—to account for instances of policy change.

PERCEPTIONS OF POLICY ELITES

It makes a difference what values, experiences, training, and commitments policy elites have when they are involved in discussions and debates about particular policy and organizational reform initiatives. Our intent is not to argue that individuals determine policy choice but that policy elites in general, including individuals among them, are significant actors in their own right in discussions of reform initiatives and that they have a nontrivial impact on the design, content, and management of reform. Thus, it is important to account for their perceptions—and the factors that influence those perceptions—in attempting to explain instances of policy reform, as suggested by a case of reform in the Gambia that will be considered in Chapter 7.

> Personalities were decisive. [Minister] Sisay was probably the only one in the government capable of successfully introducing and implementing the ERP or a similar program. His background, record, training, and relationship with the donors equipped him uniquely to head the effort, enabling him to gain the trust of the President, the public and the donors all at once. President Jawara's long relationship with the British and his general alignment with the West made him more open to the policy advice of the IMF and the World Bank. His long tenure in office and his firm hold on power gave him authority and influence. (Radelet 1988:25)

Personal Attributes and Goals

It often makes a difference who is making decisions on particular issues because individuals differ in their personal values and predispositions. Values such as the relative weight given to individual or societal "good," definitions of the public interest, and commitment to values such as democracy, rationality, modernity, and achievement can influence what specific goals for public policy are identified as important as well as how a decision maker reassesses particular needs for change. Similarly, propensities for taking risks, for seeking consensus, and for aggressiveness in confronting issues are predispositions that can influence how much change is considered appropriate and how much conflict surrounds the identification of goals. Particularly in decisions in which only a few individuals are involved, such personal characteristics can loom large in the outcome of issues being discussed.

Ideological Predispositions

Those who become active in discussions of policy reform often have acquired ideological biases that influence their perceptions of what problems are and how they should be responded to (see esp. Adler 1987). Thus, for example, ideological commitments such as those to African socialism, democratic socialism, or law and order tend to be enduring predispositions that color or influence the perceptions of particular reforms. The ideological predisposition may be diffused or focused—a strong belief that technocratic decision-making styles ought to be adopted in all situations or that land reform is the only solution to the problems of the countryside—and still influence the content of reform initiatives dealing with diverse issues.

Professional Expertise and Training

Increasingly, individuals with technical training and expertise in specific subjects are found among decision-making elites in developing countries (see, e.g., MacDougall 1976; Milne 1982; Cepeda Ulloa and Mitchell 1980). Their specialization—in economics, medicine, planning, or engineering, for example—influences how they perceive problems and what solutions they believe ought to be applied. Often, the language of discussion and debate is set by such specialists, and this may have the impact of excluding or limiting the influence of those unfamiliar with the language of, say, economics or engineering. Moreover, professional training may strongly imbue policy elites with ideas about appropriate solutions to specific problems. Whether, for example, supply distortions in basic food grains should be responded to by encouraging markets to establish price incentives or whether greater government control is required can be influenced by the particular school of thought an economist ascribes to. In some cases, the influence of professional training may amount to an ideological predisposition, as has been suggested in the case of the "Chicago boys," who determined economic policy in Chile for more than a decade and a half. More generally, professional training and experiences serve as lenses through which policy elites determine what information is relevant, what its implications are, whose views are respected or sought out, and who is engaged in the discussion of policy options. Such lenses are increasingly important as more policy-making roles are occupied by those with professional expertise.

Memories of Similar Policy Experiences

Ideological predispositions and professional expertise mean that policy elites come to discussions of policy reform with a considerable amount of perceptual baggage. Similarly, they may have accumulated experience with the success or failure or the degree of conflict and difficulty associated with making certain kinds of changes. It is not uncommon, for example, for high-level policy elites to discuss the possibility of devaluation with clear memories of the consequences—politically, socially, and economically—of previous devaluations. Similarly, current efforts to decentralize decision making in government are often colored by prior experience with the failure (or success) of such initiatives. Historical memories of this nature influence policy elites in terms of their perceptions of what works and what doesn't; what kinds of changes create the most bureaucratic headaches; which are the kind that can lead to military coups, riots in the street, or losses at the polls; or which often result in the dismissal of the official responsible for spearheading the change. Such concerns clearly influence the caution or enthusiasm with which policy elites approach discussions of new initiatives.

Position and Power Resources

Graham Allison's observation is often right in practice—where you sit frequently does determine where you stand. Policy elites come to discussions of policy reform as representatives of the organizations they head or serve and whose interests—in terms of budgets, prestige, responsibilities, and influence—they often hold dear. Their perceptions and recommendations are likely, then, to be colored by their organizational position, as well as by more general power resources such as their hierarchical position within government, their reputations as politicians and policy makers, and their access to influential others such as the president or prime minister. When such decision makers speak, therefore, they may be speaking for their ministry, their office, or the president. Considerations such as these influence their perceptions of particular reforms and they also influence the perceptions of others about the political stature and importance of the reforms.

Political and Institutional Commitments and Loyalties

Finally, policy elites are frequently also politicians and party leaders. They are often personally loyal to higher-level officials such as the president; they have often made commitments to a political party they may help lead; they are often committed to the general and more specific goals of a particular regime or its current incumbents. These factors also shape how they will perceive particular issues, how they will assess any proposed changes, and how they will weigh political and technical criteria in decision making. Policy elites thus not only often speak for bureaucratic entities, they also speak for the political leader, the party in power, or the regime.

These factors that influence the perceptions of policy elites about specific reforms are important. They may not always be knowable to outsiders, but, as evidence in our cases suggests, they help create the basic orientation of decision makers about how problems are defined and how they are most appropriately resolved. They are important in defining the background of policy elites when they confront a new reform proposal or initiate it. In addition, these elites face a series of contextual factors that shape the options available to them.

THE CONTEXTS OF POLICY CHOICE

Policy elites are never fully autonomous. Instead, they work within several interlocking contexts that confront them with issues and problems they need to address, set limits on what solutions are considered, determine what options are feasible politically, economically, and administratively, and respond to efforts to alter existing policies and institutional practices. The contexts are defined by the structure of class and interest group mobilization in the society, historical experiences and conditions, international economic and political relationships, domestic economic conditions, the administrative capacity of the state, and the impact of prior or conterminously pursued policies. While these factors are often considered to be constraints on policy elites, they can also open up opportunities for the introduction of change. These contextual factors are important because they often act at the intersection of state and society to set the agenda for policy elites, shape their perceptions of what is desirable and possible in efforts to change policy or institutional behavior, and influence the implementation and sustainability of reform initiatives. The contexts of policy choice frequently influence the perceptions, options, actions, and effectiveness of policy elites and thus are critical in explaining the emergence and unfolding of reform initiatives. Together with the perceptions of policy elites, they create the broad parameters of the policy space for any given reform initiative.

Societal Pressures and Interests

The way in which societies are divided and organized, the extent to which economic, cultural, religious, regional, and value interests are mobilized, and how efforts to affect authoritative decision making are manifested are contextual factors that have clear implications for policy choice and change. Policy elites are rarely insulated from the pressures brought to bear by organized interests in society. Frequently, in fact, they operate daily with mental maps of politically relevant divisions, organizations, class structures, and interests in their societies. They are generally well aware of an existing class structure, of important political alliances, of who is politically relevant and who is not. Thus, even when such interests are silent and unmobilized, they still play a role in shaping the perceptions of policy elites about what is feasible. More visibly, class and interest groups are often active in pressing particular issues on decision makers for action. In many developing countries—even where they are not well organized or effective in setting public agendas—they set limits on the options available to policy makers through the use of power resources such as votes, clientelistic links with government officials, control over economic resources, and ties to the military or the bureaucracy. Moreover, even when unable to influence decision making, they often intervene during implementation processes to extract resources from government or stymie efforts at change (see, e.g., Migdal 1988). These organized interests, including the specific and corporate interests of the military and civil service, are the mechanisms through which society is able to penetrate the state and shape the activities of policy elites.

Historical Context

Beyond the explicit and implicit power relationships, organizations, and interest structures in society that influence the policy process and help shape the options available to decision makers and implementers are a number of factors related to the historical circumstances particular to each country. For example, in many developing countries a legacy of colonialism has shaped the public service, has engendered enduring international economic and political relationships, and has helped define regional and ethnic divisions as well as forms of national, provincial, and local governance. The struggle for independence or later conflicts and political compromises may have defined the role and nature of the state in efforts to achieve economic development. Equally important are collective historical memories of national experiences such as wars, revolutions, invasions, coups, depressions, and the triumphs and myths surrounding great national leaders and periods of nationalist assertion and expansion.[12] These definitions and events form a backdrop of basic orientations of the state that help establish what is considered to be appropriate policy, what is an appropriate role for the state, and what values are appropriate for legitimizing policy choices. Their influence is often subtle but nevertheless real in indicating which issues and options can be considered and which are effectively off-limits because they violate norms, practices, or conditions that are embedded in the historical evolution of particular societies.

International Context

Linked closely with the historical context of Third World development is the great importance of each country's relationship to international economic and political conditions. Developing countries continue to be dependent upon and vulnerable to economic conditions such as the prices of the basic commodities they produce, the foreign exchange value of the goods they export and import, and interest rates at which they borrow capital abroad and repay debts. These factors have created complex relationships with a large variety of multilateral and bilateral institutions, many of whom have major interests in altering existing policy and organizational practice within developing countries. Dependency relations generally extend beyond those of economics to include political and military alliances that also can shape responses to policy problems. So important are these international factors that they often play a very large role in setting the agenda for policy reform initiatives, a situation particularly true of the 1980s.

Economic Conditions

Much of the economic context for development is set by international factors that are generally beyond the control of developing country governments. Linked to this, however, are domestic economic factors that also define the conditions surrounding efforts to initiate and sustain policy reform. Although they may not be directly related to the substance of any particular reform, they can significantly affect the timing and success of efforts to bring about change. The structure and productivity of agricultural and manufacturing sectors, the extent of government involvement in the economy, levels of inflation, the performance of public enterprises, exchange and interest rate structures—such factors can be critical to enhancing or diminishing opportunities for initiating policy changes and in affecting the potential to sustain reform.

Administrative Capacity

Limits are set on policy options, not only by such politically visible factors as interest groups and international economic vulnerability, but also by more mundane but still general factors such as a government's administrative capacity. This is important because it determines which policies or organizational changes can be pursued effectively. The availability of human resources, skills in particular areas, and the way the public sector is organized and how it interacts with regional and local systems of administration are important background considerations that may shape the options available to policy elites and, after decisions are made, the capacity to implement and sustain them. Such factors cannot be taken for granted in a large number of developing countries where the administrative system is characterized by wide-ranging clientelistic networks or where the capacity to penetrate to local levels with effective service delivery systems is very weak. The capacity of a government to achieve certain kinds of reforms may be seriously limited by the inability of its administrative system, or significant parts of it, to perform effectively.

Other Policies

Policy changes are introduced into situations in which prior policies have created conditions and expectations that affect the viability of new responses to public problems. Moreover, they are introduced in environments in which they are affected by other policies, pursued conterminously, that fundamentally shape their ability to achieve the goals set for them. For example, any effort to alter agricultural productivity at the sector level will be affected by macroeconomic policies relating to exchange rates and interest rates. The context of policy reform initiatives, then, includes the opportunities and constraints placed upon available options by a given policy environment.

Conclusions

Policy elites play major roles in the process of policy and organizational change. Because of this, the skills, values, and experiences they bring to reform situations are important, for they shape perceptions of what problems need to be addressed through public sector action and how they should be addressed. In addition, however, policy elites are rarely far from the influence of interacting contexts that shape their perceptions of possibilities and options and that influence the decisions they make and the capacity to pursue them. In this way, our model emphasizes that the state does not float freely above society but incorporates basic values, traditions, collective memories, conflicts, and divisions. This model makes it possible to understand policy elites as actors with ongoing concerns about policy, historically determined orientations about the role of the state in development and the scope of its responsibilities toward society, and perceptions of the constraints and contextual realities they face.

Based on our initial set of variables, we are able to assert that policy elites can have particular goals for the activities of the state. These goals are formed by a shared ideology or approach to problem solving that can be derived from the embedded orientation of the state, from the historical development of state activities and the way in which the state's role has been defined, from particular positions in government, and from personal values, ideological predispositions, professional training, and experiential learning. We can also assert that policy elites incorporate the concerns and orientations of a particular regime and are concerned to ensure its survival through their actions. Third, policy elites are never fully autonomous but are always variably constrained by societal pressures and interests, historical and international contexts, domestic economic realities, and bureaucratic capacity and compliance. These perceptions and conditions create the general context within which policy elites maneuver to craft solutions to major societal problems.

Admittedly, this view may easily overemphasize the positive and active contributions of policy elites to the creation of policy and policy change. Policy elites are not invariably heroes nor are their choices ever likely to be disinterested.[13] Reform is not necessarily viewed by them as beneficial, and they may actively try to subvert initiatives for change as well as promote them. Moreover, they can make mistakes in the policies they prescribe in terms of their economic, political, and social impact. In addition, the discussion thus far has left unanswered important questions about when policy change is likely to occur: under what conditions will policy elites have greater independence to initiate and shape responses to important policy issues? Under what conditions is change more or less likely to occur? What kind of change—incremental or radical—is likely to be pursued? These questions pose issues about the circumstances surrounding particular policy initiatives. Such circumstances can vary over time and among policy issues, accounting for different dynamics in how the issues are considered, what role policy elites assume, and the capacity of societal forces to influence decisional outcomes. Circumstances, as well

41

as the criteria adopted by policy elites in making decisions and the impact of policy characteristics, are specific to particular instances of reform and are therefore considered in detail in subsequent chapters.

In Chapter 3, we present a series of generalizations about decision making in the Third World. At this very general level, the chapter provides a broad overview of the structural and ideological factors that have, in the past, dictated that governments in developing countries assume considerable responsibility for the process of economic development and that have resulted in a characteristic pattern of centralized decision making. In turn, these factors work to increase the importance and visibility of policy elites in making decisions about reforms. The chapter also provides greater detail about the characteristics of those individuals and groups who tend to be involved in policy making and about the forms through which they attempt to influence the decision process. Subsequent chapters will turn from broader contextual issues to focus on specific reform initiatives.

CHAPTER 3

Generalizing
about Developing Country
Policy Environments

Decision makers in developing countries assume central roles in initiating, shaping, and pursuing public policies. They are frequently the most important actors in placing issues on an agenda for government action, assessing alternatives, and superintending implementation. The actions of developing country officials tend to be much more visible and central in determining outcomes than are the activities of national decision makers in many Western industrialized countries. In this chapter we examine the role of public officials in developing countries and Western industrialized nations in the policy-making and implementation process in order to establish the differences in their situations, and most specifically the relatively greater centrality of public officials in developing countries. In this book, we have set out to describe and analyze the influence, scope, and limitations of the roles assumed by these policy makers and managers in the introduction and pursuit of reform initiatives. In this chapter, we explore the structural and ideological reasons why decision makers assume such central positions in the politics of reform. We therefore present a series of generalizations about the policy environment in developing countries to serve as a background for the analysis of specific instances of reform in subsequent chapters.

In Chapter 2, we argued that specific reform initiatives do not emerge in a void, nor are they decided upon in isolation from the preexisting perceptions, experiences, and values of policy elites or conditions of the political economy. In fact, the broader context within which particular reforms are considered provides insight into the choices that are made and the processes through which change is pursued. What is important to know about the general policy environment is often subtle. Policy-making and implementation processes in many developing countries look superficially like they do in Western industrial societies. However, when looking at something as complex as decision making, a finely tuned understanding of the environment and the factors that influence the interactions among the principal players and institutions is critical. In developing countries, such insight is particularly important because structural and ideological conditions are often very different from those familiar to persons who have lived and worked only in industrialized countries.

The potential for misunderstanding the process of policy making and implementation is illustrated in a description written by an American who worked for three years as a senior adviser in a developing country ministry. Although the meeting described is a composite of several, the adjustment to a different framework for thinking about the decision process is well illustrated by his retrospective reflection on his experiences.

> One can imagine the adviser as he pondered the meeting. None of the "right" issues had been discussed, according to the theories of resource allocation and techniques for decision making in which he had been trained. No one had asked about marginal returns, alternative investments, or trade-offs or whether the project was consistent with national development priorities. Instead, the questions were along the lines of, "What did this region get last year? Do they really need three Land Rovers? Who is going to run the program? Who is going to establish the budget?" These all appear to be minor questions in view of what is taught in courses in microeconomics or in decision theory. Sooner or later, the adviser must modify his assumptions about what is central to project performance. As he does, the reality behind the policy discussions—a set of conditions, personalities, and circumstances critical to a particular environment affecting the outcome of Government programs—will become clear. After that, the decision making process will become comprehensible and rational. (Thomas 1982:116–17)

Our focus is on the similarities that exist among developing countries that tend to enhance the influence of policy elites and to explain their concerns. There are, of course, singularly important differences among the more than one hundred countries that compose the developing world, and any effort to understand policy initiatives in particular countries must be based on an appreciation of the specific historical, institutional, political, and economic contexts of each. Thus, we acknowledge the limits of the generalizations we present and the many exceptions to them. Nevertheless, we believe that as a result of a set of structural and ideological conditions, there are important similarities among developing countries that affect how policy and institutional changes are initiated, decided upon, and implemented. In particular, they are conditions that enhance the role of policy elites and managers in the policy process.

Decision makers within government emerge as central actors in the politics of reform because of the very characteristics of developing countries—uncertain information, poverty, pervasive state influence in the economy, centralization of decision making. These characteristics in turn are a result of a legacy of colonial rule, the nature of state-building and nation-building activities, and structural vulnerability to international and domestic economic and political forces. The generalized picture we develop, then, is one of centralized and pervasive states with roots in structural conditions, along with considerable vulnerability to present economic and political circumstances. This picture is useful for understanding the concerns of decision makers, such as the assumption of autonomy, the fear of economic and political vulnerability, and the knowledge of uncertainty. These themes are developed in the following pages.

Characteristics of Developing Countries: Structures of Uncertainty

Decision makers in developing countries face a set of informational, demographic, and economic characteristics that increase their prominence in the policy process at the same time that they limit their ability to make well-informed decisions about the development of their countries. These conditions are apparent in a quantitative profile that describes general demographic and economic characteristics of these countries. Each of the quantitative indicators has real consequences for the tasks assumed by decision makers, as we suggest later.

The availability of information and access to it have long been associated with power. As governments are required to make increasingly complex decisions that affect the economic viability of whole societies, availability and access have increased in political importance (see, e.g., Cepeda Ulloa and Mitchell 1980; MacDougall 1976; Milne 1982; O'Donnell 1973). In developing countries, information, critical in the decision-making process, is generally in short supply and is often unreliable.

A shortage of data means that policy makers have much less information than they need and that what they have is often of questionable reliability. As a result, they must frequently rely more on intuition and experience than on solid information when making decisions. Intuitive decisions tend to be heavily subjective, a characteristic well described by Oliver Saasa.

> Those traditional models that emphasize rationality [in decision making] are clearly inappropriate for developing countries. . . . The information that is available to the policy-makers may not only be inadequate but could also be highly unreliable both at the more objective, quantifiable level and at the subjective level of data concerning societal value preferences. . . . Given the non-availability of adequate and reliable data in these countries, policy-makers lack the capacity successfully to project their plans into a highly unpredictable future. (Saasa 1985:314)

The problem of inadequate data also means that challenges to government decisions are easier, in the absence of concrete evidence, and likely to be more politically oriented. As a result, political power tends to be the central determinant of policy outcomes and implementation. At the same time, as we will see later, decision makers in developing countries are required to decide on a much wider range of issues than is characteristic of their counterparts in more developed countries.

Not only is information problematic, the conditions of underdevelopment exacerbate the uncertainties facing decision makers. Low income, reliance on agricultural production, and the emergence of more complex urban societies often add up to large demands made on the public sector and limited resources with which to respond to them. The widely used term *developing countries* connotes a series of important similarities among a large group of countries.[1] Basically, of course, the term refers to a group of countries with low GNP per capita compared to industrial market economies. Although virtually all of these countries have made progress in achieving economic growth in the last twenty to forty years, there is still an identifiable gap that separates them from the industrialized countries.[2] According to the World Bank, in 1988 the forty-two countries it classifies as low income had an average per capita GNP of $320; the thirty-seven lower-middle-income countries, $1,380; and the seventeen upper-middle-income countries, $3,240; while in the nineteen countries classified as high-income economies, per capita GNP was $17,080 (World Bank 1990:178–79). Poverty, then, defines basic conditions in most developing countries.

The share of agriculture in GDP in developing countries also sets them apart from more industrialized countries. This share varies from 35 percent in low-income countries, to 22 percent in lower-middle-income countries, to 10 percent in upper-middle-income countries, as compared to 3 percent in industrial market economies. At the same time, agriculture and other raw materials are extremely important to the economies of all developing countries, not only for the extent of the labor force involved, but also because of their importance in their international trade. In low-income countries in 1986, for example, 44 percent of merchandise exports originated in the primary sector. In lower-middle-income countries, it was 72 percent; and in middle-income countries, 41 percent. This indication of the importance of the primary sector in the economies of developing countries takes on added meaning because, frequently, exports are dominated by one or two commodities, international prices for such commodities tend to be highly volatile, and, for many of them, prices tend to decline over time relative to manufactured goods. The result is extensive vulnerability to world market prices and their trends over time.

Most developing countries continue to be predominantly rural, but they are also experiencing important population and economic changes associated with the emergence of more complex urban societies. As agriculture declines as a proportion of GDP, urban-centered services and production increase. In 1988, in low-income countries, 75 percent of the population was rural; in lower-middle-income countries, 44 percent was rural; in upper-middle-income countries, 38 percent of the population was rural; while in high-income economies, 22 percent was rural (World Bank 1990:238–39). In the developing world, the countries that are most rural tend to be located in Africa, also the site of many of the poorest countries in the world. In the mid-1980s, for example, the urban population in Africa ranged from about 2 percent of the total population in Burundi to 54 percent in Mauritius and 56 percent in South Africa. Asian countries had anywhere from 2 percent of their populations in urban areas, the case for Bhutan, to 64 percent, in South Korea.[3] Latin American countries generally have the most urban populations, ranging from 27 percent in Haiti to 85 percent in Uruguay in the mid-1980s, as well as having the largest portion of countries in the upper-middle-income category. With changes in the structure of production and the distribution of the population, the percentage of GDP generated by services tends to rise, from 32 percent in low-income countries, to 46 percent in lower-middle-income countries, to 50 percent in upper-middle-income countries, to 61 percent in industrial market economies (World Bank 1988:226–27). These trends are illustrated in figure 3.1. More urban societies require greater outlays for public services, protection, and social insurance, thus increasing demands on government budgets.

The conditions of underdevelopment that particularly characterize those countries in the low-income and lower-middle-income categories, but also those in the upper-middle-income category—low per capita income, agriculture-dependent economies, large rural populations, the emergence of more complex societies—are important to the work of policy makers and managers. They increase expectations that the principal job of policy makers is to address the critical issues of stimulating

47

FIGURE 3.1
Structure of Production at Varying Stages
of Economic Growth

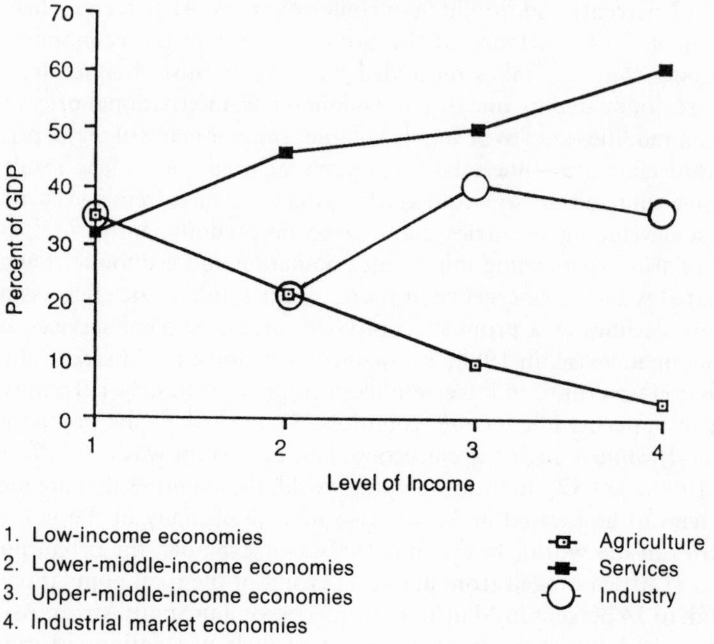

1. Low-income economies
2. Lower-middle-income economies
3. Upper-middle-income economies
4. Industrial market economies

-□- Agriculture
-■- Services
-○- Industry

Source: World Bank, World Development Report 1988, Table 3, pp. 226–27.

economic growth and distribution and rapidly expanding social welfare services to the needy population. This job description is ambitious, and the skills it requires are extensive. At the same time, however, conditions of poverty and reliance on relatively primary products mean limited resources with which to carry out the ambitious objectives of development policy making. The availability of those resources will also vary widely, depending on climatic, technological, and international trade factors.

For much of the period after the Depression of the 1930s and World War II, policy makers in the large majority of countries attempted to deal with problems and uncertainties such as these by expanding state control of the economy. Few would now dispute the statement that the state intervenes much more actively in the economies of developing countries than in Western industrialized ones. Edward S. Mason summarized the dominant approach followed in most developing countries (and its limitations) in 1958.

48

In those countries actively seeking development—and this is almost the whole of the underdeveloped world—government tends to be the principal agent of development. Not only is the share of government in total investment large, but public action tends to impinge on the development process at many points. But finally, we would do well to recognize that there is frequently a large gap between what government is trying to do and what in fact gets done. (Mason 1958:12)

Over the years, state intervention in the economy has tended to increase, to the point that it is possible to argue that "the role of the state in most contemporary developing economies is pervasive" (Perkins 1988:4). There are four principal ways in which this control is established. First, "the public sector often dominates capital formation. . . . This is true across a range of countries that consider themselves both socialist and capitalist" (4). Second, state-owned enterprises dominate many key sectors of developing economies. Third, nationalized enterprises frequently control banking and finance. Fourth, "even when the modern sector is privately owned and managed, private owners and managers are generally dominated by government controls" (4–9).[4]

Given the large role assumed by the state in economic management and development initiatives, it should not be surprising that for many of the developing countries the public sector is the largest employer, and in some cases the employer of last resort. This is particularly true in Africa, where parastatal organizations play a very large role in many economies. For example, in Zambia, employment in parastatal organizations (not including regular government service) represented 28 percent of total wage employment in the country in the 1970s (Haslet 1976:6). In Kenya, at the end of the 1970s, parastatal employment was equal to total employment in the central government, itself a very large employer (Republic of Kenya 1979). International Labor Office (ILO) data show that public service employment in some developing countries increased three to four times faster in the 1970s than in industrialized countries and two to three times faster than the growth rate of the general population (World Bank 1987:102). Thus, developing country governments not only control critical levers in the economy, they also directly affect the livelihoods of a significant proportion of the population. Decisions made by policy makers and managers therefore assume major importance for economic conditions at both household and national levels in those countries.

Information is limited, needs are great, resources are scarce, and responsibilities are extensive. These structural characteristics that place decision makers in critical roles in developing countries are reinforced by the extensive centralization of decision-making responsibilities. In almost all developing countries, national governments, highly centralized

TABLE 3.1

Indicators of Mobility and Information Flow by Country, Classified
by Level of GDP

	Low Income	Middle Income	Industrialized
Passenger cars per 000 pop.	2.0	26.8	356.5
Newspapers per 000 pop.	16.4	50.8	331.3
Radios per 000 pop.	92.8	153.8	1,085.8
Adult literacy percentage of pop.	51.0%	65.2%	98.9%
AGE DISTRIBUTION OF POPULATION			
Percentage of pop.			
0–14 years	37.2	41.0	22.4
15–64 years	58.7	55.3	66.0
65+ years	4.1	3.8	11.6

Source: World Bank, World Bank Tables, vol. 2, Social Data (Washington, D.C.: Johns
Hopkins University Press for World Bank, 1984), Social Data Sheet 2, pp. 148–49.

in large capital cities, make most of the decisions that affect people down
to the most remote village. One indicator of the relative importance of
central governments compared to local governments is the share of public
sector employment accounted for by each. Data presented by Smoke
(1988:3) show that in the Organization for Economic Cooperation and
Development (OECD) countries, local government averages 11 percent
of total public sector employment. In a number of member countries,
the figure runs as high as 20 to 25 percent. This stands in contrast to
developing countries, where the share of public sector employment accounted for by local government averages 4.5 percent.

Centralization of decision-making responsibilities tends to increase the
government's power and decrease its accountability to the population.
This is so for several reasons. First, we have already seen that the population of most developing countries is heavily rural. A population that
is both scattered and remote from government is less likely to have an
important influence on government than an urban population. Second,
knowledge of what government is doing is difficult to acquire. Dramatic
differences in access to communications are demonstrated in table 3.1,
which shows the passenger cars per thousand of population, the newspapers circulated per thousand, and the radios per thousand of population, for low-income, middle-income, and industrialized nations. These

data suggest that the population of developing countries, particularly that in rural areas, gets much less information as to what government is doing than their counterparts in the industrialized nations.

Poverty explains much of this situation, because it tends to be highly related to levels of literacy and school enrollments. In the early 1980s, for example, adult literacy was 51 percent in low-income countries and 65.2 percent in middle-income countries, compared to 98.9 percent in industrialized countries (World Bank 1984:148–49). The figures for secondary education are even more striking: the enrollment ratio for low-income countries was 34 percent of the appropriate age group; for middle-income countries, 49 percent; and for industrialized countries, 93 percent (World Bank 1988:280–81).[5] Low levels of education limit the extent and complexity of communication among the population about the issues and problems facing the countries. This can easily translate into feelings of powerlessness among the least informed and most isolated sectors of the population.

Finally, the age distribution of the population is significantly different in developing than in industrialized countries, and this tends to reinforce the aloofness of decision makers from their societies. Table 3.1 shows that significantly larger proportions of the population in low- and middle-income countries are fourteen years of age or less. This means that the politically aware and active percentage of the population is also lower in developing countries than in industrialized ones. A large rural population, limited communications, low levels of literacy, and a limited adult population tend to mean that a much larger percentage of the population is out of touch with what is happening, especially when government is strongly centralized. This inevitably enhances the role of policy makers while tending to isolate them from critical information about what is occurring in their societies.

Centralization of decision making generally has structural roots in the colonial past. Despite variations among regions and countries, most developing countries had centralized political systems imposed on them from outside for significant periods of their history. These systems were centralized to enable colonial powers to ensure the stable rule that was essential for the exploitation of the colonies (Migdal 1988; Young 1986). Further, most have been subject to a form of economic domination by one or more of the industrialized countries (Smith 1986; dos Santos 1970). Finally, almost all gained independence more recently than the industrialized nations. Most of the countries in Asia gained independence in the 1940s and 1950s, while in Africa, most countries became independent only in the 1960s. This pattern of recent emergence from colonial domination is not true for Latin America, where most countries became independent in the early nineteenth century. For many, though, the emergence from domination to full recognition as members of a world community has taken place only in the last forty years. The era of independence started not only with limited resources, but also with traditions of centralized and nonrepresentative government.

For these countries, a primary challenge at the moment of independence was national integration (Young 1986; Young 1976; Frankel 1978). In Africa and many Asian countries—India is a good example—multiethnic societies had been pieced together and controlled by colonial regimes; frequently, they existed as nations on maps and in international relations but not in the identities of their populations (see, e.g., Jackson and Rosberg 1986; Migdal 1988; Kasfir 1986). With independence, government leaders became preoccupied with holding these diverse societies together and forging national political and economic systems. Centralized power and decision making was, for them, almost an imperative, as decentralization raised the clear threat of political dissolution and conflict.

The structural and historical conditions of underdevelopment that have been reviewed here tend to increase the role of government in the economy and to centralize decision making in national governments. These characteristics in turn enhance the influence of decision makers in government, increasing the range of issues they deal with and the impact of their decisions on their societies. The location of the population, a shortage of highly trained people, and the legacy of colonialism have promoted highly centralized political systems with limited communication with their populace. This translates into a very different policy-making and implementation environment than is found in Western industrialized nations.

Ideological Paradigms
and Legacies of the Past:
The Role of the State in Developing Countries

As we have seen, the state in most developing countries has assumed a major role in guiding the course of economic and social development; decision making has tended to be highly centralized and to deal principally with the most extensive issues concerning economic growth and welfare. In turn, the responsibilities of policy makers have been correspondingly large and influential. This situation, derived in large part from the structural and historical conditions just reviewed, is also buttressed by strongly held ideas among policy makers about the appropriate role the state ought to assume in guiding the course of development.

Many developing countries gained independence at a time when governments all over the world were expanding the range of activities considered appropriate for states to undertake. For example, in the United States, the experience of the New Deal, a formative period in the country's history with clear implications about the relationships between the state and society, as well as World War II and the emergence of the country as a world power, increased the size and centrality of government to economic and social systems. The Soviet Union became a world power at the same time, while in China a major revolution redefined the relationship between state and citizenry. The welfare state in the United States and the rise of communism as a major anticolonial force and a model for revolutionary development emerged as powerful ideas just as the process of independence began for many countries.

After World War II, the anticolonial movement in Africa and Asia gathered force. India, whose independence struggles had captured worldwide attention in the 1930s, was a leader of the movement. When India achieved independence in August of 1947, the country became a symbol for other colonies. It became the model for those trying to gain independence or chart national policy in newly established countries; India's leaders became model statesmen to a generation of leaders who helped achieve independence in other countries. Not incidentally, India had a group of articulate economists who created a planning commission and argued for the necessity for central planning in a developing economy. An early chairman of India's Planning Commission, D. R. Gadgil, wrote in 1955, for example, that it was "only a very rich country like the United States of America which [could] afford to talk of free enterprise and even indulge in it and not suffer economically" (see Mason 1958:5). This view became influential among many leaders of newly independent developing countries. In fact, many of them had been trained at the London School of Economics in the 1930s, when the dominant ideology had been that of state socialism.

This development model, as strongly articulated in India, was adopted by other countries and their leaders, particularly the ex-colonies of Asia, Africa, and the Caribbean region. Kwame Nkrumah, the Ghanaian leader and a major figure in the African anticolonial movement, was deeply influenced by the Indian experience, as was Sukarno in Indonesia, to name only two. In Latin America, where the independence struggles of Asia and Africa were less relevant, the postwar years witnessed the widespread adoption of an import-substituting model of development that called for stimulation and guidance by a strongly interventionist state.

The most influential view of the 1940s, 1950s, and 1960s, then, indicated that the only way that new states, short of capital and human resources, could make rapid economic progress was for the state to allocate those resources. It was also argued that because there were severe limits on the numbers of trained people, the best educated had to be attracted to the central government to manage the economy. Moreover, it was frequently argued that the only way in which a state with an impoverished populace could keep profit-seeking entrepreneurs from exploiting the poor was for the state to take on many economic responsibilities to ensure greater equity than a capitalist society could provide. The state thus took on a large regulatory role, on the assumption that this would help prevent capitalist exploitation of the poor. Frequently, particularly in former British colonies such as India, Pakistan, Ghana, and Kenya, the state's capacity to assume this role was considerable because it had inherited a powerful elite civil service from the colonial period.

Interest in this model of state-led development was not exclusive to developing countries. A literature and academic field of development economics and of political development emerged in Western academic circles also. This literature was consistent with views and practices in developing countries that planning, central economic management, and state-building were important factors in spearheading rapid economic growth. Consistent with these views, international agencies such as the World Bank, the United Nations Development Programme, and major bilateral donors insisted on giving aid to the central governments that were assumed to be "engines of development." Soon, for a country to be considered worthy of aid, it had to have a development plan, and this in turn stimulated the widespread growth of national planning agencies.

In practice, planning as a way of achieving efficient and equitable allocation of scarce resources became the norm for most of the developing world. From the 1950s until the late 1970s, most aid agencies were unwilling to support development projects that were not included in the national development plan and, for them, a five-year plan became the sine qua non identifying a well-run developing country. Inevitably, there emerged a literature on the techniques of development planning.[6] The World Bank's Economic Development Institute began offering courses in planning, and the UNDP held conferences on planning. Thus, Western theory and practice fully supported the political and economic choices of the developing countries in the three decades that followed World War II.[7] An important consequence of this experience was that in many of the ex-colonial nations, particularly the British and French colonies, the brightest and best-educated people were attracted to the civil service, which, given the development model that was adopted, became the repository of some of the most powerful positions in these nations. Other than the top political leaders, politicians were often considerably less powerful than civil servants and were frequently bypassed by them in making public policy (Abernethy 1988).

A logical concomitant of planning was regulation, licensing, and price controls. In the 1950s, many developing countries introduced systems regulating the private sector. Permits were necessary to start businesses; approvals were necessary to get raw materials; imports were licensed and regulated through the allocation of foreign exchange, high tariffs, and import taxes; and exchange rates were kept at artificial levels that resulted in overvalued local currencies. Even exports were controlled and taxed in some cases. Prices of critical goods were also regulated. Basic food commodities were often sold at subsidized rates through government ration shops in the name of equity.[8] Rather than allow market mechanisms to control foreign exchange, it was usually distributed bureaucratically in the name of high-priority development activities. Each of these activities created government agencies with the power to allocate critical resources that were in short supply. Ultimately, the state-led development model created large and expansion-oriented governments and high levels of public sector employment.

State-owned enterprises, along with subsidies and benefits provided to private entrepreneurs, were a mechanism for assuring that critical goods were produced domestically (see, e.g., Trebat 1981; Saulniers 1988). Frequently, power, transport, and heavy manufacturing were produced and controlled by the state and their products or services provided to the public at heavily subsidized rates. Extraction of natural resources was more often than not handled by public enterprises. In many countries, state trading corporations or boards also handled significant portions of commercial retail trade. Most of these enterprises operated at a loss, but they seemed to serve critical political functions and to be consistent with national economic goals that, at the time, were seen as more important than economic efficiency. For example, in a study of food policy in East Africa, Thomas (1982) noted that commercial retail trade was controlled by Asians, but that national goals included Africanization as a top political priority. Policy makers were therefore fully willing to establish state corporations to handle the purchase, movement, storage, and commercial sales of basic food commodities in order to ensure that these critical functions were controlled by Africans.[9] Moreover, the existence of many state corporations and boards provided the opportunity to spread the benefits of independence among the many ethnic groups represented and to provide a balance of political power—and thus to help achieve another important government priority, national integration (Thomas 1982).

Aid donors supported the establishment and operation of state-owned enterprises and many semi-autonomous agencies outside the regular structure of government. After some years of experience, many donors had come to despair at the prospect of getting bureaucracies in developing countries to work in the way the donors deemed appropriate; they came to believe that the answer was to avoid line bureaucracies (Abernethy

1988). The donors actively promoted the formation of boards, authorities, and state corporations for many years. Moreover, the foreign aid system buttressed the growth of the state. The major flows of resources, whether bilateral or multilateral, were channeled through the government system. Even private aid—only a fraction of public aid—often had to be approved by the government of the receiving country. In many cases, aid represented a significant source of income for the country, and the fact that it all flowed through the central government served to strengthen state control over the development process and the economy.

If the widely adopted model placed the state in the role of the dominant and orchestrating agent of development, it assumed that role despite some significant shortcomings. State planning and regulation of the economy require large quantities of highly trained technical personnel. As already noted, human resources were in very short supply in most developing countries. The combination of limited human resources and high demands for these resources in the central government had the effect of concentrating talented people in the central government and giving them a stake in the persistence and expansion of its power. Moreover, although the stated objectives of state leadership of the economy were efficiency, equity, and the efficient use of scarce human resources, the activities assumed by the state began to provide significant benefits to the economic and bureaucratic elites who ran the systems. As the state grew and its control over economic resources increased, so also did the capacity of politicians and public officials to use these resources to reward loyal supporters, to put together political coalitions, and to provide benefits to favored individuals. State control of the economy yielded political control, privilege—previously the province of the colonial masters—and personal gain.

Frequently, the planners and the elites who managed the central government were trained abroad, and their work and personal life gave them little understanding of the poor who formed the bulk of the population. In fact, state actions often did little to promote the welfare or economic interests of much of the population, especially those in rural areas. To the contrary, terms of trade between agriculture and industrial sectors in most developing countries strongly favored industry.[10] Rural populations were taxed to support the development of the urban and industrial economy. In many ways, the more dependent they became on the market, the more likely their interests were to be subordinated to the strong state (see esp. Hyden 1983; Bates 1981; Grindle 1986a; Migdal 1988). In response, the poor often tried to create barriers to protect themselves from exploitation, such as parallel markets to circumvent government control and strategic retreats into subsistence. Ironically, then, the more power became concentrated in the central government, the less able it became to assert control over large segments of the population. This was particularly the case with many very rural countries.[11] As a result of this phenomenon, the state in many developing countries became uniquely powerful while at the same time strikingly vulnerable.

Power and Vulnerability: The Concerns of Government

We have presented an image of a powerful state, one that controls instruments that enable it to influence and manipulate the economic system. It is centralized and subject to relatively little scrutiny from much of its populace, which often tends to be remote geographically, educationally, and informationally from the centers of national power. Internally, it directs its officials through powerful hierarchical controls. Such governments can employ the powers of government to limit freedom of the press or their critics or to create new programs or activities in response to the wishes of powerful individuals with a freedom that must be envied by the leaders of many industrialized country governments. Nevertheless, power over the state apparatus does not necessarily ensure the strength of the regime. Developing country governments are frequently very vulnerable to challenge.

In the absence of established systems and traditions, constitutional or other, reinforced by adherence over time, that regulate political competition and changes of power, the legitimacy of state actions is always open to dispute. Challenges to the right of regimes to remain in power can emerge easily. The view that coups take place with great regularity in developing countries is probably overblown, but it is based on the record of vulnerability of these regimes (Jackson and Rosberg 1986; Decalo 1976; Lowenthal and Fitch 1986). Compare, for example, the situation of the president of the United States with that of the president of the Philippines. In 1990, both countries had broadly similar constitutions, and both had pluralistic political systems. However, the Philippines has had four different constitutions since independence in 1946, compared to one in two hundred years for the United States. There have been regular elections in both countries, but in the Philippines, President Aquino faced five coup attempts during her first four years in office. She therefore had to be constantly alert for attempts to overthrow her government and had to make repeated concessions to those in the military who were her chief adversaries. President Bush faces no such threat. He is virtually certain to complete his four years in office and can compete for reelection under a well-established system, a certainty Philippines presidents cannot look forward to. On the other hand, President Aquino had considerably greater capacity to allocate government resources and control the instruments of government at her command. A U.S. president might well view this capacity with envy.

The issues that decision makers in developing countries are most concerned about therefore tend to differ significantly from those of policy makers in industrialized countries. For example, in developing countries, national integration remains a central concern of policy elites. Ethnic, religious, and ideological conflicts continue to threaten the integrity of the state and continue to require the close attention of national leadership. The task of state-building continues to be a fundamental preoccupation of the developing country governments (Young 1986; Migdal 1988). Issues such as the role of the military or the development of legitimate constitutions, as well as national development, are also of deep concern to most governments. Although it is frequently observed that, with independence, colonial law-and-order governments had to become development-oriented public sectors, a closer look at the actual tasks of these governments suggests that the role of maintaining civil order and state integrity continued to be, in fact, a primary preoccupation. Beyond maintaining the integrity of the state, such governments must also maintain the regime in power, and reliance on constitutional legitimacy and process is not sufficient to accomplish this. Therefore, the policy deliberations and reform decisions of public officials must constantly take into account the vulnerability of the regime and the effect of any change in policy on its political fortunes. Much of decision makers' attention is devoted to attempting to satisfy and manipulate critical elite groups such as the military, the bureaucracy, leaders of ethnic groups, and religious leaders. This problem of maintaining a coalition of support is also a source of vulnerability for many governments that otherwise appear very strong, given the instruments of policy they control and the hierarchical authority they wield.

Finally, many governments exist in a climate of real uncertainty. We have mentioned the frequent absence of established political systems that provide reliable means for sharing and changing power and the constant vulnerability of economic systems. Because they are often dependent on international markets for a few primary commodities, or because their manufactured exports are often destined for markets in one or two large countries, changes in prices, consumer preferences, or import restrictions in high-income countries can have a devastating economic impact. Economic vulnerability was exacerbated in the 1970s and 1980s because of high energy prices, low commodity prices, and rising international debt.

To political and economic factors, of course, must be added the natural environment of uncertainty. While natural disasters are probably no more frequent in developing countries than in industrialized ones, they generally impose higher costs in developing countries because the infrastructure is of lower quality and more vulnerable to earthquakes, floods, or storms, and thus the consequences in human suffering tend to be greater. Disasters such as famine are more frequent because of the fragility of economic systems and of the basic physical and social infrastructure; and over the last twenty years, military conflicts have been far more prevalent in developing countries. What may be most important is that economic vulnerability and the shallow foundation of legitimacy on which many governments rest means that a disaster of any significance leaves them open to severe challenge by their opponents. Rarely do industrialized nations' governments fall as the result of conflict or disaster, but such occurrences have regularly been the basis for serious challenges to the existing regime in many developing countries. Few policy elites are unaware of this vulnerability.

Policy Elites: Who Are They?

We use the term *policy elites* throughout this book to refer to those who have official positions in government and whose responsibilities include making or participating in making and implementing authoritative decisions for society. Depending on what particular policy is being considered, the composition of the relevant policy elite will be distinct. If the issue is reorganizing a ministry of health, the most prominent actors are likely to be the minister of health and her principal division chiefs. In contrast, a devaluation is likely to involve a policy elite composed of the president or prime minister, the minister of finance, the director of the central bank, and probably a small corps of high-level technocrats. Despite these differences in the makeup of the policy elite for specific issues, some generalizations can be made. In a situation in which government is unlikely to be broadly representative and power tends to be highly centralized, the number of authoritative and influential positions in government tends to be limited, and those who play important roles in the policy process often have much in common.

HEADS OF STATE AND MINISTERS

Central among those in government who have important policy-making roles are the head of state and the executive bureaucracy. Given the importance of maintaining the government in office in a context of great uncertainty, the head of state tends to be heavily involved in almost all important decisions. In fact, the more vulnerable the regime, the more likely it is that decision making will involve the president or prime minister, or a close associate, adviser, or political deputy, usually in the office of the president. Such advisers often have long histories of close association with the chief executive, and their loyalty may have been cemented through political, professional, social, and even kinship ties.

In addition to the head of state and his political household, members of the cabinet are closely involved in making important decisions. Some ministers have close political, economic, or personal ties to the executive, but may also have been selected for their technical and managerial skills to fill important positions such as that of finance minister. Sometimes ministers represent a coalition of powerful elite groups. In many African countries, it is necessary for the major tribal groups to have a member in high echelons of government. Regional representation in the cabinet may also be important in countries where regional differences are cause for political tensions. Other high-level decision makers include the heads of some of the more powerful state-owned corporations, semi-government agencies, and other such bodies. The heads of such organizations are influential in part because of the economic or political importance of the enterprises they lead, but also because they may represent ethnic, regional, or economic elite interests in government. At times, they have been drawn from the president's personal household (Thomas 1982: 126).

The Executive Bureaucracy

As indicated, the executive bureaucracy in most developing countries plays a very significant role in the policy process. In many former colonial countries of Africa and Asia, the civil service is particularly powerful, because it was built on the colonial model of a small elite group primarily responsible for political and economic affairs in a country (Abernethy 1988). Although a national political structure emerged to take formal power in the independence process, the civil service still offers a career that attracts ambitious and well-trained people because it is secure and provides opportunities for real power and influence. In Latin America, a strongly institutionalized civil service never developed, except occasionally in isolated pockets such as the foreign service. Bureaucratic positions are filled by appointment, and careers may last only as long as the incumbent administration or regime, although many bureaucrats retain executive positions for long periods (Grindle 1977). Despite the more political and less permanent appointment process, the highly centralized nature of decision making means these officials are as powerful as high-level civil servants elsewhere. They may, however, be more dependent on the political favor of ministers and chief executives.

In those countries where there is a formal civil service, it usually has power rivaling that of the political establishment. Its power is derived from its capacity to operate the government, from its status, and from the fact that, while the political leadership may change, the civil servants remain in place and generally know the complexities of governing more fully than do the political leadership. In many countries they sit in the senior positions in ministries and run the organizations on a day-to-day basis. They are frequently the ones who deal with aid donors and take charge of planning and budgeting. In some cases their staffs do whatever analytical work is done, and they see that proposed changes are cleared through the political system.

In countries in which ministers are drawn from the legislature, much of their time is spent interpreting government policies and actions to the legislature, a role that leaves much of the policy initiation and supervision to their nominal deputies in the civil service. This system has provided stability and government continuity in situations of extensive political instability and regime change. Efforts to democratize the civil service in some countries have changed its complexion in recent years, lowering barriers to entry, increasing its size, and lowering the standards of the service (Abernethy 1988). Where this has occurred, the power of the civil service vis-à-vis the political system has been reduced. In Pakistan, for instance, President Bhutto broke the Civil Service of Pakistan into several more specialized services, making it possible to alter high entry standards and to more than double its size. In Kenya after independence, many expatriates were either retained in the civil service or were hired from the outside. Over time, however, and certainly by the mid-1970s, most of the civil service had been Africanized. Expatriates were found only in advisory positions, and admission to the service had acquired important political objectives.

As governments became increasingly involved in managing their economies, and as the problems faced by governments increasingly came to require expert analysis and advice, the number of technocratic roles in government also increased dramatically. This trend became noticeable in the 1970s and extremely apparent in the 1980s, when issues of macroeconomic management and extensive interaction with donor agencies over issues of debt and structural adjustment dominated government agendas. In many cases, presidents, prime ministers, and ministers, as well as their staffs, were required to understand the language and analytic techniques of economists in order to deal with critical economic problems facing the countries. Expertise, particularly in economics, became an added reason for centralizing power and decision making, and those without such expertise often found themselves excluded or marginalized from policy discussions (Cepeda Ulloa and Mitchell 1980).

LEGISLATORS

Notably absent in most discussions of policy making in developing countries are elected representatives. Legislatures exist in virtually all such countries, generally the result of a constitutional mandate and a desire to demonstrate democratic legitimacy. Legislators often play extremely important roles in holding fragile political systems together by ensuring that local, ethnic, or class interests figure in resource allocation decisions and in mediating political conflict (see Kasfir 1986; Nelson 1979). However, the arena in which these activities occur is generally not policy making but implementation, when decisions about specific resource allocations can be influenced and regional, ethnic, class, or other interests can be served directly. Legislators also tend to be marginalized from policy making because of their backgrounds, lack of experience in managing government and dealing with international organizations, and lower levels of education compared to members of the civil service or executive bureaucracy. At times, bureaucracies will use legislative approval to legitimize their actions but will keep the legislators distant from actual decision-making councils. Legislators may have the capacity to raise questions, and occasionally they can impose vetoes on some actions, but rarely do they have any sustained decision-making power compared to the executive or the public bureaucracy. Usually, they are informed and actions are legitimized by them only after decisions are made. There are many examples of governments having to ride out protests in the legislature, but usually "they" come to accept what has been decided before "the government" moves ahead with its plans.

SOCIETAL INTERESTS

Thus far, we have focused our attention on the critical role assumed by policy elites in the decision-making process. However, their preferences and activities are not immune from the power and influence of societal interests. In every society there are groups that wish to influence the actions of government in their favor. These may range from the desire of a specific group to win favors for its enterprise to citizens who have ideologically based views on questions over which the state apparatus has great influence. How these interests exert pressure on government for the actions they want is an important part of the process of government. In this realm there are often important differences between developing country and industrialized country governments. These differences derive from the fact that organizational interests and specific groups are much more institutionalized in the industrialized countries, and the dispersion of power within government, particularly through active legislatures and regulatory bureaucracies, offers more formal access to interest groups. Whatever the issue, interest groups play an identifiable and significant role in articulating citizen and organizational interests in the industrialized states. In developing countries, in contrast, the link between societal interests and the decision-making process is more elusive.

Extensive organized interest activity tends to be less clearly defined in developing countries than in the industrialized democracies of the West. Large portions of the population—peasants and urban shantytown residents, for instance—are generally not organized for sustained political activity. Many authoritarian regimes in the Third World actively discourage representation of societal interests through formally constituted interest groups. In some cases, elite organizations—the ubiquitous national chamber of manufacturers or the national agricultural society, for instance—may be well organized and vociferous, but in fact they wield their real political influence behind the scenes in informal interactions with political leaders, not through votes or more visible lobbying activities. In other cases, the most important economic interests in a society may not even be formally organized. In some cases, organizations will lack access to policy makers or even the capacity to control their followers or to exert pressure on the decision-making process. Elsewhere, organized groups may actually be dependent clientele organizations of bureaucratic agencies or of particular political leaders, with little capacity to press a policy agenda on their patrons in government.

Most important, societal interests are often likely to be represented through informal processes rather than through more public forms of lobbying. A relatively closed decision-making process and elite-centered politics leave wide scope for pressures to be exerted on the policy-making process through informal and nonpublic channels. Political understandings with the military about the changes that will be tolerated in development policies or budgetary allocations, unspoken recognition of the disruptive capacities of organized groups or economic interests, the implicit power of foreign interests, and private deals struck in informal encounters with political leaders often loom large in explaining the political rationale for particular policy choices. This suggests that formal structures for the representation of interests, formal rules, and formal organizations tell only part of the story. "Interests" clearly exist in developing countries, of course, but the extent to which they are or can be formally constituted to represent goals of a membership, and their capacity to gain access to the state, need always to be specified empirically. In many cases, "barriers to entry" are high, and any assumptions about democratic responsiveness need to be scrutinized carefully.

Business Interests

Which interests are policy elites most likely to be aware of and most likely to respond to? Any list drawn up to answer this question would probably include industrial elites, religious leaders, the military, the press, and labor. Often, however, the power of these groups is distinct from what would be expected based on the experience of industrial countries. Business and commercial interests are a good example of this. In industrialized capitalist societies, these tend to be the best-funded and best-organized interests. They tend to be less organized and less powerful in many developing countries. The traditional statist orientation of many governments generally includes a serious suspicion of private business and the profit motive. As a result, business organizations are often viewed as self-serving and antiegalitarian. Uma Lele, in her study of rural development in Africa, comments on the public view of private food traders, for instance. "There is a widespread belief that traditional trade channels are inefficient, exploitative, and generally anti-social" (Lele 1975:101). In parts of Africa and Asia, this attitude is reinforced by the low status accorded to those in business. This attitude is considerably less true in Latin America, where the economic elite is composed of wealthy and even aristocratic entrepreneurs who disparage politics and public officials. Outside of Latin American, business people tend to be less educated and less powerful than their counterparts in industrial societies, and they are often seen as engaged in activities that are destructive of the common good of society. Having pointed out the relatively limited power of business as an organized interest, especially in many parts of Asia and Africa, it must be made clear that individual business people do carry enormous influence, but more as specific individuals than as a group. Through long-established success and accumulated wealth, some gain power and influence, but these are based on individual circumstance more than on organized business as an interest group.

Religious Elites

Religious elites are powerful in many developing countries and are able to wield considerable influence on policy choices. Obvious examples are the Catholic church in Latin America and the Islamic leaders in the Middle East (see, e.g., Levine 1981). In divided societies where religion is at the heart of the conflict, the role of the clergy in encouraging or discouraging religious conflict is often critical. Religious elites also play major roles in discussion of nonreligious issues. On issues such as birth control, the church (both Catholic and Islamic) has strong opinions that tend to affect public policy. In the Philippines, the church has been an important participant in the debate on land reform. Religious leaders may also have strong views on who should govern the country. They are unlikely, for example, to want to see a member of a religious minority become head of state.

The Military

With a very few notable exceptions—Mexico, Costa Rica, Kenya—any discussion of powerful groups in developing countries must take note of the influence of the military. In many countries—in a majority of African states in the 1980s and Latin American states in the 1970s—the military has held the formal reins of government. In these, military officials occupy the most important decision-making positions and are therefore critical members of the policy elite. Even where the military does not hold formal decision-making positions, it is often an essential and frequently dominant member of governing coalitions. Further, the politically active military often becomes so at the behest of civilians and is frequently maintained in power through considerable civilian support. This relationship is often referred to as "civil-militarism." Because of its political importance to the establishment and survival of governing coalitions, the military has the capacity to influence the allocation of government resources and to act also as a veto group on specific public policies for a wide variety of objectives, even in regimes with a well-established tradition of civilian rule. Thus, a military regime is only the most visible form of military involvement in decision making (Grindle 1987; Bienen 1978; Crouch 1986; Stepan 1971). The military frequently participates in politics in the role of a central pillar of a stable dominant coalition, as under the Somoza regime in Nicaragua, or in the role of an essential partner in unstable governing coalitions, as in the Philippines, or in the role of a moderator of civilian politics, as in Brazil during some periods of its history. Civilian policy makers who ignore the preferences and concerns of the military, or of important factions within it, frequently regret the oversight.

Organized Labor

The power of organized labor differs significantly among countries, although the fact that organized labor interests tend to represent a "labor elite" of those with steady jobs, regular pay, and access to benefits, and the fact that most organized labor is urban-based, means that policy elites are generally aware of its concerns and capacity to make demands on the political system. Organized labor working in the formal sector is paid considerably more than the majority of laborers and is a relatively small and privileged group. Prominent among its organizations are those of public sector employees such as teachers, health workers, police, and workers in state enterprises. Because of the political importance of these groups, they are likely to have influence out of proportion to their numbers.

The Media

In many developing countries, the media represent an important elite group, and their actions can have a significant effect on the decisions made by government, although their influence is undoubtedly less than the media in democratic industrialized countries. This is because governments tend to be less open in developing countries and because governments often control critical resources desired by the media. Governments often have their own radio and television stations, although there may be private stations as well. Most developing nations have several important newspapers, and these are usually independent of government, but governments have been active in trying to control or influence the press. This may take the form of censorship, imprisonment of newspaper editors or publishers who are too critical of government, or a more subtle form of pressure, control of advertising or newsprint.

Those Who Look Elsewhere for Influence

Large segments of the population in developing countries are not represented in discussions of policy. In fact, much of the participation in policy discussions that occurs in more open democratic countries is replaced in developing countries by more particularistic or clientelistic participation of low-status groups during policy implementation. Citizens and groups excluded from the closed decision making that occurs within ministries or executive councils in capital cities have much greater capacity to approach implementing officials who control day-to-day allocation of resources with demands, petitions, bribes, or other forms of pressure. This tends to increase the extent to which processes of policy implementation are highly political in developing countries (Grindle 1980). Bending the rules, seeking exceptions to generalized prescriptions, proffering bribes for special consideration, having a friend in city hall— these are immensely important aspects of political participation in developing countries and often become more important the more closed the policy-making process is. Moreover, political elites and policy makers often recognize, at least implicitly, the importance of the policy implementation process because of the vulnerability of the regimes they serve. Policies may have implicit goals (to provide payoffs to those who can strengthen regime stability) as well as explicit goals (to achieve the stated goals of the policy). Similarly, clientelism often serves to hold a tenuous political regime together, a regime that must continue to provide specific benefits where it is not accorded widespread legitimacy (see, e.g., Bratton 1980).

The other form through which the unrepresented make their interests known is public protest. When the public begins to see itself harmed by government action, and in the absence of established groups to represent its interests to the government, public protest is often the only outlet for making demands known to government. Such protests may come from an identifiable group, like workers in a particular industry, or a broad cross-section of the aggrieved. The riots against the removal of subsidies on food commodities in Egypt in 1977 and 1979, Morocco in 1981 and 1984, Zambia in 1986, and the Dominican Republic in 1984, or the protests in Algeria in October 1988 against austerity programs that were increasing the cost of living and eliminating jobs, are examples of the types of protests that changes in government policy can engender. The critical fact is that groups adversely affected by policy may have little formalized structure through which to make their concerns known, and therefore they resort to public protest. Dissatisfaction with government action often takes the form of direct confrontation with a government that is already vulnerable, for the reasons indicated earlier. This tends to make the stakes in public protest very high.

Conclusions

The picture that emerges from a review of policy elites and the groups that have access to them reiterates the patterns described earlier when structural and ideological legacies surrounding state actions were examined. Centralized and relatively closed decision making, informal processes of interest representation, and vulnerability of regimes mark the environment in which policy elites work. These factors also add to their power and simultaneously isolate them from critical information about societal preferences and tolerance for policy change. For these reasons, the preferences and belief systems of policy elites become critical political variables in decision-making contexts. Generally, belief and value systems do not dictate policy choices; instead, they shape and color the way new information is processed. Thus, "decision makers tend to fit incoming information into their existing theories and images. Indeed, their theories and images play a large part in determining what they notice" (Jervis 1968:455). Moreover, a general belief or attitude may make an individual more sensitive to information supporting his predispositions than to information contradicting them (Odell 1982:63). In this way, policy choices are often heavily influenced by broad notions about what constitutes development and what the role of the state ought to be in development. At the most general level, definitions of development affect the choice of development strategy. For example, industrialization, import substitution, export promotion, basic needs, and integrated rural development have, at various times, been adopted as beliefs about what development means and how it is to be achieved. These beliefs, at times adopted under the influence of donor assistance and technical advice, have played important roles in the choice of overarching development strategies. Notions of what the appropriate role of the state ought to be are often strongly statist and anti–private enterprise, as has been noted. Sometimes this has its roots in a broadly socialist ideology, but more frequently it is a view of the unique role the state must play in a country struggling to modernize rapidly. In the past, this has included a specific preference for state enterprises, planning, control over the economy, and the state as an enforcer of equity. In addition, there is frequently a strongly held notion of rational decision making that is apparent in a high priority placed on official policy as set forth in a plan or in a speech by a head of state, despite the fact that officials acknowledge that such pronouncements only partly account for policy choices. More recently, in the 1980s and into the 1990s, much of the emphasis on policy reform has had significant implications for long-held notions about the role of the state and for the activities undertaken by policy elites. Many reforms have called for a diminution in the size and economic role of the state and a decentralization of decision making. When the market replaces the state as the allocator of scarce resources, whether in planning; the allocation of permits, licenses, or foreign exchange; or permission to start a new enterprise, the stakes for government involve ideological predispositions as well as economic and political power.

In this chapter, we have argued that policy elites within government play much more decisive roles in most developing countries than they do in Western industrialized nations. In practical terms, this suggests that reformers need to be centrally concerned with the attitudes, perceptions, and actions of these elites, since they will be fundamental to any efforts to initiate and sustain reform. These officials are not necessarily isolated from societal interests, but the environment of underdevelopment, the legacy of a statist orientation to development, and the ambiguous cues derived from an incompletely organized political society tend to increase the weight of their power and preferences. These same factors, of course, can also increase their vulnerability to mistaken choices because the information they have available to them on social, economic, and political conditions is often vague, ambiguous, and very incomplete. Add to this the vulnerability of the regimes they serve, and it becomes apparent that the stakes for decision makers in policy reform initiatives can be extraordinarily high. For practitioners and reformers, knowledge of such contextual factors is centrally important when the discussion moves from a general consideration of policy making and implementation to a more specific consideration of efforts to introduce significant policy and institutional changes. The space for introducing specific changes is in part bounded by general contextual factors. In Chapter 4, we begin to address the politics of reform.

CHAPTER 4

Setting Agendas:
Circumstance, Process,
and Reform

O n December 27, 1971, a press release from the prime minister's office in Ghana announced a massive devaluation of the national currency against the dollar.[1] The decision to devalue, reached by the prime minister and affirmed by his cabinet, resulted from a growing perception among these high-level officials that the country faced a major balance-of-payments crisis. The decision was made under considerable pressure from the IMF and other creditors and on the basis of technical analyses provided to the chief policy makers by a small group of domestic and foreign economic advisers. It followed a four-year period in which the subject of devaluation was rarely mentioned within government councils and, when mentioned, was dismissed as a measure either unnecessary or inappropriate for the economic ills of the country. In fact, the influential minister of finance, J. H. Mensah, had only acknowledged the need for "a downward adjustment in the exchange rate" on December 20, after steadfastly opposing such a move despite a mounting sense of crisis within high-level circles in the government (quoted in Killick, Roemer, and Stern 1972:40). The Busia government, elected in 1969, had favored policies to increase government investments in development programs, especially in rural areas, and to liberalize a rigid and corrupt import control system while continuing to maintain an overvalued cedi (the national currency). Many government officials continued to believe that

Ghana would find a solution to balance-of-payments problems through economic growth.

This view, which had begun to erode by mid-1971, was firmly rejected between October and December, when the prime minister became increasingly convinced that a severe economic crisis faced the country. By late 1971, high-level government officials agreed that the time had come to confront serious structural problems in the country's economy. A crisis existed, the prime minister stated in addresses to the Ghanaian people on December 27 and again on December 31, and it required strong medicine, however unpleasant the taste. Eventually, the taste of the medicine was most bitter for these decision makers. On January 13, 1972, the government of Prime Minister Busia was overthrown by a military coup; in justifying their action, military leaders gave as one reason the decision to devalue and to throw the country's economy into even greater turmoil.[2] Among those who found themselves in jail or under its threat were many of those who had participated in the discussions about devaluation.

Among the decision makers who discussed and debated the issue of devaluation between October and December—the prime minister, the minister of finance, the president of the central bank, a small number of other cabinet officials, and a small group of technical advisers—there was increasing concern about the gravity of the economic situation in the country. Ghana was caught in a situation of rapidly rising imports and falling international prices for cocoa, a product that accounted for some 60–70 percent of export earnings. The Bank of Ghana was unable to meet its credit obligations. Of course, foreign exchange problems were not new to this consumption-based economy in which little savings and investment activity could be discerned. However, in the past, the problem had been masked by the availability of foreign exchange reserves, large-scale borrowing from abroad—including the extensive use of suppliers' credits—and a timely boom in the cocoa market. But now, the reserves were exhausted, the external debt was very large, suppliers were refusing to extend more credit and were demanding payment for bills past due, and the cocoa boom was over. From an average of $790 per ton in 1970, cocoa fell to $470 per ton in 1971 (and to $360 per ton in the first months of 1972). The government's Cabinet Standing Development Committee warned of a serious impending trade imbalance.

The IMF and creditor countries, which had reached short-term rescheduling agreements with the government in 1966, 1968, and 1970, were now refusing assistance unless major reforms in economic policy were put in place. In October, the government was informed by the British government that no economic assistance or debt relief would be forthcoming without real Ghanaian commitment to putting its economic house in order. If such reforms were made, government officials believed that foreign assistance would be forthcoming, even if they had no firm commitments from the IMF, the British, or other major donors. Officials within the Bank of Ghana, a technical advisory committee, and the cabinet moved from a position of opposition to devaluation to one of acceptance, largely on the basis of economic indicators, the concerns of their advisers, and the warnings of their foreign creditors.

The sense of crisis among high-level officials developed without extensive evidence of violence, protest, or demand making by domestic political actors. A strike by port workers in September 1971, opposing aspects of 1971/1972 budget measures announced in July, was the only clear public statement of dissatisfaction with the government's policies; students did not protest in the streets, workers did not riot, and political violence did not escalate. Nevertheless, public opinion was increasingly critical of the government's performance. In particular, urban labor groups, the urban middle class, and the military were becoming more vocal in their criticism of the government's policies, rising inflation, and frozen wages. In part, their dissatisfaction reflected a series of unwelcome measures that were introduced in the 1971/1972 budget. Interest rates were raised, students were charged fees for university attendance, government agencies were expected to become more efficient in the use of foreign exchange, a profits and remittance tax was imposed on foreign firms, salaries and perquisites of civil and military servants were severely cut back, and a development tax to raise additional revenue was imposed on the population.

By the latter half of 1971, therefore, public grumbling—but not mobilized protest—about economic conditions had become widespread. While generally more sensitive to the economic dimensions of the crisis than to their political ramifications, the prime minister and the cabinet did include a number of sweeteners in the devaluation package for cocoa farmers and others. The government was also aware that the devaluation might have severe repercussions in terms of public support if it was announced at the height of the pre-Christmas buying season. As a consequence, the announcement of the devaluation was postponed for five days after the decision had been reached.

The case of devaluation in Ghana highlights the importance of circumstance in explaining how, why, and when decisions are made. In this case, the perception of crisis is clear. Beginning in mid-October, high-level officials, with the minister in the lead, began to accept that dire consequences would result if they did not act and if they did not make major changes in the economic management of the country. In the months leading up to the acceptance of this view, there was disagreement among officials about the severity of the economic situation and the appropriate policy response to it; by mid-December, they were all in agreement that a crisis existed and that devaluation was a central part of any solution. They also agreed that something had to be done, despite high economic and political stakes; for them, failure to act would lead to almost certain disaster, the bankruptcy of the government.

Crisis is an often-invoked reason in explanations of the adoption and pursuit of major changes in public policy. In fact, while many of the theoretical formulations considered in Chapter 2 are more useful for understanding policy stasis than policy change, most theories incorporate the idea of a relationship between circumstances of crisis and instances of policy change. In class analytic models, for example, theorists argue that a crisis allows the state to take on more autonomy from societal actors and to introduce measures that may infringe on the power and interests of dominant social classes. For public choice theorists, a crisis offers a unique opportunity to break through the hold of rent-seeking behavior to consider larger issues such as "the national interest." In a bureaucratic politics approach, crisis is the condition that often sets off bureaucratic "games," defining the stakes and presenting opportunities for personal and bureaucratic competition and bargaining. For those who adopt a state interests approach, a crisis is an opportunity for state elites to define new strategies for addressing major problems of development and to take an active role in putting together supportive coalitions for reform. In all these approaches, then, crisis presents a "moment" or an opportunity for bringing about significant changes in public policy. Crisis, it appears, is instrumental to reform.[3]

Certain kinds of policy issues—a devaluation, say—tend to get on decision makers' agendas only when crisis conditions exist. Other kinds of policies—to decentralize, for example—emerge almost uniquely under politics-as-usual circumstances. In our framework, we have chosen to focus on the dynamics of two distinct agenda-setting contexts rather than on the types of policies that tend to emerge within these contexts. The reasons why particular policies regularly tend to arise under distinct circumstances can then be put in analytic perspective. Agenda-setting circumstances can illuminate broad categories of policies and allow for comparisons among them; assessing individual types of policies provides less of a basis for generalization and comparison, at least as a starting point for analysis. Moreover, there are also categories of policies—revising price structures, introducing sectoral investments, altering trade incentives, for example—that can occur under either crisis or politics-as-usual circumstances. Here, we attempt to go beyond specific policy types to the dynamics of the circumstances that surround their emergence as issues on a policy agenda.

The experience of devaluation in Ghana, as well as several other cases considered in this study, affirm this general statement. But these cases do more than affirm the possible truism that crisis generates reform. They help us respond to a difficult conceptual issue—how do we know a crisis exists?—and they provide insights into what crisis means in terms of the process of decision making and the kinds of decisions that it is likely to generate. In this chapter, the circumstances of crisis that surrounded several of the policy reform cases are compared with circumstances of politics as usual that provided the context for several other cases. The comparison illuminates the distinct dynamics of agenda setting and decision making when a crisis is perceived to exist and when it is not.

In Chapter 3, we suggested the centrality of policy elites and of the state more generally to policy initiatives in developing countries. Here we wish to indicate how the circumstances surrounding a particular issue shape the opportunities for reform and the process of decision making about adopting policy and institutional changes. Central to our argument is the assertion that circumstances of crisis or noncrisis have very clear implications for the dynamics and process of decision making, but they do not directly determine the outcome of that process, the content of the reform initiative. In all our cases of crisis-ridden reforms, circumstances influenced the stakes and timing of reform, but policy elites, however pressured they felt, always had options available to them, including the options of not acting or of experimenting with alternatives to extremely high-risk actions. Moreover, policy elites had considerable scope for shaping the specific content of changed policies and institutional arrangements and thus had significant influence in determining the outcome of decision making, even under conditions in which it appeared they had "no choice" but to act. In Ghana, for instance, policy makers came to believe that devaluation was the only option available to them, but they had clear choices in terms of the amount of the devaluation, the package of other policy instruments to be introduced with it, and the way in which the actions were introduced to the public. These choices that accompanied the general decision to devalue shaped much of its scope, timing, and public reaction.

In the pages to follow, we first consider cases of policy change under circumstances of perceived crisis for the insights they offer into the definition of crisis and the dynamics that surround agenda setting and decision making under these conditions. We then turn to cases in which policy change is attempted under circumstances of politics as usual. We find that reform also occurs under such conditions, but that its dynamics are distinct.

Crisis-ridden Policy Changes

The case of devaluation in Ghana illuminates a problem of definition that plagues efforts to explain policy change—how do we know when a crisis exists? The problem is difficult because, unless clear criteria are adopted, explanations of change can easily become tautological: major policy changes are introduced because there is a crisis and, therefore, a crisis exists when major policy changes are introduced. In most cases, the existence of a crisis cannot easily be established through the description of an objective situation; instead, the fact of crisis remains in the eye of the beholder. This was true in Ghana. The economic situation in the country was bad and deteriorating through much of 1971. Indeed, for over a decade there had been serious structural imbalances in the country's economy and its relationship with the international economy. Per capita consumption was declining. Yet, the existence of a full-blown crisis was not acknowledged until the October–December period of 1971. It was during this period that the prime minister became convinced that the economy was in serious trouble and that short-term internal adjustments or additional foreign assistance could not resolve the foreign exchange problem. It was at this time that the other high-level decision makers, including the minister of finance, who had long opposed any consideration of the need to devalue, came to share an appreciation of the gravity of the economic situation. Similarly, although the decision makers recognized to some degree the economic and political risks involved in devaluation, they came to believe that far greater problems would be encountered if they failed to act.

In this and other cases, then, a crisis existed because (1) decision makers perceived that one existed; (2) there was a general consensus among them that the situation of crisis was real and of a threatening nature; and (3) they believed that failure to act would lead to even more threatening economic and political realities (Hampson 1986:17). Our cases indicate that policy makers often become convinced that a crisis exists as a result of two interrelated factors. First, the gravity of a situation is frequently borne in upon them by events and actors outside of government—a riot, a dramatic fall in the international price of a major export commodity, or pressure from international agencies, for example. This kind of external reminder often puts the issue on the agenda for government decision makers.

Second, policy elites are often helped along the path to the perception of crisis because of the information made available to them by their own staffs of technical experts or by the technocrats of international agencies pressing for changes. Increasingly, as was suggested in Chapter 3, policy makers have access to and are better able to understand such information. Increasingly, they are asked to make difficult decisions based on complex or sophisticated information and advice. In a typical case of balance-of-payments problems, such as in Ghana, for example, analyses made available to policy elites signal the degree of current foreign exchange problems and budgetary deficits and project future trends. In our cases, this kind of technical information was important in convincing policy elites that they faced a crisis and in suggesting options for addressing the crisis. Such perceptions defined the circumstances surrounding the discussion of policy changes and shaped the nature of the decision-making process. They did not, however, determine what changes would be adopted, how "good" or "bad" the decisions would be, or how appropriate they were to the particular problem being faced.

THE PROCESS OF DECISION MAKING

When a perception of crisis surrounds the consideration of policy changes, considerable pressure develops to "do something" about a problem if dire consequences are to be avoided—or so decision makers believe. In particular, when policy elites perceive a crisis to exist, the decision-making process is distinct from noncrisis situations in terms of the pressures for reform, the stakes involved in change, the level of decision makers involved, the degree of change considered, and the timing of reforms. Our cases clearly indicate that perceived crisis sets in motion a process of decision making characterized by pressure to act, high stakes, high-level decision makers, major changes from existing policy, and urgency.

Pressing and Chosen Problems

In the case of devaluation in Ghana, decision makers were keenly aware of the concerns and pressures from outside of government about the economic situation of the country. Among the most explicit pressures on them were the demands and expectations of international creditors. The British, for example, refused new balance-of-payments relief unless the Ghanaian government reached an agreement with the International Monetary Fund. In turn, the IMF was clear in insisting that major policy changes had to be undertaken before debt relief could be seriously discussed. Domestically, labor unions were clear in their desire for wage increases, and urban middle-class groups were increasingly dismayed by economic conditions in the country and opposed to the policy measures in the budget that affected them directly. The military was bitter about a 12 percent cut in its budget and the ending of a number of important perquisites such as vehicle allowances, free utilities, and subsidized rents. This was a situation in which the problem was a "pressing" one.

Circumstances of crisis tend to bring pressing problems to the attention of policy elites. Albert Hirschman (1981:146) has suggested that pressing problems are those "that are forced on the policymakers through pressure from injured or interested outside parties"; in contrast, chosen problems are those that decision makers "have picked out of thin air" as a result of their own preferences and perceptions. In several of our cases, actors outside of government played significant roles in placing issues for debate on the government's agenda. In Ghana, the international creditors were particularly important in pressing the need for reform on the policy makers. In the case of agrarian reform in the Philippines, insurgent forces and international donors were among those pressuring a frequently reluctant government to consider this policy (Thomas 1986). In the case of structural adjustment in Korea, the threat of the loss of U.S. PL480 food assistance was a significant factor pressing the government to consider changes (Haggard and Cole 1987). Moreover, pressing problems encouraged policy elites to perceive a crisis, and the pressures added to their sense of urgency about the problem. Those pressing for reform did not necessarily determine how the policy elites would respond to a particular problem, but only that they would feel the need to respond in some way. The pressures did not always push in the same direction, either. In Ghana, the international creditors wanted devaluation, austerity, and trade liberalization. Domestic groups pressed for increased government spending and cheap imports. Nevertheless, in most cases, policy elites would have been more reluctant to act, or would have acted less decisively, if the problems they were considering had not been pressed upon them by those outside of government.

Stakes

Circumstances of crisis surrounding the emergence and consideration of a particular policy issue also systematically raise the stakes for policy elites (see esp. Hampson 1986:16–17). This was true in Ghana. Convinced that a dire economic crisis faced the country, Prime Minister Busia and the other decision makers were clearly concerned about a major economic value, the future creditworthiness of the government, and the economic conditions that would prevail if the supply of imports were to be cut off. For them, the future development of the country was at stake, as well as their own reputations as managers of the economy and as leaders of a popularly supported political party. Thus, for them, the stakes involved fundamental conditions of economic stability and growth and the legitimacy and durability of their hold on political power.

77

In other cases, also, a situation of perceived crisis appeared to raise the concerns policy elites had about macropolitical conditions such as political stability, legitimacy, and regime vulnerability and led them to assess carefully the political and economic consequences of the options available to them. In Indonesia, perceived crises about the availability of domestic supplies of rice repeatedly raised concern among policy elites about the political volatility of food shortages or high prices for staple goods among the urban population (Timmer 1987a). In the Philippines, agrarian reform proposals were clearly assessed in terms of the very high stakes of political legitimacy and the vulnerability of the regime to both popular and elite opposition (Thomas 1986). In Korea, the stakes involved in economic reform involved not only important U.S. assistance but also the legitimacy of a newly elected regime (Haggard and Cole 1987).

Status of Decision Makers

Conditions of crisis tend strongly to move the level of concern upward in the decision-making hierarchy of government, while situations in which the crisis threat is low tend to remain at lower hierarchical levels. This distinction is clearly related to the level of threat to macropolitical conditions of stability and legitimacy and macroeconomic conditions of stability and growth; the higher the perceived stakes, the more likely that high-level officials will take a personal interest in the decision. Ghana is a good case of this. In Ghana, technical advisers had for some time been concerned about the economic situation and its trend toward a full-blown crisis. The prime minister, however, was content until the summer and fall of 1971 to leave economic management in the hands of his minister of finance. Only after he became fully convinced that a crisis existed did the prime minister take over control of economic policy making from his former economics czar. Moreover, it was only after October 1971 that the analyses of the economic advisers began to receive serious attention at the cabinet and prime ministerial levels. Similarly, in Costa Rica, the significant reorientations of the country's development strategy were decided upon by officials at the highest level in government (Doryan-Garrón 1988).

Innovation or Incrementalism

Distinct circumstances also alter the perceptions of decision makers about the causes and consequences of a particular policy issue and the remedies for the problem. Crisis-ridden reforms tend to emphasize major changes from preexisting policies. That is, prior policies are often considered to be fully implicated in the causes of the crisis; thus, they must be rejected if the crisis is to be overcome. Moreover, policy elites may feel under considerable pressure to appear to be taking decisive action in response to a dire situation. In Ghana, after avoiding devaluation as a no-win policy for four years, the government decided on a major change in 1971. In fact, the situation of crisis moved the government in the direction of a larger devaluation than economic conditions appeared to warrant.

> The crisis atmosphere had its effects on the technical work leading to devaluation. Most obviously, it forced a hurried pace of analysis. . . . Although it was necessary to quantify the outcome as well as possible, the advisors knew, and told the politicians, that a devaluation of 50% or more (in the cedi-dollar rate) was a shot in the dark, an act both of faith and of desperation. Since everyone knew they were dealing with very uncertain parameters, the tendency of the technicians was always to err on the side of greater force: use conservative estimates of responses and opt for larger devaluations. (Killick, Roemer, and Stern 1972:48–49)

In other cases, crisis situations moved policy elites toward major reformations of existing policy. In Costa Rica, a development strategy that focused on import substitution had been in effect since the early 1960s; it was reversed in the 1980s as a result of a severe economic crisis. Policy elites, who had been discussing the appropriateness of a new development model for some years, were hesitant to make more than incremental adjustments in existing policy to encourage a more outward-oriented development strategy until a crisis offered an opportunity to take more decisive action. (Doryan-Garrón 1988). Indonesia systematically altered its strategic approach to rice-pricing policy in response to crisis situations—in one instance as a result of a domestic and international shortage of rice and in another as a result of severe and sudden budgetary shortfalls (Timmer 1987a). Korean policy makers dismantled an extensive government apparatus supporting import substitution as the state adopted a fundamentally different approach to development through export promotion (Haggard and Cole 1987). Thus, although the stakes are high for the decision makers in crisis-ridden reforms, policy elites are also pushed in the direction of major reform initiatives when a perception of crisis exists. Innovation rather than incrementalism is likely to result.

Timing

Finally, the timing of policy response can be altered by circumstance. Under conditions of perceived crisis, decision makers often believe they have little alternative but to act, however much they might wish to avoid making difficult and risky decisions. They will not be without power or room to maneuver, but their control over timing may be significantly reduced. In Ghana, the prime minister believed that the government had to act before it had to repudiate its debts or before suppliers cut off imports. The case of rice price reforms in Indonesia is also a good example of how the timing of change is affected by crisis conditions.

> The changes reflected the government's concern about the impact that food prices would have in urban areas and that imported rice and subsidized prices had on the management of the budget. The specific policy options adopted indicated the government's confidence in the technical advice it received from a team of food policy analysts. The timing of the changes, however, reflected broader political concerns about food prices during periods of perceived economic crisis. (Timmer 1987a:3–4)

THE CONTENT OF POLICY

While the perception of crisis clearly affects the pressures for change, the stakes of reform, the identity of the decision makers, and the extent and timing of the changes considered, it does not necessarily result in either predictable or recommended policy changes. Policy elites in Ghana did eventually decide to devalue, a policy option favored by the international creditors and the government's own corps of economic advisers. The country was in a precarious international situation and in desperate need of the relief the government thought had been promised by the IMF and other creditors; policy elites believed, in fact, that the country had become economically dependent on the approval of the international actors. At the same time, the government was facing increasing domestic criticism of its management of the economy and was under pressure by domestic groups to increase incomes and development investments. Ten years of declining per capita consumption could be expected to take a toll on the popularity of the Progress party government that had been democratically elected in 1969. The policy elites who agreed to the devaluation believed that such a measure would infuse the government budget with additional resources and consequently would allow them to raise crop prices for cocoa farmers and to introduce a wage hike for urban workers. From these perspectives, then, the decision to devalue was not without a political rationale.

Yet, what is apparent on closer inspection of the Ghana case is not that the government responded to pressures from domestic and international sources, but rather that it tried to deal with the economic situation in other ways and then prevaricated so long before taking decisive action. For an extended period in 1970 and 1971, there were disagreements within the government about what were appropriate policy measures; alternative proposals were also put in motion to encourage better performance of the economy. In particular, the budget for 1970–71 was an effort to use government investments and changes in tariff policy to stimulate growth in the economy, especially in rural areas. The budget, a "bold, blunt statement that put into practice many of the Progress Party's campaign promises, included a 53 percent increase in expenditures in the development budget" (Denoon 1986:156). As the principal actor in formulating the government's economic policies, Minister of Finance Mensah was instrumental in convincing most top-level officials that balance-of-payments problems were of a short-term nature. This view continued to prevail through July of 1971, when the 1971–72 budget, crafted by the minister of finance in isolation from advice and debate in the cabinet, was unveiled.

> The Finance Minister framed his two budgets on the assumption of continued high cocoa prices and he steadfastly and explicitly refused to recognize the limits of available foreign exchange and fiscal resources. His most important economic policy, import liberalization, was implemented without its essential concomitant, an effective import price to reflect the scarcity of foreign exchange. Once he had set the Government on this path leading inevitably to a crisis, the Minister refused to change direction until the crisis was unavoidable. (Killick, Roemer, and Stern 1972:47–48)

Devaluation was systematically resisted as a viable option until the fall of 1971. Moreover, having eventually made the decision to devalue, the decision makers still had complete autonomy to decide by how much (not a trivial issue, given the nature of the interests involved) and had some range of choice concerning the timing and public justification of the announcement. They also had considerable scope for including sweeteners in the devaluation package, such as raising cocoa producer prices, increasing the minimum wage, doing away with the much-resented development tax, and eliminating import surcharges. The history of decision making in Ghana indicates that policy elites actively searched for alternatives to devaluation and then crafted a devaluation package that they thought would prove economically useful at the same time that it would be politically feasible. This scope for action left them considerable room for making mistakes. This last point was apparent in the devaluation—its extent went beyond that required by the economic situation. Moreover, the public was unprepared for the devaluation, and the Busia government proved inept at handling public explanations of the measure.

In this case, the decision makers were clearly constrained by the political and economic situation facing them. But neither the crisis (which they believed eventually forced them to act) nor the pressures (which pushed them in divergent directions, in any case) fully determined their actions. Caught in a difficult situation, perhaps even a no-win situation, the decision makers attempted a variety of approaches to the crisis and put off decisive action as long as possible. Even in these circumstances, however, they were devoid of neither room to maneuver nor the capacity to disagree about appropriate responses. The personality of the minister of finance, and Busia's uncertainty about what course of action to take, form a leitmotif within which the devaluation decision unfolded.

> Mensah's peculiar work habits, his imperious self-confidence, and his contempt for his peers in the cabinet created problems during the period of crisis decision making which culminated in the December devaluation. . . . At the time, Mensah was the czar of Ghanaian economic policy. No one, even Busia, openly contradicted him. (Denoon 1986:154, 156)

An even clearer example of the way in which crisis situations account for characteristics of the process of decision making but do not determine the content of the decisions is that of agrarian reform in the Philippines.[4] In this case, developing a vigorous agrarian reform policy was rejected, but there was nothing inherent in the situation that necessarily preordained this choice. A different group of decision makers facing the same circumstances could have decided differently. In the aftermath of the "people's revolution" that brought Corazon Aquino to the presidency, policy elites could have acted forcefully to promulgate an extensive agrarian reform program and to respond to demands for greater equity in rural areas. For the first eighteen months of the new government, the popularity of and support for President Aquino was high among many domestic political groups, and international lenders were firmly behind an agrarian reform initiative and willing to provide financial support for it. The "moment" for reform might have been seized with considerable prospect of success at this point. Even later, the government might have pursued an aggressive agrarian reform program as a way of undercutting the appeal of the National People's Army in the countryside and solidifying popular support for the government among the peasants. Instead, after much rhetoric in favor of agrarian reform but a series of delaying actions in doing anything about it, Aquino chose to negotiate a ceasefire and amnesty with the insurgent forces rather than to move ahead with a reform program.

It is, of course, easy to understand the government's reluctance to undertake agrarian reform in the face of opposition from large, commercially oriented landlords, Aquino's personal ties to the landed elite in the country, and the constant challenge to her authority from the military. The fact remains that she could have supported an agrarian reform effort and could have used the opportunity as a bold gesture to gain support, yet she chose instead to attempt to negotiate with the NPA. In this case, either outcome can be explained by the circumstances, suggesting the importance of who is assessing the situation and making the decision.

In Ghana and the Philippines, policy elites were agreed that crises existed, and that some action needed to be taken. Yet the scope and nature of the decisions made were not preordained by the crisis. In Ghana, decision makers actually increased the degree of crisis through prevarication; in the Philippines, at least for a period of several months, Aquino could have used the crisis as a high-risk opportunity to reshape productive relationships in the countryside fundamentally and to enhance her own power. At least through 1989, however, policy elites in the Philippines rejected land reform as too destabilizing politically and economically and sought to deal with crises of economic distribution, insurgency, and political support in other ways. It is important to emphasize, however, that they could have acted differently. The process of decision making did not fully determine the content of the decision.

Politics-As-Usual Policy Changes

It is not surprising that the perception of crisis is often responsible for placing an issue on the agenda of government decision making. Nor is it surprising that decisions to make significant changes in public policies are frequently surrounded by an atmosphere of crisis. There is considerable theoretical consensus that crisis provides policy elites with greater autonomy to make choices and that the pressures upon them often push in the direction of significant change. Empirically, also, there is substantial evidence that crisis and reform initiatives are significantly correlated. Among our cases in which a perception of crisis existed among decision makers, all but one of them resulted in significant changes in major policies. Clearly, the stakes are higher, the risks are greater, and attention is more focused when such moments of crisis occur. Situations of perceived crisis appear to be instrumental to major policy changes—although, as we have seen, crisis itself does not dictate what solutions will be chosen nor the form in which they will be introduced.

Noncrisis situations can be expected to generate much less impetus for reform. In fact, much of the theoretical literature reviewed in Chapter 2 indicates that change is not likely to occur at all under conditions of politics as usual. According to this literature, stasis rather than change is the outcome of normal politics, and, in the absence of crisis, most theory is much more able to explain why reform does not occur than to account for its incidence.[5] Marxist, public choice, rational actor, and bureaucratic politics models all focus on the constraints on change and provide a series of logically compelling explanations about why "things are the way they are." Marxist theory indicates that the link between given class alliances and the biases of policy in favor of dominant classes are persistent and inexorable in the absence of crisis. Public choice theory posits a parceling out of state resources to specific rent-seeking groups and a set of assumptions about rational self-interested behavior under normal politics that inevitably leads to an inability to alter policies once they have been considered entitlements by their beneficiaries. Rational actor models build on concepts of uncertainty and risk to explain that change must be understood in terms of satisficing and incrementalism. In the bureaucratic politics approach, normal routines and processes of decision making predominate unless a crisis brings an issue to decision makers' attention and triggers a set of games having to do with position, power, and influence. Each of these models predicts that reformist initiatives will not be successful unless some kind of crisis situation is perceived to exist.

In our cases, however, there is substantial evidence that efforts to change existing policies and institutions do not subside or disappear simply because there is no perception of crisis among policy elites. Reform initiatives appear to be more or less continuously on government agendas. At any given time, a series of ideas about changing existing practice is being debated, studied, discussed, and considered within bureaucratic agencies, legislatures, and groups of interested publics. Many of these ideas are placed in front of decision makers and acted upon. Nevertheless, there is also considerable evidence that circumstances of politics as usual result in processes of agenda setting and decision making that are distinct from those that prevail under circumstances of perceived crisis. Planning reform in Colombia is a case in point.[6]

Planning reform in Colombia got on the agenda in the 1960s when a new administration took over the reins of government and was seeking to enhance the role of the state in guiding the process of economic development. Previous administrations had ignored and weakened the planning institution; the task for reformers was to develop and enhance the prestige of the institution and to attempt to build a nonpolitical image for the planners so that they could have influence in a multisectoral decision-making process, cutting across other agencies and regions and affecting public enterprises and the workings of the central government. A principal concern, then, was the bureaucratic position of the agency and its ability to work with—not in spite of—other ministries and agencies that were inclined to be highly suspicious of competing sources of power. Promoters of the enhanced role of planning in government were therefore very concerned about strategy; they were less concerned initially about the actual exercises undertaken by the revitalized agency. In particular, promoters of planning had to address the problem of how to "plug planning into the operational goals of government . . . and overcome planning's reputation for failure" (Mallon 1986:1–2).

A foreign adviser arrived in Colombia in 1966, shortly after a Liberal party government had been elected, in order to help promote planning reform. Planning as a function of government had withered under the previous Conservative party government; the new president was interested in seeing the institution responsible for data collection and analysis revived and integrated into national policy decision making. The intention of the president, the foreign adviser, and his chief counterpart in the Colombian government was to make planning the serious heart of development policy making in the country. They developed and pursued a conscious strategy that included (1) carving out an important and useful role for the national planning agency as a source of information; (2) gaining access to policy makers and encouraging them to rely on the information and analyses provided by the agency; (3) building support among prominent technocrats and important officials within the bureaucracy in order to have wide access to decision makers of different political persuasions; (4) involving influential members of society in support for the idea of planning, especially if such individuals and groups might come to power in the future; and (5) strengthening the competence, image, and staff spirit of the agency as a means of attracting and retaining good people to work within it. Overall, this strategy was one of building a coalition of support within the government and among influential individuals and groups in society.

More specifically, internationally recognized scholars were invited to lecture at the agency, considerable efforts were taken to attract university professors into the agency, and attempts were made to carve out a niche for the institution as the technical secretariat of the Economic and Social Committee of the cabinet. This committee had been identified by the reformers as the most efficient policy-making body in the government, and they had enthusiastic presidential support for assuming a role in its activities. Although the agency was formally charged with producing a national development plan, this became a very secondary priority to demonstrating the institution's more immediate usefulness to the government and specifically to the cabinet committee. As a result, the agency did a considerable amount of planning without ever writing a plan. As it evolved, the principal job of the agency became that of assuming responsibility for defining standards for evaluating development initiatives and coordinating the other agencies in project appraisal.

The Process of Decision Making

The circumstances that surrounded this effort at reform were far from those of a perceived crisis. Planning reform was an initiative introduced by a new administration as part of a general effort to improve the performance of government and especially to improve the efficiency of foreign assistance channeled into the country through the Alliance for Progress. Although reformers, including a newly elected president, shared a desire to improve the technical basis for policy decision making in Colombia, they never believed that dire consequences would result if the desired changes were not adopted. Likewise, they did not feel under great pressure to "do something" about a situation. There was no perception of threat or impending disaster and little sense of high stakes and risk in the decision-making process. Rather, their task—as they defined it—involved working within the established system over an extended period of time to convince, cajole, and win support for change. The circumstance of politics as usual in Colombia affected the process of reform because it influenced the source of pressures for change, the stakes and the level of decision makers who would be involved in promoting reform, the degree of change considered by decision makers, and the timing of reform.

Pressing and Chosen Problems

Chosen problems are those that policy elites select more or less autonomously as priorities or goals to be achieved. Such problems are often identified on the basis of the policy makers' own perceptions of what constitutes a problem for government or society. In Colombia, although the Alliance for Progress had promoted the importance of planning since its inception in the early 1960s, various administrations apparently felt free to take up the initiative or ignore it. In 1966, a new administration chose planning reform as one among several initiatives it wished to see introduced during its tenure in office. This chosen problem, like others, was part of a longer menu of changes that the government desired and felt relatively free to promote according to the reformers' own preferences.

Although some noncrisis reforms are pressed upon decision makers by those outside government, most politics-as-usual reform initiatives present policy elites with significant opportunities to take up the issue or not. Even when such reforms have important proponents outside of government who seek to influence decision makers, officials appear to have considerable scope to respond seriously or not to those pressing for change. In Colombia, the Alliance for Progress was important in urging planning reform on the government and in providing financial incentives for it to do so; but to a significant extent, policy makers chose the initiative in response to their own preferences, just as the previous administration had ignored it. The promoters of the idea came from within government, and they sought to use alliance funding and the presence of a foreign adviser to pursue their ideas.

In an initiative to decentralize decision making in Kenya, a similar situation of outside pressure—in this case from the U.S. Agency for International Development—led to similar responses of political officials: in one administration they chose not to promote it; in the next, they chose to pursue the initiative. The divergent preferences of these two different administrations were shaped by their broader political goals and concerns about ethnic support bases in society (Hook 1986). Thus, in contrast to crisis-ridden reform initiatives, under politics-as-usual situations policy elites appear to have greater autonomy to decide whether or not to push for policy and institutional change, and the decision about taking up a reform comes largely from within government.

Stakes

The stakes in noncrisis-ridden reforms tend to be those related to bureaucratic and clientelistic power relationships. In such cases, bureaucratic agencies may be actively engaged in supporting or opposing the reformers, and reformers will no doubt give considerable attention to thinking of strategies for ameliorating opposition, winning over supporters, and avoiding possible sabotage of their plans. These were clearly the preoccupations of the planning reformers in Colombia, whose primary bases of both support and opposition were within government, located among the ministries and agencies that could support or sabotage the rebuilt planning agency. In Kenya, support and opposition to decentralization emerged within the ministries and at various levels of the civil service. Interests outside of government were neither appealed to nor mobilized (Hook 1986).

Such reforms rarely threaten major societal interests, although the clienteles of bureaucratic agencies may become involved as supporters or opponents of the changes. In Colombia, reformers sought allies within the academic community and among potentially influential political actors who were not allied with the Liberal government. For the reformers, the stakes may involve their potential career trajectories and jobs; if they are successful in introducing their projects, for example, they may become more influential in national policy making and enjoy enhanced salaries, greater prestige, or more secure job tenure. The stakes also involve the power, prestige, and budgetary resources of bureaucratic agencies or bureaus; success can mean greater influence in sectoral policy making, opportunities to expand, and more resources to use for a variety of goals, including those of rewarding friends and supporters with jobs or project-related benefits.

In contrast, stakes such as the survival of a regime, overall political stability, economic stability, or the tenure of high-level politicians are rarely, if ever, at risk in politics-as-usual reforms. In Colombia, reformers had diverse reasons for wanting to succeed, not the least of which was a desire to introduce better policy-making practices in the country, but none of them believed that macropolitical or macroeconomic conditions were at stake if they were unsuccessful. When circumstances of politics as usual prevail, the stakes for reform tend to involve issues of bureaucratic power, the career potential of reformers, and micropolitical concerns related to patronage and clientelism.

Status of Decision Makers

In Colombia, the president helped place the issue of planning reform on the agenda; he was also a loyal supporter of the reformers' efforts. He was not, however, actively engaged in developing strategies or making decisions about the scope or pace of change. Instead, because there was little perception of threat to macropolitical or major economic conditions, decision making about the reform remained at lower hierarchical levels, involving in this case technocrats such as midlevel directors and managers in the bureaucracy. The initiative for reform was considered more or less a routine matter, introduction of which would improve overall government decision making and performance, but the absence of which would not threaten the longevity of an administration, regime, or leadership group. On a day-to-day basis, presidents and high-level administrators did not devote much time to bringing about the changes desired by reformers.

Innovation or Incrementalism

Under noncrisis conditions, change is often incremental, with considerable scope for trial and error or scaling up if initial efforts provide positive results. The capacity to implement changes concerns decision makers in these cases, and improving this capacity tends to prolong the duration of the reform. In general, in these reforms there is greater potential for the initiative to become sidetracked by other issues or pushed to the bottom of the policy agenda by more pressing issues. More bureaucratic maneuvering and concern with possible sabotage or resistance is characteristic of reforms undertaken under circumstances of politics as usual. In the case of Colombia, reformers developed and pursued a strategy of having the notion and utility of planning gradually accepted and inserted into actual decision-making situations.

Timing

As we have seen, the proponents of planning in Colombia were under no great pressure to "do something" about reform in the short term. In fact, their strategy clearly depended on the availability of time and their own capacity to select appropriate moments for pushing for reform or lowering its salience. In the case of decentralization in Kenya, the initiative languished for two years before changed political conditions introduced an opportunity for reform (Hook 1986). In general, when noncrisis circumstances surround a reform initiative, more time is available to decision makers for studying the implications of change, and policy elites are able to determine the extent to which it will be actively pursued. When moments appear to be propitious for reform, they can encourage its pursuit but then place the issue on a back burner when conditions seem to be adverse to success. In fact, institutional reforms in Colombia, Argentina, and Kenya were shelved for long periods of time when little political support was available for pursuing them. While such conditions provide policy elites with greater control over the timing of reform, they may also rob them of the pressured political environment that can act as a stimulus to change.

These characteristics of politics-as-usual reforms tend to reinforce one another in actual policy-making situations. The interrelationship of lower stakes, less high-level involvement, and timing is particularly clear in a case of urban water management reform in India. According to an official involved in this case,

> No domestic actor considered [water management] to be something which required urgent and forceful action. Because of its low problem status, it was considered unnecessary to raise the matter to the political level at either the center or the state. Bureaucracies within the central and state agencies had, over the years, developed sufficient understanding of what were politically possible alternatives and of the time-frame in which they would become implementable. This was not considered an issue that required forcing onto the higher political level, or that was likely to be accepted within the kind of short period the World Bank had in mind. (Bajpai 1988:8)

THE CONTENT OF POLICY

The theoretical literature on how policy and institutional change comes about strongly suggests that reforms pursued in noncrisis situations will not be successfully introduced. Indeed, some of the characteristics mentioned above—in particular, incrementalism and timing—mean that major and rapid changes should not be expected under conditions of politics as usual. Nevertheless, our cases indicate that, although changes are generally incremental and the introduction of reform often slow, politics-as-usual reforms are not necessarily doomed to failure. Reform appears to occur as well under noncrisis conditions as under the more frequently accepted circumstance of perceived crisis, but the process by which it is introduced and adopted is significantly different. Moreover, circumstances of crisis or politics as usual appear to be independent of the success or failure of reform initiatives. In Colombia, for instance, the new planning agency gradually inserted itself into national decision-making processes.

Similarly, in Kenya, circumstances of politics as usual meant a long and slow process of institutional change that, after ten years of effort, appeared to have had some modest success. In 1976, the Kenyan government, at the urging and with the financial backing of USAID, agreed to develop a program of planning and administrative decentralization.[7] The project was initiated even though program documents offered no definition of decentralization, and no one in the government appeared to have definite ideas about what should be done. However, the more central concern was whether anyone at the top levels in government wanted such a program. Although a few strategically located people— such as the minister of planning—believed that economic decisions made at the local level would foster more rational policies, President Jomo Kenyatta had pursued a successful policy of centralization since independence in 1962. His strategy was to increase the central government's capacity to provide benefits to his fellow tribesmen and therefore help sustain the political regime. As a result, by the 1970s, 95 percent of the development budget was controlled from Nairobi. A policy of decentralization conflicted with political and bureaucratic interests in maintaining central control of economic resources.

In the early period, when there was no political support and little bureaucratic interest, the approach taken by decentralization project personnel was to build up a constituency for reform. This meant finding important groups in national and local administration and interesting them in activities that could advance the goals of the project. They had very limited success with this endeavor. For example, one idea was to get the central ministries to disaggregate their spending. The vice-president was persuaded to send out a letter to this effect to the concerned ministries. However, no subsequent attempts were made to implement this project. Simply because a high official ordered a particular action was no guarantee of compliance when there were disagreements in government about the direction of decentralization policy and when it threatened the power of the central ministries.

With Kenyatta's death in August of 1978, a change occurred in the political relevance of decentralization. The new president, Daniel arap Moi, needed to build his own constituency of support and saw decentralization as a way to distribute benefits that would increase loyalty to him. As a result, efforts at decentralization became politicized, with the Office of the President becoming very involved. Even with increased implementation efforts, the central role assumed by the president's office in decisions on decentralization conflicted with the perceptions and interests of the ministries (Smoke 1988). Thus, in spite of continued high-level support, progress toward decentralization was sporadic and slow. It appears that projects such as decentralization have long gestation periods when political and bureaucratic incentives for adoption are weak. Nevertheless, some progress was made. By the mid-1980s, some 15–18 percent of spending was controlled by local governments, local bureaucracies had become stronger in response to their new responsibilities, coordination of resources for development projects was modestly improved, and a rolling process of annual planning was in operation. While such changes are modest compared to the major changes decided upon in Ghana, Korea, Costa Rica, and Indonesia, they are not insignificant and may have important long-term consequences for development in a particular country.

There is no guarantee, however, that circumstances of politics as usual will result in even modest changes in institutions or policies. In the rural primary health care initiative in Mali, for example, the characteristics of noncrisis-ridden reforms were instrumental in bringing the program to an end after only four years.[8] The Mali Health Project (MHP) was the result of a chosen problem. The MHP originated in 1975 at the request of the Mali government, which was seeking funds for medical inputs from USAID. This agency, however, was less interested in medical inputs than it was in introducing a major renovation of the country's health care system. After more than two years of study, a plan was drawn up that reflected USAID's interests more than those of the government of Mali. The resulting rural health program of primary care units based on village health workers and a network of village dispensaries was to be introduced in two regions of the country that were distant from each other and difficult to reach. It took two days to reach each project site from the capital city, Bamako, and direct travel from region to region was impossible. This travel/communication problem was compounded by the insistence of the Malians that the project team be located in the national capital rather than in a regional capital.

In addition to these logistical problems, bureaucratic infighting weakened the project. It was never clear who project personnel were responsible to or which authority, the Mali government or USAID, had the final say on project matters. Though AID lost interest in the project in terms of its content shortly after the contract was signed, it continued to be very involved in administrative matters. AID officials were present at all meetings between project personnel and their Malian counterparts, a practice that the Malians saw as inappropriate interference in the project. Not only did the poor relationship make for considerable administrative confusion, it also left the project without much protection in disputes with other Malian agencies or ministries. The MHP was placed in a weak ministry, a constraint compounded by its placement within the weakest part of the ministry, the Division of Public Health. If changes in laws or regulations were needed, cabinet approval was required. With such a weak ministry, this process took too long and was oftentimes unsuccessful.

Further bureaucratic concerns affected the trajectory of the project. There was a shortage of doctors, and most of them did not want to work outside Bamako. The project also had to deal with a severely understaffed Malian civil service. The government simply lacked enough trained personnel, both in health and in general skills. The lack of an atmosphere of crisis and the extensive bureaucratic stakes involved affected the timing of the project. MHP required that counterparts be assigned to work with foreign advisers, but the Malians did not assign the chief counterpart until six months after the project started. At the same time, the Malians had considerable interest in the project inputs. At the local level, this meant the steady paychecks that came from the project; at the regional and national level, it meant access to vehicles and medical supplies. Given such problems, there is good reason to understand why the project was not extended beyond its initial four years.

The cases of reform in Colombia, Kenya, and Mali demonstrate similar dynamics in terms of where the initiative for change emerged, how the stakes were identified, the status of the reformers, the extent of change introduced, and the timing of reform. They had divergent outcomes, however, in terms of their success or failure. As with the crisis-ridden reforms reviewed earlier, process does not appear to determine outcome.

Conclusions

In many of our cases, the perception of a crisis situation provided an opportunity to introduce significant changes in public policies. Crises, as we have argued, appear to offer an important moment for reform. But

even in our cases of politics-as-usual reform, changes that were successfully introduced appear to have been accomplished in part because moments in national politics opened up opportunities for reformers to pursue their projects. In Colombia, for example, a new administration
assumed control of the executive branch with an agenda of reforms it
wished to introduce during its four years in office. One of these reforms
involved resuscitating the planning function of government. In Kenya,
the death of Jomo Kenyatta, who, as president, had consistently worked
to centralize political and bureaucratic power in Nairobi, opened up an
opportunity for new political leadership to introduce institutional
changes in government. Among these was a new interest in decentralization, in large part because the new president believed that decentralization would increase his political capacity to distribute resources to his
own supporters. With changing political circumstances, opportunities for
pursuing reforms—in both cases, ones already on a latent agenda—were
introduced. In contrast, the experiment with health policy reform in Mali
was planned and pursued in the absence of any apparent opportunity or
moment for reform. Similarly, in the case of urban water management
reform in India, no unusual circumstances intervened to give some impetus to the reform. It may well be that reform projects appear to require
such moments if they are to be introduced successfully.

We have argued that situations of crisis and politics as usual affect the
magnitude and timing of reform initiatives. Some confirmation for this
perspective comes from viewing policy changes in a particular sector in
a particular country over a long period of time. In such cases, the kinds
of changes that are introduced under crisis and politics-as-usual conditions can be seen to differ systematically. In the case of pricing policy
for rice in Indonesia, to be explained in greater detail in Chapter 6, a
series of policy changes was made over the course of twenty years, beginning in the 1960s. Changes in official prices for rice were recommended by a team of policy analysts and responded to concerns about
the economic impact of such prices on urban consumers and the budget.
This technical analysis, however, is insufficient to explain the introduction of different kinds of reforms at particular moments. During periods
when policy elites perceived the potential for politically destabilizing price
increases or shortages of rice, the food logistics agency, BULOG, introduced significant changes in its orientation in price policy. In interim,
politics-as-usual periods, reforms tended to focus on improving the operation and efficiency of the agency.

The circumstances surrounding the introduction of policy reform initiatives suggest who the decision makers are likely to be, what pressures
they are likely to be under, and how much change they are likely to
contemplate. As will be suggested in greater detail in Chapter 8, the

insights that obtain from understanding agenda-setting circumstances can be useful in generating strategies for enhancing the potential for reform to be successfully initiated. These agenda-setting circumstances not only set the boundaries for what is likely to occur, they also open up opportunities for influencing the process of reform. Before assessing more fully how agenda-setting circumstances can define room for changing the boundaries of policy space, however, it is important to consider how the framework structures thinking about the processes of decision making and implementation. In the next chapter, the criteria that decision makers apply to issues of policy and institutional change will be the focus of attention. We will see that at the level of the perceptions of policy elites, these criteria differ depending on whether circumstances of crisis or politics as usual prevail.

CHAPTER 5

Making Decisions:
The Concerns of Policy Elites

What kinds of issues do decision makers think about when they assess possibilities for changing existing policies or organizational practices? Do they apply any criteria—technical, political, ideological—to guide them toward certain choices? Decision-making situations are almost always complex, and cues about which choices are to be preferred tend to be numerous and conflicting. For any given decision, policy makers may be pushed in divergent directions by specific societal and bureaucratic interests, their own preferences and understanding of the issues involved, the historical and international context within which the problem has emerged, and a variety of other concerns and influences.

In this chapter, we address the issues that policy elites appear to consider when they assess options for change. Our cases are helpful in sorting out the broad range of concerns of policy elites because they indicate that a fairly consistent set of decision criteria explains the choices made. They also display a fairly consistent hierarchy of concerns of decision makers about the impact that their choices will have. Circumstances of crisis or politics as usual play an important role in ordering this hierarchy of decision criteria. Thus, we focus on what appear to be the overriding concerns of decision makers and attempt to demonstrate how the broad orientations of policy-making elites, the contextual factors that help shape those orientations, and the circumstances surrounding specific reform initiatives interact to explain the content of decisions. We return, then, to a central theme of this book: the importance of policy elites in the policy process and the way in which state and societal in-

TABLE 5.1
Criteria for Choices about Policy and Institutional Reform

"Lenses" of Policy Elites	Concerns Influencing Decisions	Influential Actors
Technical advice	Information, analyses, and options presented by advisers, experts	Technocrats, ministers, and other high-level bureaucrats; Foreign advisers
Bureaucratic implications	Career objectives of individuals; Competitive position of units; Budgets; Compliance and responsiveness	Ministers and other high-level bureaucrats; Middle-level bureaucrats; International bureaucrats and advisers
Political stability and support	Stability of political system; Calculus of costs and benefits to groups, classes, interests; Military support or opposition	Political leadership; Dominant economic elites; Leaders of class, ethnic, interest associations; Military
International pressure	Access to aid; loans, trade relations	IMF, World Bank, USAID, other multilateral or bilateral agencies; Governments of former colonial powers; International banks

terests interact in producing—or inhibiting—policy and organizational changes.

Criteria for Choices

In the twelve decision-making cases we investigated, decision-making elites filtered policy options through at least four lenses: the technical advice they received, the impact of their choices on bureaucratic interactions, the meaning of potential changes for political stability and political support, and their concern about relationships with international actors (table 5.1). These lenses appeared to help them assess the risks and benefits of alternative courses of action and to order their thinking about how, and often why, reform should occur. As they applied these different criteria, some appeared to gain in importance, while others became less salient. In the following pages, the cases are used to help explore the factors considered by the decision makers and to explain their relative importance under different sets of circumstances.

TECHNICAL ADVICE

Making decisions in increasingly complex and interdependent economic and social systems has come to include the extensive involvement of technical specialists. Especially in the 1980s, when developing country governments were severely pressed to address difficult macroeconomic problems in their dealings with international lending agencies, the role of technical expertise, particularly in economics, became increasingly important (see, e.g., Milne 1982; MacDougall 1976; Cepeda Ulloa and Mitchell 1980). As we suggested in Chapter 3, few governments have resisted the trend to incorporate corps of technical advisers into middle- and high-level positions, and many governments have increasingly appointed ministers, secretaries, and undersecretaries with professional training—economists, agronomists, educators, engineers, and health professionals, for example. Ministers of finance, planning, and budgeting, and directors of central banks are rarely without degrees in economics and technical teams that they rely on for analysis and advice. In turn, presidents and prime ministers have appointed kitchen cabinets of economic advisers and have often elevated important technical ministries to preeminence in national policy making. Political leaders may need to justify decisions—particularly those that are unpopular—in terms of their technical "correctness" and may therefore increase the visibility of their technical advisers.[1] In countries in which the process of decision making is highly centralized in the executive, much policy discussion may be relatively closed and even secret. Such characteristics tend to increase the importance of technocrats in decision making. These new technocratic elites also include a variety of foreign advisers from international agencies, consulting firms, universities, and governments. The 1980s accelerated the trend toward technocracy in almost all developing countries.

It is not surprising, then, that decision makers in our cases considered the advice they received from domestic and international corps of technical advisers. Ministers with technical training and advisory teams of experts figured not only in the cases of macroeconomic reform but also in those that concerned sectoral policy and organizational changes. The technical advice was often imbued with ideological content, indicating the important role that ideas have in defining "correct" paths to development—decisions to adopt import substitution or export-led growth are good examples of this influence, but so also are decisions to emphasize the planning function in government or the role of markets in setting prices. Technical analyses and technical advisers were particularly prominent in shaping decisional outcomes in Korea and Indonesia; decision makers in these cases responded to the technical input they received and applied it to the problems they sought to solve. Moreover, it was they who determined that the technical advisers would play an important part in assessing options and recommendations. For example, in Korea, the military government that assumed power in 1961 and its civilian successor systematically increased the power of American-trained economists in decision making and relied on their advice about macroeconomic and market-oriented policy reforms. Their work was then critical to the export-led growth policies that were adopted by both these highly centralized governments (Haggard and Cole 1986; Haggard, Kim, and Moon 1987). In Indonesia, efforts by technical advisers helped legitimize the role of policy analysis in price policy in agriculture and were a critical factor influencing the minister of trade, the director of trade research, and the food logistics agency in designing policies for agricultural development (Timmer 1987a, 1987b).

More generally, what the advice was, how it was packaged by the technical advisers, how well it was understood by the decision makers, and how much confidence they had in the advice of the advisers appear to have been important in determining the content of specific decisions. Thus, the technical advice was not automatically accepted but was rather a lens or filter that was applied by decision makers. Their predispositions in terms of the characteristics considered in Chapter 2 were intervening variables that shaped receptivity to and application of the technical advice they received. Thus, in the case of technical advice and the receptivity of decision makers to it, the background characteristics of the policy elites appear to be important. The case of Ghana reflects well the complex way in which technical information feeds into actual decision-making contexts by affecting the perceptions of the decision makers.

> At the end of 1971, the governor of the central bank called an emergency meeting to discuss ways of meeting the economic crisis. No one from the Ministry of Finance attended, underlining the antagonism between the minister and the rest of the economic decision makers. Without his assessment of the economic consequences of the decision, the prime minister and cabinet decided to undertake a major devaluation in opposition to the position of the minister of finance. It later became clear that the cabinet was not well-equipped to evaluate the complex economic information given them in reports that were intended for an audience of trained economists at the central bank. Simpler memos with fewer recommendations should have been prepared to offer clear alternatives to the cabinet. (Roemer and Stern 1986)

In Ghana, technical lenses fit imperfectly, for they appeared to confuse the perception of decision makers, contributing to a poorly informed decision to devalue. The case of development strategy choice in Costa Rica provides clear evidence of the way the ideas of technical specialists can shape the perceptions of policy elites.

> The most structured and ideologically coherent criticism of traditional conservative ideas of the 1940s came from the "Centro de Estudios de los Problemas Nacionales" . . . the core of ideas which was to orient Costa Rica's development after 1948 emanated from the Centro. . . . [By] the late 1950s, the initial ideas of the Centro slowly sinking down and more than a decade of establishing the ground for industrialization set the stage for an import substitution strategy. (Doryan-Garrón 1988:91–92, 100)

On a more specific level, policy choices can be shaped by the relative power of technical advisers. This was true in the Ghana case, in which the power of the minister of finance waxed and then waned in the period leading up to the crisis; in Korea, where technocrats were largely unheeded by policy makers until regime changes in the 1960s brought them to greater dominance; and in Costa Rica, where the minister of planning and the head of the central bank varied in their influence over time and relative to each other. "Prior to the late 1984 appointment of a very prestigious economist to the Central Bank Post (Eduardo Lizano), the new Minister of Planning, Juan M. Villasuso, wielded the most influence. '1984 was indeed my year' [he stated in an interview]. . . . However, by early 1985, with Eduardo Lizano in full control of the Central Bank and Jorge M. Dengo serving as Economic Team Coordinator, another drive towards more conservative spending policies was pursued" (Doryan-Garrón 1988:32).

BUREAUCRATIC IMPLICATIONS

As indicated in Chapter 2, decision makers frequently represent bureaucratic constituencies. Integral to the choices they make are concerns about how particular changes will affect the power, prestige, budget, and clienteles of the ministry, agency, or bureau they represent (see, e.g., Foltz and Foltz 1988). When policy changes require changed behavior from bureaucratic agencies—greater efficiency or more equitable treatment of low-income beneficiaries, for example—issues of administrative capacity, compliance, and responsiveness are often important to policy elites. Moreover, when reforms imply organizational changes within ministries or agencies, the rivalries, competencies, and morale of the organizations they lead may well weigh on decision makers' minds as they consider options. In addition, bureaucratic leaders are generally concerned with how proposed changes affect their own career options (Grindle 1977).

Thus, a second criterion that emerged in the cases indicates how policy elites are influenced by the bureaucratic politics that surround the selection of policy and institutional changes. With regularity, decision makers within government were concerned with making decisions or supporting positions that would enhance the fortunes—in terms of budgetary resources, influence over programs, prestige, or clienteles—of the bureaucratic entities they led or were part of as well as contribute to their own career opportunities. The advocates of reform in Colombia, for example, were concerned that their efforts to rebuild the planning agency would generate a bureaucratic backlash from long-established ministries that felt threatened by the increased power of the planners. In Mali, public health officials anticipating salary bonuses, vehicles, and other perquisites raised few objections to the health sector reform "so dear to USAID's heart," even when they had serious reservations about its replicability (Gray et al. 1990:35). In the reorganization of the Ministry of Agriculture in Kenya, the permanent secretary was careful to assess and evaluate how his subordinates would respond to the changes (Thomas and Grindle 1988a). In the Philippines, some policy options were rejected in the search for a viable agrarian reform program because policy makers and their advisers were concerned about the lack of administrative capacity and motivation that existed inside the agrarian reform ministry (Thomas and Grindle 1988b).

In fact, in the case of Mali, the health project faltered and then died largely because bureaucratic concerns came to dominate decision making. But these cases also provide evidence that decision makers' criteria are often intertwined. In the Kenya decentralization case, for example, bureaucratic politics influenced the acceptance of reform, but so did a major political change that altered the support group most important to the regime. Moreover, concerns about the impact of reform on bureaucratic organizations can be triggered by expectations about political reactions. For example, in India, the refusal of a number of bureaucratic entities to assume responsibilities for urban water management reform was endemic because public officials were well aware that the reforms pressed upon them by the World Bank could easily incite political instability if they were pursued (Bajpai 1988). No agency wanted to take responsibility for a politically unpopular policy that would damage its reputation and make achievement of its normal responsibilities more difficult. In this case, bureaucratic buck-passing was engendered by concern about extrabureaucratic implications of reform.

POLITICAL STABILITY AND POLITICAL SUPPORT

Decision makers often represent the interests of particular organizations. They also respond to concerns about the political support available to the regime they represent or to its leadership. How particular decisions will affect the coalitions that sustain the regime in power, how policy changes can help develop new coalitions of support, and how particular clienteles will be affected by proposed changes often weigh prominently in their decisions. In fact, in a considerable amount of scholarly work, the goal of maintaining the regime has been adopted as a way to explain a wide range of policy decisions as well as to account for why certain policy options are off limits because they impose heavy costs on important groups in the society (Ames 1987; Krueger 1974; Lindenberg 1988). The importance of maintaining the regime is also used to explain how government actions are employed as pay-offs to maintain the loyalty of important groups or interests (Bates 1981; Haggard 1985; Srinivasan 1985; Bennett and DiLorenzo 1984). It is understandable that such criteria are often salient to decision makers because of the fragility of the coalitions that support incumbent regimes in many developing countries and because of the limited legitimacy that makes them vulnerable to the performance expectations of supporters (Ames 1987). At the broadest level, Robert Bates (1981:4) has argued that regime maintenance becomes the single most important factor in explaining the perpetuation of economically irrational development policies. "Governments want to stay in power. They must appease powerful interests. And people turn to political action to secure special advantages—rewards they are unable to secure by competing in the marketplace."[2]

Consistently, policy elites in our cases were concerned about how various options would affect political stability, political opposition and support, and the political use of policy resources. Thus, policy reform options were assessed by decision makers in terms of how reactions to them would affect the longevity of the regime in power or the particular leadership group wielding authority. Explicitly political criteria were applied to decision making, and they indicated the importance of building or maintaining coalitions of support for incumbent political elites. In Mali, for example, "the project sites were selected on the basis of political criteria. The Malians had recently fought a 'soccer war' with Burkina Faso (then Upper Volta), and wanted to have a presence in the border area. [In another area], the government wanted to . . . forestall any shifts in political loyalty" (Cash 1987).

The relationship of reform to political coalitions was of primary concern to decision makers in the Philippines: "Adoption of an agrarian reform was considered by some leaders of the government to be central to weakening the appeal of the insurgent National People's Army, but the fact that top leadership saw it as potentially disruptive of its support coalition meant that it was consistently given low priority in the government's policy agenda" (Thomas 1986).

Similarly, decision makers in Ghana were highly concerned about how devaluation would affect the groups thought to be important to maintaining the regime—cocoa farmers and urban elites (Roemer and Stern 1986). In Korea, decision makers believed that rapidly improving economic performance was a critical ingredient in building legitimacy for a new regime. In the case of decentralization in Kenya, President Kenyatta withheld support from the initiative because of the political utility of centralizing public resource allocations for rewarding his tribal support group. The subsequent administration found decentralization more attractive because it allowed the president to use policy resources to build up new constituencies of support (Hook 1986). Water management reform in India, involving fee increases for users, was resisted because of concern about adverse political reaction (Bajpai 1988). In designing Costa Rica's stabilization and structural adjustment programs to meet the demands of international agencies, administrations of the 1980s sought to rotate the costs of adjustment over time among different social groups in order to maintain the country's much-vaunted political stability (Doryan-Garrón 1988). Political concerns such as these were an inescapable aspect of decision making in all the cases.

INTERNATIONAL PRESSURE

As we indicate in Chapter 7, policy changes of the 1980s were marked by the role of international actors, including the vulnerability of developing countries to international economic and political pressures (see, e.g., Bacha and Feinberg 1986). During this period of severe international economic crisis, foreign donors, governments, and a variety of international agencies put extensive pressure on developing country governments to make recommended changes (Cohen, Grindle, and Walker 1985; Goldsmith 1988). With badly needed economic resources at their command, they sought leverage through a variety of mechanisms in order to promote changes in macroeconomic and sectoral policies. The power of these international actors was enlarged in part because they often command extensive technical expertise that can influence decision makers. Such issues as choice of technology and institutional reform were also pressed upon governments and often became conditions for "rewards" from international actors. In fact, in some explanations of policy choice, developing country governments are portrayed as having little or no choice but to acquiesce in the demands and recommendations of such powerful bodies as the International Monetary Fund and the World Bank (see, e.g., Payer 1974).

Indeed, a fourth factor that was regularly considered important by policy elites in our case histories was the role of international actors and international economic and political dependency relations in determining the outcome of decision making about reform. In South Korea, the U.S. ambassador withheld PL480 food aid in 1963 to pressure the government to adopt a stabilization plan and to hold elections (Haggard and Cole 1986; Haggard, Kim, and Moon 1987). The health sector reform initially suggested by the Mali government was taken over and radically redefined by USAID; in Jamaica, export promotion resulted from strong advocacy by the World Bank and the interest of government officials in receiving U.S. and World Bank assistance (Gray et al. 1990; Veira 1988).

As indicated in Chapter 4, however, these cases suggest not that policy elites have no choice when confronted with pressure from international agencies, but rather that decisions tend to reflect concern about the role of the international actors and how various options would affect relationships with them. The salience of pressure from international actors varies over time, and often in conformance with the perceptions of the policy elites about other concerns (see, e.g., Krasner 1978; Mares 1985).[3] In cases such as Korea and Ghana, decisions that reflected international pressures were taken after long periods of resisting or ignoring those pressures because policy elites had other priorities (Haggard and Cole 1986; Roemer and Stern 1986). In the Philippines, international pressure was a concern of decision makers but was not decisive in whether to pursue agrarian reform or not (Thomas 1986).

The cases also indicate how international actors become engaged in bureaucratic interactions in developing countries. In the Latin American cases of planning reform, for example, resources made available through the Alliance for Progress were used effectively within bureaucratic agencies to enhance the prestige and bargaining power of the agencies (Mallon 1986). In India,

> The Finance Ministry's general approach towards foreign aid is to maximize its volume on the most concessional terms available while minimizing external interference with established national policies. . . . [In the case of water management reform] the point repeatedly made by the Indian authorities was that . . . the [World] Bank was welcome to present its point of view for discussion . . . but that India could not accept wholesale policy change leveraged on particular projects. . . . Detailed discussions between the Bank, the Finance Ministry, and the Ministry of Works resulted in a compromise. (Bajpai 1988)

Technical analysis, bureaucratic interactions, concerns about political stability and support, and international leverage were factors that emerged repeatedly in the explanations offered by insiders in reform experiences to explain a variety of outcomes. These factors, summarized in table 5.1, emerged as a fairly consistent set of criteria that decision makers applied to specific options for policy and institutional change and that shaped their thinking about how to proceed on specific issues. How they were applied and how seriously they were considered tended to reflect the background characteristics of the policy elites—their ideological predispositions; their professional training, bureaucratic responsibilities, and political commitments; and their experience with similar choices in the past—as well as the interlocking general contexts related to historical and international conditions and bureaucratic capacity. This multiplicity of influences and concerns helps explain why decision makers, who appear in our cases to be serious and relatively well informed, frequently make mistakes in judging the political and economic consequences of the choices they make.

The Salience of Decision Criteria

Because of the consistency with which the four criteria emerged in the cases, they provide a first cut on the kinds of issues that decision makers consider when they assess options for policy and organizational change. Nevertheless, it is clear that the importance of each of the lenses through which specific decisions are viewed varies over time and among policies. A second cut on the concerns of policy elites can be made by considering the factors that appear to determine the relative importance of various criteria. In order to explain their variable salience, the characteristics of the agenda-setting process for specific issues provide important cues. Are policy elites considering a particular issue under circumstances of perceived crisis, or are they operating within a context of politics as usual? Answers to this question will signal the relative priority of distinct decision criteria for decision makers, indicating which lenses are most important to them under particular circumstances. Agenda setting and decision making are thus closely intertwined.

We believe that, overall, the cases suggest that crisis-ridden reforms are adopted or rejected most frequently in conformance to the priority of maintaining political stability, and that politics-as-usual reforms most frequently reveal the priorities of political support and bureaucratic implications. Technical advice and international pressures often figure as important factors considered, but they are generally subordinated to the political and bureaucratic concerns of decision makers. Additionally, we believe that we can make a distinction between macropolitical concerns (involving the implications of reform for broad categories of regime supporters and opponents and its implications for regime stability and survival) and micropolitical concerns (involving the implications of reform for narrower constituencies and clienteles, more short-term rewards for such support, and the political or bureaucratic fortunes of specific in-

TABLE 5.2
Macropolitical and Micropolitical Concerns of Policy Makers

Circumstances of Agenda Setting	Political Concerns of Decision Makers
	MACROPOLITICS
Perceived crisis	Legitimacy of the regime; Survival of the regime; Survival of the institutions of government; The "national interest"; Broadest categories of support groups (classes or sectors); Availability of policy resources to build major coalitions of broadly defined groups; "High politics"
	MICROPOLITICS
Politics-as-usual	Meeting parochial demands of interest groups; Availability of policy resources for "parceling out" to narrowly defined groups in exchange for political support; Clientelism; Short-term interests of political elite; Career aspirations of individual politicians; "Low politics"

dividuals). Crisis-ridden reforms tend to raise the salience of macropolitical concerns, while politics-as-usual changes often invoke micropolitical concerns.

The distinction between macropolitical and micropolitical concerns is not always clear-cut, for in politics-as-usual circumstances, overall political stability may be achieved by paying close attention to narrowly defined clienteles and responding to the short-term interests of specific groups. Nevertheless, we believe the distinction is useful in a general sense because it provides insights into the categories of political concerns that are relevant to decision makers. As summarized in table 5.2, macropolitical concerns, most prevalent under crisis situations, mean that policy elites pay particular attention to how reforms will affect the legitimacy of the regime they serve, longer-term political and economic goals, major definitions of "the national interest," class alignments, and the overall survival of the regime. Micropolitical concerns, most relevant in the non-crisis-ridden reforms, include concerns about the more parochial demands of specific interest groups, the use of policy resources to maintain clientelistic relationships, the parceling out of policy resources to ensure political control, and the more short-term interests of political elites (Hampson 1986; Doryan-Garrón 1988). The distinction between macropolitics and micropolitics suggests that the definition of politics by policy elites shifts under two different agenda-setting circumstances.

The following three hypotheses generalize from a limited number of cases of policy and institutional change about the hierarchy of concerns that appear to be relevant to decision makers.

Hypothesis 1:
In crisis-ridden reforms, decision making tends to be dominated by concern about major issues of political stability and control. Technical analysis, bureaucratic interactions, and international pressures often assume importance in these decisions but usually remain subordinate to concerns about the stability or survival of the regime in power or the longevity of its incumbent leadership.

Hypothesis 2:
When noncrisis-ridden reforms concern policy issues, decisional outcomes tend to be dominated by micropolitical and bureaucratic concerns. Technical input and international pressure are important, but not decisive, in explaining policy choice under these conditions. Major issues of political survival and support building are usually not salient to decision makers.

Hypothesis 3:
When noncrisis-ridden reforms concern issues of organizational change, decision making tends to be dominated by bureaucratic concerns. International pressures often emerge as part of bureaucratic interactions in these reforms. Technical input and concern for political survival are usually not salient to reform decision makers.

Table 5.3 summarizes the hypothesized linkages between circumstances in which agendas are set and criteria for making decisions. In the pages that follow, we use specific cases to illustrate each of these hypotheses. The cases of structural adjustment in Korea and health care in Mali indicate the differences in the salience of criteria that emerge under distinct circumstances of perceived crisis and politics as usual. The case of development strategy change in Costa Rica is an interesting illustration of how changing circumstances can alter the decision criteria of policy elites. Finally, the case of reorganization in the Ministry of Agriculture in Kenya indicates the salience of bureaucratic concerns in organizational reforms.

TABLE 5.3
Agenda Setting and Decision Making

Circumstances of Agenda Setting	Characteristics of Decision Process	Policy Elites Most Concerned About . . .
Perceived crisis	Frequently, problems pressed upon decision makers by interests outside of government; High political and economic stakes; Small groups of high-level decision makers closely involved; Major changes from prior policy (innovation); Sense of urgency to act, "do something"	Macropolitical issues such as legitimacy, social stability, costs and benefits to major national interests, duration of regime in power
Politics-as-usual	Frequently, problems "chosen" by decision makers for action; Low political and economic stakes; Middle- and lower-level officials involved, dependent on high-level support for action; Incremental changes in existing policy or institution; Little sense of urgency, with promoters of reform able to control extent of emphasis on change	Bureaucratic issues such as careers, budgets, compliance and responsiveness of implementers, incentives to modify bureaucratic behavior and procedures; Agency power within government; Micropolitical issues such as clientelism and narrow coalition building

Structural Adjustment in South Korea

Between 1960 and 1966, governments of South Korea adopted far-reaching policy reforms that ultimately reoriented the country's strategy for economic development.[4] Critical changes—a large devaluation and stabilization package, followed by new policy instruments to increase government revenues and encourage export-led growth—were made between 1964 and 1966. These changes confirm the characteristics of crisis-ridden reforms. Policy makers were keenly aware of a need to do something to improve the economic situation of the country. They were also under considerable pressure to make significant changes—from the military, the government's corps of reformist technocrats, leftist students, and the U.S. government. Two bad harvests of rice and barley in 1962 and 1963 created harsh food shortages and rising food prices in 1963 and 1964. Threats by USAID personnel to withhold PL480 food aid added to the sense of crisis within the military government in power between 1961 and January 1964 and its successor, the elected government of Park Chung Hee. The stakes were high for these regimes because they needed to consolidate power and legitimize their leadership. As tends to be the case with crisis-induced reforms, the decision makers were a small circle of high-level officials in a superministry—the Economic Planning Board—and the cabinet. The magnitude of the changes was significant and amounted to reversing the previous development strategy of import substitution. Thus, the changes in policy cannot be considered incremental. Moreover, most of the policy changes were accomplished within two years, corresponding to the urgency felt by the decision makers to respond to what they considered a crisis in the country's development.

The sense that a crisis existed, although clearly encouraged by the food shortages of 1963 and 1964, was not simply the result of an objective appraisal of economic indicators. Indeed, the Korean economy had been in difficult straits throughout much of the late 1950s and early 1960s, and pressure from the United States to reform economic policy had been a constant in Korean decision-making conditions since the late 1940s. The Syngman Rhee regime, however, successfully resisted or ignored pressures to alter existing policies that gave strong emphasis to import-substituting industrialization through a wide variety of benefits for domestic entrepreneurs. The U.S. government appeared to be in a powerful position vis-à-vis the regime, but in fact, it was not able to dictate policy.

> The significance of U.S. support for the Rhee government can hardly be overstated. AID financed nearly 70% of total imports between 1953 and 1961 and 75% of total fixed capital formation. In return for aid, the U.S. sought various economic policy reforms. . . . The reforms sought by the Americans over the fifties cut directly against Rhee's political interests, however. Rhee and his Liberal Party maintained power and financed their political activities through the distribution of patronage and various economic rents. . . . The aging nationalist proved skillful at manipulating Korea's strategic significance to maintain the flow of economic and military support. . . . Even when the United States began to reduce its aid commitments and succeeded in coupling aid with an annual stabilization program, it could not secure Rhee's commitment to a coherent and consistent planning effort. (Haggard, Kim, and Moon 1987:8–9)

In the early 1960s, however, political leadership changed, a new regime needed to consolidate power, and the perception that a crisis in economic development existed found greater credence among decision makers. The moment seemed more propitious for policy reform.

In many ways, then, it was the collapse of the Syngman Rhee regime in 1960 that opened the way for the adoption of stabilization policies and the initiation of important economic reforms. In the latter Rhee years, a broad range of policy instruments was used to increase the political control of the Liberal party. For example, licensing of all sorts, receipt of foreign exchange, and import-export business were all tied to the political machine, with Rhee having a direct hand in the allocation of many of these resources. Reformist technocrats in government were routinely ignored and circumvented as policy instruments were used to respond to the political rationality of rewarding important clienteles and support groups rather than to an economic rationality emphasizing efficiency and performance.

Violent student protest against Rhee's style of rule, poor economic performance, and complaints of a rigged election led to the demise of the regime. It was replaced by a short-lived civilian government that undertook economic reforms with only limited success. Then, a coup in May 1961 brought the military to power. The new military government, although split between older generals and younger, more radical colonels, was reformist in orientation and responsive to the broad concerns of the student protesters. Both groups found common ground in their concern to improve economic performance, in order to justify the coup and legitimize military leadership that had assumed power extraconstitutionally. The military government, in power between 1961 and 1964, centralized political power and economic policy making in the executive and consciously increased the relevance of the reformist technocrats in decision making. Regime change and a leadership group oriented toward reform thus opened the way for significant policy changes.

Beginning in the spring of 1963, the government began to make key economic changes to respond to what it identified as severe problems in the economy. In May 1964, under the civilian government of the former military junta leader, Park Chung Hee, policy makers agreed to a large devaluation. Stabilization measures, pressed upon the government by the USAID mission in Seoul, followed closely in the wake of the devaluation, as did tax and interest rate reform and policies whose goal was to expand exports and increase savings. Soon, with a change of American assistance personnel, export promotion as a development strategy assumed greater importance, and stabilization as an objective of macroeconomic policy receded in importance. The decisions to adopt such far-reaching reforms were not easily made. Many Koreans had grown up under tight trade controls and import allocations and were familiar with an economy that limited business flexibility and paid high rents to those who ran and benefited from the controls.

In the mid-1960s, however, several reasons came together to overcome resistance to change. First, Park encouraged an environment favorable to reform and placed great emphasis on "getting things done." This urgency to improve economic performance was instrumental in elevating the importance of technocrats in government. As early as 1961, American-trained Koreans in the Ministry of Finance, the Ministry of Reconstruction (Planning), and the state-owned banks were convinced of the benefits to be gained from macroeconomic and market-oriented policy reforms; however, at that time, they were not in positions of power. The deputy prime minister, head of the Economic Planning Board, brought these young technocrats up through the ranks, often skipping them past more senior people. These technocrats were supported by economic advisers in the USAID mission, who sent a clear message to the Korean government to adopt their advice, or U.S. aid would be cut back over the short term and gradually phased out over the longer term. The leadership thus faced a major loss of assistance at the same time that the bad harvests of the early 1960s created inflationary pressures and the prospect of significant balance-of-payments problems. Export growth was advocated by the technocrats as a way out of these economic problems and as a way of reducing vulnerability to external pressure; it was adopted by Park, who recognized the need to change policies.

These factors clearly encouraged the adoption of reforms, but it is unlikely that the domestic and foreign technocrats would have been listened to so carefully if it had not been for Park's concern about consolidating and legitimizing his power. Thus, concomitant with a variety of policy reforms came other measures that helped ensure their pursuit. He moved quickly to shift potential opponents out of government and to create loyalists through a series of promotions. Park had barely won the election of 1963, and he came to identify economic growth as the factor that would enable him to strengthen his power and give him broader political support. Domestic political opposition to such drastic changes should have been expected, but the political opposition was fragmented. Students were still active, but the left had been squashed under the military regime, and, as the new policies came into effect, business slowly came into the government's camp. Toward the end of 1965, the success of the new policies helped convince many that export growth was really happening, creating an *ex post* confirmation of the strategy.

The Korean case demonstrates the influence of the decision criteria that have been identified. Policy makers in South Korea in the early and mid-1960s shared an orientation toward reform, created in part by their dissatisfaction with the policies of the Rhee government and more general concerns about economic growth, efficiency, and getting things done. This general orientation increased the visibility of the technocrats and made the policy makers open to their advice about appropriate instruments for reorienting the country's development strategy. A greater emphasis on centralized decision making further increased the weight of the technocrats' advice. Bureaucratic politics was also a factor of concern to the policy makers as they increased the power of the economic bureaucracy and used government positions to increase political support and limit the capacity of corruption and clientelism to stymie agreed-upon reforms. Political stability and support were clearly goals the leaders wished to achieve, and much of their adhesion to the new departure in policies can be ascribed to the belief that the impact of the reforms on the economy would increase their political base of support and aid them in consolidating power. The impact of international pressure was pervasive, both as a contributor to the sense of crisis and as a criterion that influenced the decisions made. American advisers and American threats were clearly taken into consideration in the assessment of reformist measures.

The case suggests that the importance of the four lenses through which policy makers viewed proposed changes varied. Indeed, as indicated in hypothesis 1, the military and civilian governments were preeminently concerned with the issues of political stability and support and evaluated policy options in terms of their potential to contribute to these goals. Their receptivity to advice from both domestic and foreign technocrats, as well as their concern about the possible actions of the Americans, also contributed to the decisions that were made, but these factors were always subordinate to political concerns. Bureaucratic interactions appear to have been of least salience to the decision makers, in the sense that they did not appear to constitute a major constraint but rather an instrument that could be manipulated to promote the adoption and effectiveness of reform. Significantly, the predominant concern over the political impact of the reforms tended to center on macropolitical effects, that is, concerns about the legitimacy and longevity of the regime headed by Park. This can be contrasted with the situation under the Rhee government—problems were increasingly grave, but decision makers did not behave as if they believed a crisis existed—when political concerns tended to focus on micropolitical pay-offs of policy resources to specific and more narrowly defined clienteles.

Decision criteria, at least in the Korean case, do appear to assume different salience for decision makers. We believe this is related to the circumstances under which particular reforms are considered. Korean decision makers in the early to mid-1960s believed that economic and political crises faced their country. Pressing problems, high stakes, and urgency not only contributed to the fact that the changes considered were major departures from prior policy but also meant that these changes were carefully evaluated in terms of their potential political impact on the regime and its incumbents. The case of Mali's health reform, presented in Chapter 4 and briefly recapitulated below, indicates a significantly different ordering of elite priorities. We believe these priorities are related to the politics-as-usual circumstances that placed health reform on the agenda for government decision makers.

HEALTH POLICY REFORM IN MALI

As will be recalled from Chapter 4, health care reform in Mali was a chosen problem, and no particular event or stimulus could be identified as providing a propitious moment for reform. Decision makers were at middle and high levels in the Ministry of Health, a relatively weak ministry within the government, and the stakes for top-level leadership in the government were low. No particular crisis or sense of urgency stimulated rapid response or the complete rejection of existing policy. In fact, it took two years to develop the plan, and its content was largely drafted by USAID personnel and consultants in the absence of any real involvement on the part of the government. In the reform initiative, the dominant concerns of policy makers and implementers were with the problems and benefits that would accrue to the ministry and its personnel if the change were pursued. Thus, bureaucratic infighting (which involved considerable tension with USAID), reluctance of technical personnel to commit themselves to the change, and the desire to acquire project resources such as vehicles, supplies, and regular paychecks figured prominently in decision making. More explicitly political criteria were applied in the selection of sites, but the concern for political support building did not appear to incorporate the macropolitical concerns of national political leaders. Bureaucratic and micropolitical concerns seemed to dominate decision making in this case, and technical concerns appear to have played more minor roles in determining decisional outcomes. Contrary to hypothesis 2, however, the importance of international actors for the Malians was great.

Based on the examples of reformist initiatives in Korea and Mali, the salience of decision criteria applied by decision makers does appear to vary with agenda-setting circumstances. If this is plausible, then the priorities among decision criteria should change when the dynamics of agenda setting change. This situation appears to have occurred repeatedly in the case of Costa Rica. Between 1948 and 1986, that country made four major transitions in development strategy. Major changes occurred when policy elites believed a national crisis existed; their decisions were generally dominated by concerns about the macropolitical consequences of change. When the crisis was considered to have passed, policy changes conformed to the model of politics as usual, and more micropolitical criteria were used to evaluate options.

DEVELOPMENT STRATEGY REFORMS IN COSTA RICA

The four shifts in development strategy in Costa Rica correspond to the tenures of specific administrations.[5] In the first shift, which occurred in 1948–49, the state assumed greater control over the economy by nationalizing the banks, which limited the traditional power of importers and coffee exporters. A new strategy of modernized primary export-led growth was promoted through policies to encourage agricultural diversification. This strategy was significantly altered between 1959 and 1963 when Costa Rica joined the Central American Common Market and adopted a strategy of import substitution. Then, in 1972, the "entrepreneurial state" was created, and with it, efforts to deepen the structure of the country's import-substituting industrialization were pursued. Between 1982 and 1986, this strategy was rejected in favor of a liberalized export promotion strategy.

In each case, policy makers perceived a developmental crisis that stimulated the search for alternative solutions. Table 5.4 summarizes the changes and the elements of crisis that were perceived by the state elites under the four strategy shifts. The changes generally appeared on the policy agenda of government decision makers as pressing problems, and the stakes were considered to be high by policy elites, involving their ability to hold a broad supportive coalition together and to maintain the regime in power and/or the incumbency of the political party they represented. In each case, decision makers included the president, the minister of finance, the minister of planning, and the director of the central bank as well as corps of advisers—both political and technical—in government and the political parties. Finally, the changes in policy were innovative rather than incremental.

Of course, a wide variety of factors helped put strategy changes on the agenda of government action in Costa Rica, and a series of factors is useful in explaining the content of the policy changes made. In each of them, however, decision makers sifted through a series of decision criteria in crafting the content of the strategy shift. For example, each shift required a new vision or definition of development and how to achieve it. New development ideologies were adopted by policy makers, often as a result of the work of technical specialists, and these in turn contributed to their receptivity to advice from domestic and foreign technocrats. A good example of this was the shift to import substitution, in which the work of Raúl Prebisch and others from the UN Economic

TABLE 5.4
Development Strategy Shifts in Costa Rica

	Date President			
	1948–1949 José Figueres	1959–1963 Mario Echandi	1972–1978 José Figueres	1982–1986 Luis Monge
Strategy adopted	Modernized primary export-led growth	Import substitution	Entrepreneurial state; Deepening of import substitution	Export-led growth
Elements of crisis perceived	Dominance of traditional oligarchy encouraging economic and political instability; Emergence of new economic sectors without access to decision making; Potential for violence	Sharp drop in coffee prices, adverse prices for bananas, cocoa; Other Central American countries embarked on industrialization process; Crisis of primary export-led growth strategy	Deterioration of CACM; Increased vulnerability to foreign capital; External disequilibrium	Sharply declining GDP and real per capita GDP; Rapid escalation of inflation; Unemployment; External debt; Exhaustion of import substitution
Moments for reform	Aftermath of civil war; New constitution; New administration	New administration; Different party in power	New administration; Different party in power	New administration; Severe economic crisis perceived by populace
Principal changes adopted	Nationalize banks; Implement social and labor legislation; Tax on capital; Agricultural diversification; Introduction of economic bureaucracy	Join Central American Common Market; Incentives to domestic production; Strengthen power of state economic bureaucracy to allocate resources	Creation of Costa Rican Development Corporation	Stabilization; Dismantling of entrepreneurial state; Structural adjustment

Source: Doryan-Garrón 1988.

Commission for Latin America played a key role in reorienting policy and encouraging the ascendance of a corps of technocrats within government. Similarly, in the shift initiated in 1982, technical analyses of the origins of the country's economic crisis played a key role in the emergence of a new development strategy.

Development strategy shifts also corresponded to major shifts in coalition partners in Costa Rica. In each case, decision makers appeared to have consciously attempted to incorporate new groups into the elite structures of the economy and the government while undercutting the power of those representing the most negative aspects of the previous strategy. In the late 1940s, for example, José Figueres consciously sought to undercut the power of agro-exporters, importers of manufactured goods, and financiers and banks while incorporating small agricultural producers and a new class of agro-industrialists into economic and political power (Doryan-Garrón 1988:13–14). Luís Monge sought to build national consensus around a new development strategy in the 1980s and was followed by Oscar Arias, who worked actively to promote "an equilibrated, balanced path towards an export-led strategy where adjustment costs would be rotated among different sectors, where the key would be gradualism, and where the country's social stability would be a major concern" (Doryan-Garrón 1988:41).

The role assumed by international conditions and actors also weighed in the minds of decision makers, particularly during the development shifts of 1959–63, when decision makers were principally concerned about the activities of other Central American countries, and the shift initiated in 1982, in which Central American regional instability, USAID, the IMF, and the World Bank all increased in salience for decision makers. As with other cases, however, these international concerns did not necessarily determine policy outcomes. Indeed, even in the midst of a major economic crisis in the 1980s,

[President] Monge delayed signing another IMF Stand-by Agreement [in 1987]. To do so, he needed World Bank and USAID support because of a crossed conditionality mechanism. . . . The IMF requested the simultaneous signing of a Structural Adjustment Loan (SAL) with the World Bank and negotiations with the Club of Paris. The World Bank made signing the IMF agreement a pre-condition. USAID listed both as conditions for greater economic aid. This complex situation allowed the administration to delay the IMF agreement, mainly done in order to obtain World Bank and AID support in a stance against the more severe IMF restrictions regarding social policies. . . . In this case, then, the government used cross conditionality to play off one international agency against the others. (Doryan-Garrón 1988:35)

The elites' concern with macropolitical factors during crisis decision making is important in explaining all of the strategy shifts. In Costa Rica, state elites were actively involved in efforts to establish a national consensus on the importance of change, and crisis situations appeared to have provided them with additional autonomy to influence the content of the new strategy. In the 1980s, for example,

> President Monge's landslide victory in 1982 also reflected a consensus for change and for the new President to have full control over the Executive, Congress, and local governments. Electoral support, in addition to the agreement with the opposition, created a political and economic environment where domestic political pressures were lessened. Aided by the macropolitical environment brought on [by] the crisis, state elite decision makers can construct their own ideas about how to deal with the crisis. (Doryan-Garrón 1988:159–60)

If we examine what occurred between major strategy choices in Costa Rica, however, the priorities and autonomy of decision makers appear to have been significantly different. During periods when elites did not agree that a crisis existed, pressure groups took on added weight in decision making, and micropolitical factors tended to dominate decisions about policies and resource allocation. Moreover, after strategy shifts occurred, the bureaucratic power of individuals within the president's economic team was often related to incremental adjustments in the dominant strategy. Frequently, for example, the views of the director of the central bank conflicted with those of the minister of planning. In the Monge administration, the ascendance of, first, the director of the central bank, then the minister of planning, and then the central bank director once again, led once more to adjustments in the overall export promotion strategy. One example of the influence in the shift in circumstances is the administration of Rodrigo Carazo between 1978 and 1982. Even though Carazo advocated a change in the country's development strategy, politics-as-usual circumstances stymied efforts at instrumenting major innovations.

> Within the framework of a stable economy, fairly high GDP growth, and cheap foreign loans during his first three years in office, Carazo did not face the opportunities for change (nor the dangers) which a crisis provided. Without this sense of crisis, micropolitical motives, distributional coalitions and short-sighted electoral politics became the everyday reality of Costa Rican society from early 1978 to early 1981. Carazo appeared to have the will and the beliefs necessary to bring about a change in development strategy, but he needed a push from a crisis situation. (Doryan-Garrón 1988:159)

This Costa Rican case is instructive in linking changes in agenda-setting circumstances to distinct decision criteria of policy elites and in indicating that the autonomy of decision makers to craft policy solutions varies with such circumstances. It appears that, even though the stakes are higher for decision makers under crisis-ridden circumstances, their autonomy to develop solutions is increased. If their autonomy to define solutions is greater, however, so is their capacity to misjudge the political acceptability of proposed reforms. Concern for the macropolitical impact of change is a logical consequence of this high-risk situation. A very different set of factors emerges in the final case considered here, that of a ministry reorganization in Kenya in which concerns about bureaucratic interactions were most salient to decision makers.

REORGANIZATION OF THE MINISTRY
OF AGRICULTURE IN KENYA

The third hypothesis predicts that decision makers will be primarily concerned about bureaucratic politics in instituting organizational reforms and will be little concerned with technical analysis and issues of political survival. This case is well illustrated by an effort to reorganize the Ministry of Agriculture in Kenya in 1978 and 1979.[6] Ministry reorganization in Kenya was facilitated by an important political moment; thus, although this politics-as-usual reform principally involved bureaucratic concerns and bureaucratic implications, it occurred in part because the bureaucracy was embedded within a broader political context.

In August 1978, President Jomo Kenyatta, Kenya's only president since independence in 1963, died. Kenyatta's long period of leadership was based on political support derived from his role as the leader of the national movement for independence and on his strong power base in the Kikuyu tribe, the largest tribe, which represented approximately 25 percent of the population. There were widespread apprehensions in Kenya and abroad as to the potential conflicts that might occur in the struggle for succession. It was therefore a source of pride to Kenyans when the vice-president, Daniel arap Moi, succeeded to the presidency in a smooth constitutional manner. Moi, a Kalenjin, came from one of the smallest tribes in the nation and had no independently established power base. According to the constitution, the new president had to call an election within sixty days of succeeding to office. To win this election, Moi had to consolidate his presidency and to build his own, non-Kikuyu power base. He moved quickly to use the power of appointment to accomplish this. Among his first acts were to appoint a new cabinet, to select new heads of Kenya's many parastatal organizations, and to reorganize the senior civil service.

The Ministry of Agriculture, one of the most powerful ministries, was affected by these changes. It had the largest number of employees and the largest budget of all government dependencies because of the importance of agriculture to the country's economy. Agriculture constituted 42 percent of Kenya's GDP in 1977 and accounted for 90 percent of total exports. Agricultural land holding was the basis of power and wealth for many of Kenya's upper class. In addition to the ministry, there were over twenty parastatal organizations in the agricultural sector. The minister or the permanent secretary of agriculture chaired most of the boards of directors of the parastatals. In addition, there were several powerful private organizations such as the Kenya Farmers Association that acted as lobbies in the sector.

President Moi appointed a new minister and permanent secretary (PS) of agriculture in 1978. Shortly after taking up his assignment, the new PS noticed that virtually every problem or issue came directly to his office. His work load was overwhelming, and priorities were often dictated by external circumstance. Because of constant claims on his time, he usually was not able to start on each day's large accumulation of files until well after the end of the official working day. He was soon quite concerned because he was finding himself constantly reacting to questions that were brought to him, but he was rarely able to control problems or initiate solutions.

To understand the situation better, he undertook a review of the functioning of the management of the ministry. He spoke with all the principal officers to get their explanation of how they conceived their roles and their views of how the ministry should work. He also consulted a foreign management adviser who had been working in the ministry for about a year and a half. What he learned confirmed his initial impressions. The various assistant secretaries did not have continuing responsibilities but awaited the assignment of specific tasks by the PS or deputy secretaries. Moreover, as he observed the functioning of his staff, the PS began to notice that there was an informal power network that ran vertically within the ministry but often across formal lines of authority. This network was based on tribal affiliations. Each officer was tied into an informal tribal-based network that often conflicted with formal lines of authority and responsibility.

After some reflection, the permanent secretary decided that the only way he could manage and control his job was to assign specific responsibilities to each of his management staff and hold each accountable for performing these roles. Each would have responsibility in his or her area for following specific issues, organizations, and topics. Each would be responsible for reporting to the PS before any issue became a problem and for warning him in advance and providing a full briefing when decisions were needed on a specific issue. Others would have continuing responsibility for monitoring the performance and issues of parastatals and either briefing the PS before he attended board meetings or keeping him fully informed if they attended on his behalf. In addition, the PS identified several areas of major responsibility such as monitoring food availability in all regions of the country and monitoring the implementation of development projects. These were to be assigned to specific officers.

The PS knew that such an organization would be controversial and even threatening because staff might resist the notion of being held responsible for a particular area of the ministry's work. He wanted to carry out the reorganization with a minimum of disruption. Consequently, he discussed the plan with all senior management staff individually, and job assignments were revised to suit individual skills and preferences. Every officer assured the PS personally that he or she supported the plan. The concept and the specifics seemed to be received enthusiastically, and everyone appeared to be willing to make his or her best efforts to implement the new system.

Nevertheless, after the PS implemented the new plan, some unforeseen problems began to emerge. The deputy secretaries, for example, resisted the new arrangements, despite their earlier verbal endorsement of the changes. In the past they had been able to assign much of the work to the assistant secretaries, and they felt that the new system shifted power to the PS. There was also resistance from some of the assistant secretaries who did not like what appeared to be a heavier work load, less free time, and being held accountable for continuing performance. The most serious problem arose because of the nature and influence of the informal power structure within the ministry. Officers often were unwilling or unable to move across these informal power networks and share information with those of other groups.

In the face of these problems, the PS took steps to enforce his reorganization. He set in motion arrangements to transfer one of the deputy secretaries and to replace him with someone he thought would be more sympathetic to what he was trying to accomplish. Unfortunately, that took a long time. Before it was accomplished the PS himself was transferred. Moi had won the election and was now securely in power; to tailor government to his needs, several shuffles of top officials took place. Thus, the PS was moved to the Ministry of Sports and Culture after less than eighteen months in the Ministry of Agriculture. The new personal secretary of agriculture had to deal with an imminent food shortage, so he did not take on the issues of internal organization in the ministry for some time. In the interim, officers generally slid back into the old system of waiting to be assigned specific tasks. The reorganization of the ministry came to a halt.

In this case, while the general context indicated a propitious moment for reform in terms of a national political environment, the decision to reorganize the Ministry of Agriculture was dominated by concerns about how change would be received within the ministry. Other decision criteria were weak by comparison. In this effort at reorganization, bureaucratic politics explains the desire of the permanent secretary to increase his power and autonomy by shifting work assignments and increasing his control over the behavior of subordinates and also the reaction of officers within the ministry to efforts to reassign responsibilities. The fate of the reform was also significantly determined by the intrabureaucratic sources of conflict and resistance that it introduced.

Conclusions

In this chapter, we have suggested that political and bureaucratic concerns tend to be uppermost in the minds of decision makers when they assess options for policy and organizational changes. Moreover, their political concerns tend to be dominated by macropolitical or micropolitical considerations, depending on how particular issues get on the decision-making agenda. Despite the predominance of political and bureaucratic criteria in decision-making situations, policy elites also often assess options in terms of the technical advice they receive and their implications for international political and economic relationships.

The cases presented here suggest that policy elites have personal orientations to the problems they address that are shaped by ideology, training, political commitments, and experience. These elites also generally have implicit understandings of the political and bureaucratic environments they confront that set limits on the options they consider and help them select among a variety of decision criteria. Policy choices do not result from the autonomous action of decision makers, but neither are they mere reflections of the power of societal groups. The cases indicate how broad contextual factors, perceptual predispositions of state elites, and circumstances of crisis or politics as usual combine to shape the preferences of decision makers. For those who seek to go beyond analysis to consider actions that can strengthen opportunities for reform, this chapter can form a basis for thinking strategically about the factors that will be uppermost in decision makers' minds and how the content of particular reforms could respond to their political and bureaucratic concerns. This is a topic that we return to in Chapter 8. In the next chapter, we use an analysis of the characteristics of particular policies to illustrate how the framework can become the basis on which to predict the ease or difficulty of implementation and sustainability of reform, and how it can be used to develop strategies for reformers.

CHAPTER 6

Implementing Reform: Arenas, Stakes, and Resources

However difficult and politically risky it is to decide to introduce a reformist initiative, the process of implementing and sustaining that decision is likely to be even more fraught with difficulty and risk. The capacity of governments to bring about sought-after changes often proves problematic because opposition can emerge from many sides and stymie efforts to implement reform. Nevertheless, the difficulty of turning decisions to alter existing policy and institutional arrangements into reality is often inadequately acknowledged in both theory and practice. Instead, policy makers and policy analysts tend to assume that decisions to bring about change automatically result in changed policy or institutional behavior.

This situation is reflected in the meager literature on implementation. In comparison to the amount written on and the intellectual attention given to policy analysis and decision making, implementation has been relatively neglected. As our cases repeatedly demonstrate, the implementation phase of the policy reform process frequently determines the nature and success of a policy reform initiative. Often, in practice, the process of implementation leads to outcomes quite different than those intended and anticipated by analysts and decision makers. Review of the literature of implementation only suggests this complexity, focuses on examples of faulty implementation, and most important, provides little guidance to those directly involved.[1] This chapter attempts to close that gap.

Our cases provide examples of both success and failure in implementation; but, equally as important, they provide examples of a range of intermediate and even unanticipated outcomes. It is this richness and variety of experience that suggests the need for a framework to help those involved and concerned develop strategies of implementation.

In this chapter, we examine the evidence, provided by our cases, that demonstrates the critical nature of implementation in the process of policy reform. To enable policy makers better to manage implementation, we develop an interactive model of implementation that contrasts with the linear model that is frequently implicit in efforts to bring about changed policy and institutional contexts for development. The approach we propose for analyzing the process of implementation also provides some tools for anticipating reactions to change, considering the prospects for sustaining a reform through the implementation stage, and assessing whether the resources to implement it actually exist or need to be augmented. Central to our argument is the assertion that the characteristics of particular reforms determine the type of conflict and opposition that surround their implementation. With this proposition as a critical component of our framework, we believe that the basis is laid for thinking strategically about the management of reform. This chapter begins with analysis and then suggests ways in which this analysis can be applied in reform situations to improve prospects for implementing and sustaining change initiatives.

The Linear Model of Implementation

A roughly linear model of the policy process is implicit in many analyses of or proposals for reform. According to this view, a proposed reform gets on the agenda for government action, a decision is made on the proposal, and the new policy or institutional arrangement is implemented, either successfully or unsuccessfully. Figure 6.1 illustrates this model in a decision tree format: the decision is seen as the critical choice and becomes the focus of policy maker and donor attention and concerns about appropriate policy analysis, while implementation is either ignored or considered to be the responsibility of another group, the managers. All too often, implementation is thought to be a matter of carrying out that which has been decided upon, and successful implementation is viewed as a question of whether or not the implementing institution is strong enough for the task.[2] If implementation is unsuccessful, the usual remedy is to call for greater efforts to strengthen institutional capacity or to blame failure on lack of political will, an explanation often propounded by external analysts and donors who see countries not carrying

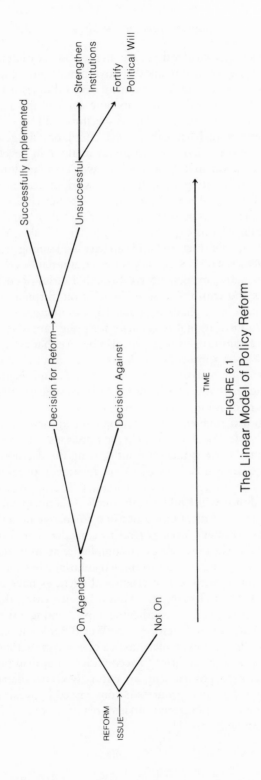

FIGURE 6.1
The Linear Model of Policy Reform

out reforms they consider desirable. In the absence of detailed knowledge about what goes on within another government and a capacity to analyze the decision process, lack of political will becomes a catch-all culprit, even though the term has little analytic content and its very vagueness expresses the lack of knowledge of specific detail.

This linear model has encouraged international agencies to support substantial efforts to strengthen policy analysis in developing countries in the expectation that good analysis will translate into good decision making and thus into good policy. The work of academic specialists has also contributed to the view that improved policy choices will result from rational policy analysis (see, e.g., Timmer, Falcon, and Pearson 1983). Operationalizing this expectation has generally taken the form of technical assistance contracts to build capacity in planning and policy analysis in many sectors. The U.S. Agency for International Development has been particularly active in such efforts through a series of contracts with U.S. universities and consulting firms. In addition, through donor programs, resources have been made available to planning agencies in developing countries to institutionalize capacity for policy analysis. While we think such innovations are desirable, we also believe that the links between the identification of appropriate policy options through analysis and their adoption cannot be assumed. Moreover, even after the decision to adopt a new policy is made, considerable evidence suggests that the real work of turning reform into reality is still ahead.

International financial and development agencies also make implicit use of the linear model of reform in their dealings with developing country governments. Their strategy for influencing the decision process is consistent, whether it is called structural adjustment, program lending, conditionality, leverage, or policy dialogue.[3] The approach is straightforward: the donor will lend or grant funds if the recipient agrees to make certain policy reforms. Once a decision to change policy is made by the recipient government, donors tend to consider that their job is largely accomplished. They may check on compliance at intervals, but in general, decision is expected to lead to implementation. Beyond the confines of any particular reform, the international agencies have at times become concerned with implementation issues. In such cases, they have emphasized the importance of strengthening implementing institutions and government commitment to reform. The World Bank's *World Development Report* for 1983, for example, makes a case for strengthening institutions in order to facilitate reform: "Faced with widespread poverty and slow economic growth, governments are naturally keener than ever to promote development. But their progress is constrained by weak institutions and management. . . . managerial capacity places an overall limit on a country's development" (p. 41).

In recent analyses, a more focused approach to strengthening institutional capacity for implementation has been articulated: "Conventional public administration prescriptions will normally not be sufficiently timely, focused or powerful to have a significant impact on the capacity of institutions to manage urgent programs of policy reform. Instead, a more specific strategy of institutional reform is required, directed at the critical agencies and functions" (Lamb 1987:4–5).

Our view of the process and of the role of implementation within it is substantially different from the linear model. Our observations over many years, as well as our research, indicate that implementation is often the most crucial aspect of the policy process and that the outcomes of implementation efforts are highly variable, ranging from successful to unsuccessful, but including also an almost limitless number of other potential outcomes. The range of outcomes results from the fact that implementation is an interactive and ongoing process of decision making by policy elites and managers in response to actual or anticipated reactions to reformist initiatives. Thus, we view these officials as potential strategic managers working within complex policy and institutional contexts who are concerned about achieving politically, institutionally, and economically viable outcomes of efforts to introduce change. We view the process of policy change as one shaped significantly by the actions of individuals in strategic locations to influence a particular change. Decision makers and implementers inevitably face opposition in attempting to pursue reform initiatives; in consequence, it is important to consider feasibility in terms of support and opposition to change, what stakes they and the governments they serve have in the pursuit of reform, and the political and bureaucratic resources needed to sustain such initiatives.[4] An alternative model of implementation can structure such an analysis.

Implementing Policy Reform: An Interactive Model

We begin with the assumption that a state of equilibrium surrounds an established policy set. This equilibrium results from the acceptance of existing policy or institutional arrangements by those who are affected—positively or negatively—by it. Efforts to alter existing policy upset that equilibrium and will elicit some response or reaction from those affected by the change. Reaction to policy change may come at any point in the process of decision and implementation. However, reactions are more than likely to occur farther into the process, since the effects of the change will become more visible as the nature and impact of the new policy become more evident. The nature, intensity, and location of those reactions will determine whether the reform is implemented and sustained.

The central element in the model is that a policy reform initiative may be altered or reversed at any stage in its life cycle by the pressures and reactions of those who oppose it. Unlike the linear model, the interactive model views policy reform as a process, one in which interested parties can exert pressure for change at many points. Some interests may be more effective at influencing high-level officials in government, others at affecting the managers of the implementation process or those who control the resources needed for implementation. Understanding the location, strength, and stakes involved in these attempts to promote, alter, or reverse policy reform initiatives is central to understanding the outcomes.

This interactive model is presented schematically in figure 6.2. In the model, pressures to put reform issues on the policy agenda come from many sources, including frequent "reform-mongering" by policy elites, and the agenda represents a stockpile of proposed changes. Some items on the agenda are acted upon, but many are not, often because of the preferences, perceptions, and actions of policy elites and their appreciation of the economic and political environment they face, as we suggested in Chapter 4. The agenda always contains many more issues than will be acted upon as well as issues that have been acted upon but not implemented.

Some issues receive active consideration by policy makers, but the point of actual decision is hard to determine precisely. The authorization process may move through one or more stages of the bureaucracy and may have to be confirmed at some level of political decision making. Once an affirmative decision is made, it may be reversed at a higher level or at some point in the implementation process, and the issues may be returned to the agenda. Thus, the ecision process needs to be envisaged as a series of formal and informal stages, with numerous actors who have distinct interests and concerns, as we indicated in Chapter 4.

The effects of a change in policy become more visible as implementation proceeds, and there are likely to be more challenges to the original conception of the reform. In this process, the characteristics of the policy will have an important influence on the nature of the reaction or response to change. In fact, the characteristics of a reformist initiative have a powerful influence on whether it will be implemented as intended or whether the outcome will be significantly different. Moreover, the distribution of the costs and benefits of a policy or institutional change, its technical complexity, its administrative intensity, its short- or long-term impact, and the degree to which it encourages participation determine whether the reaction or response to the initiative will occur primarily in a public or a bureaucratic arena. Policy characteristics also determine the

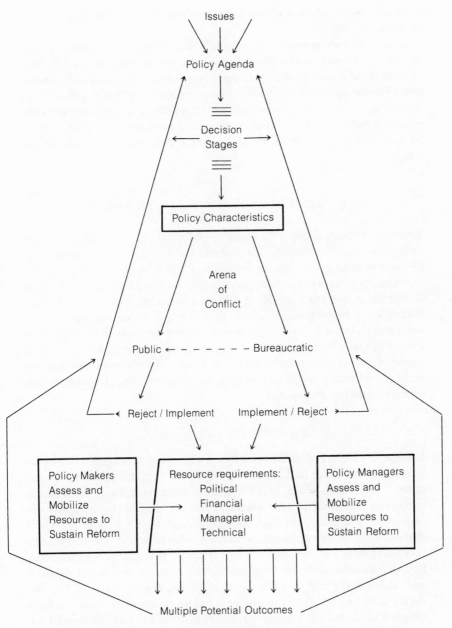

Issues

Policy Agenda

≡≡≡

Decision
Stages

≡≡≡

Policy Characteristics

Arena
of
Conflict

Public ← – – – – – – Bureaucratic

◄ Reject / Implement   Implement / Reject ►

| Policy Makers Assess and Mobilize Resources to Sustain Reform | Resource requirements: Political Financial Managerial Technical | Policy Managers Assess and Mobilize Resources to Sustain Reform |

Multiple Potential Outcomes

FIGURE 6.2
An Interactive Model of Policy Implementation

resources policy elites and implementers require if the change is to be pursued successfully.

In the implementation process, political, financial, managerial, and technical resources are likely to be needed to sustain the reform. Mobilizing these is part of the challenge to decision makers and policy managers. Those opposing the policy change may attempt to block access to the necessary resources, thus stalling the reform and returning it to the policy agenda. Choices by policy elites and managers at this stage may have an important bearing on the eventual outcome of the reform initiative.

Four Cases of Implementing Policy Reform

Four of our cases illustrate a range of potential outcomes of implementation efforts. Two of them demonstrate successful and unsuccessful implementation of policy decisions, while a third suggests that an implementing organization can substantially alter a policy long after a decision to pursue it has been made. A fourth case indicates that a reformist initiative can be removed from the agenda because those responsible for implementation are convinced that it cannot be carried through. The cases illustrate that even when reforms are implemented as intended, implementation consists of a series of choices that are made by decision makers and policy managers in response to obstacles, changing conditions, and divergent priorities.

RICE PRICING IN INDONESIA

In the mid-1960s, Indonesia established a food logistics agency, BULOG, to stabilize the price and assure the supply of rice and other basic food grains.[5] In the late 1960s, BULOG gained the confidence of key decision makers in the Suharto government, especially officials in the ministries of finance and trade, through its technical analysis of food aid wheat that allowed the government to increase sales of wheat and to generate revenues for the national budget. As a result of its technical contributions, BULOG was charged with ongoing responsibility for stabilizing the price and ensuring the supply of basic food grains, principally rice. For two decades, BULOG had to pursue its mandate of ensuring adequate food supplies while taking account of unstable domestic political conditions and working in a volatile international environment. While some of its actions appear questionable or contradictory in the perspective of the 1990s, in fact, it generally met its basic policy responsibility effectively in years of changing political and economic conditions.

In the 1960s and early 1970s, Indonesia's economy was unstable and experienced inflationary pressures. When the Ministry of Finance, under IMF pressure, tightened credit, BULOG found itself seriously short of funds to purchase necessary amounts of rice to sell at the established price. A decision, recommended by the agency's food policy analysts, to price PL480 wheat at a level that would produce revenue for the development budget enabled BULOG to maintain the rice supply. Then, in 1972, poor harvests worldwide meant that the agency came under heavy pressure to find supplies and finance rice imports. This it managed to do, just barely meeting domestic demand. By 1974, the situation changed again. Indonesia's oil revenues surged, and this relieved the constraints on buying rice to sell at subsidized prices to urban consumers. In the initial stages of the oil boom, no attempt was made to equate domestic with world market prices; by the mid-1970s, however, BULOG officials became aware of the fact that Indonesia was buying 25 percent of the international market supply of rice. In response to this knowledge, they initiated another policy shift.

The policy response to this new situation was to initiate a major effort to increase domestic production of rice through investment in agriculture and rural development and to stimulate competition in the domestic rice market. Steps were also taken to strengthen the institutional capacity of BULOG. As a consequence of the new policies and technology, rice production increased at a rate of 7 percent a year between 1978 and 1986. Despite such innovations, in 1985 a new crisis emerged. The government budget was squeezed between the continuing costs of subsidizing imported rice and declining revenues as a result of falling oil prices. When rice prices collapsed, BULOG continued to borrow to maintain a minimum rice price to protect domestic production, but at the cost of running up its debt and becoming the focus of the Ministry of Finance's concern for budgetary austerity. By this time, however, BULOG's reputation as an effective food agency enabled it to buy time to reduce its subsidies and subsequently its debt without outside intervention, and still meet its objective of rice supply and price stability in altered circumstances.

BULOG had to pursue its two policy mandates—stabilize the price of basic food grains and ensure their supply—over twenty years in frequently changing circumstances. That it was successful at doing this was a result of substantial investment in technical and managerial staff who were able to shift priorities and influence other agencies of government in changing situations. Its own growing competence and reputation meant that it became a powerful bureaucratic actor itself and an effective proponent of the policies it was charged with pursuing.

The history of BULOG illustrates the effects of time, complexity, and demands of the implementation process on those attempting to carry out a policy as intended. In 1960, Indonesia's policy makers could never have predicted the circumstances in which their policy goals would have to be pursued. It was only the capacity and commitment of BULOG that enabled Indonesia's food policy goals to be successfully implemented.

DEVALUATION IN GHANA

In 1971, a decision to devalue the currency was made after the shortage of foreign exchange became acute.[6] The decision makers, the prime minister and his cabinet, gave relatively little thought to the complexities of implementation. The decision came after a period of growing crisis.

Substantial foreign exchange earnings from cocoa exports enabled Ghanaians to become used to importing luxury items they desired in the 1950s and 1960s. As long as the international price of cocoa remained high, this consumptionist bias could be sustained. However, in the mid-1960s, international cocoa prices began a steady decline, putting foreign exchange reserves under acute pressure. When the Progress party, headed by Dr. Kofi Busia, was elected and took office in October 1969, it faced major economic problems.

In 1971, cocoa prices headed sharply downward, and deficits mounted rapidly as foreign financial institutions began to cut off credit. As Christmas approached, with its sharp seasonal upsurge in imports, the government found itself caught in a squeeze between domestic demand and depleted foreign exchange reserves. Pressured by the IMF and foreign creditors, particularly British, the government announced a 44 percent devaluation on December 27, 1971. Public response was rapid. According to observers in Ghana:

> The effect on prices was immediate and dramatic: within days the prices of imported consumer goods almost doubled or else commodities simply disappeared from the shelves for stocktaking. Even some local foodstuffs, not directly competitive with imports, were marked up by very high proportions. Retailers over-reacted to the devaluation and it was only a matter of time before market forces would bring prices down again. Nevertheless, this over-reaction helped to create a climate of opinion hostile to both devaluation and the Government. (Killick, Roemer, and Stern 1972:43)

In early January 1972 the military overthrew the Busia government, and Colonel I. K. Acheampong took over as head of state. The new government quickly revalued the currency. While other factors contributed to the coup, the public reaction to the policy of devaluation was a critical factor in making the government vulnerable and eventually in reversing the policy decision.

The neglect of implementation issues on the part of Ghana's decision makers led to the failure of their policy reform, with catastrophic consequences for the government as well. Perhaps they considered a devaluation self-implementing. If so, it was an assumption that undid the reform effort.

EXPORT-LED GROWTH IN JAMAICA

In the early 1980s, the newly elected government of Prime Minister Edward Seaga decided to make medium-scale domestic textile producers the leaders in a new strategy for export-led growth.[7]

Following his 1982 electoral victory, Prime Minister Seaga moved quickly to establish a policy of export-led growth. Shortly after his inauguration, in a speech to the nation, the prime minister informed Jamaicans: "My government has embarked on a far-reaching program, the structural adjustment of the Jamaican economy. This program is a basic requirement for the economic transformation of the country and the process of structural adjustment is strongly geared toward exports" (quoted in Veira 1988:1).

The government, in close consultation with the World Bank, decided to give first priority to promoting exports in the apparel and sewn goods subsector for a variety of reasons: the availability of cheap labor, a solidly established Jamaican apparel industry as a foundation on which to build, and favorable terms under the Caribbean Basin Initiative for Jamaican imports into the United States. The decision meant abandoning Jamaica's existing markets for apparel in other Caribbean nations in order to develop the capacity to export to the United States. This policy decision produced results quite different from those anticipated by the decision makers.

To implement this policy, U.S. consultants were hired to manage the process, with Jamaican managers and engineers as counterparts. The rationale was that such expertise was needed to obtain the best technology, to be clear on U.S. quality standards, and to gain insider assistance in penetrating U.S. markets. These consultants were to be replaced by Jamaicans after four years. At the outset of the new policy initiative, the U.S. advisers chose technologies and factory specifications that they were familiar with and that were efficient by U.S. standards under U.S. conditions. Utilization of highly modern technology for the export drive helped attract large foreign investors and manufacturers but also worked to exclude the medium-scale domestic manufacturers. Other problems quickly developed. These ranged from Jamaican labor being unused to working in large factory environments, to lack of experience in operating large machines, to high absentee rates among the young Jamaican women who were the principal workers. Given such problems, the large manufacturing operations did not perform well. To remedy the situation, the consultants initiated programs to train Jamaican workers. These included a training program for workers to familiarize them with the culture of large factories. A daycare program and a transport program for workers on night shifts were also established to facilitate the program of large manufacturers.

After six years of implementing the policy of promoting Jamaican exports, the foreign consultants remained in control of the policy. Little progress had been made in developing Jamaican exporters, and Jamaica lost most of its traditional garment export markets. In the process of implementation, those responsible made choices that altered the intent of the initial policy decision, added considerably to the cost and complexity of the policy, and failed to address Jamaica's needs for employment and a strengthened domestic manufacturing sector. It was a case of the implementers determining a policy, and the policy outcome being very different than decision makers had originally intended when they decided to assist medium-scale domestic textile producers.[8]

URBAN WATER SUPPLY IN INDIA

In India, clean drinking water, as well as an adequate domestic water supply, is universally accepted as an important goal of development.[9] Nevertheless, given the competing claims of other policy sectors, social infrastructure projects are often accorded low priority. Moreover, gaining access to water tends to be regarded as an individual activity, not a collective one. In addition, water is generally perceived to be a free good in India, and there is considerable resistance to paying for it.

Although most of the funding for new water supply systems in India has come from domestic resources, the World Bank also provided assistance for water projects beginning in the 1960s. In the early 1980s, in response to a shift in its policy worldwide, the World Bank made clear that it would no longer support programs that subsidize consumers. Therefore, officials notified India that the bank wished to enforce the conditions in existing project agreements that called for payment for water by consumers but that had never been enforced. The bank also made clear that future financial support for water supply projects was contingent upon collecting the costs of operating water systems from the consumers.

In spite of considerable reluctance on the part of the Indian government, it did agree to undertake a review of the policy concerning revenue collection in future projects. This review revealed near unanimous opposition at the various levels of government on the part of officials who perceived the introduction of user fees to be unenforceable. However, the review also revealed a consensus that the management of the sector should be improved, and steps were initiated that were expected to lead to better management of water development. Nevertheless, despite pressure from the World Bank, the policy of charging users was never put into effect because officials of the Indian government were convinced it was unimplementable.

In the case of the pricing of the domestic water supply in India, the views of the implementers proved to be decisive. We cannot consider the water price policy reform a complete failure, however, just because it was not carried out as originally anticipated. The reform initiative did lead to substantial improvements in the implementation of water development.

These cases suggest that categorizing efforts at policy reform implementation misses a large range of intermediate or unanticipated outcomes. They point out the complexity of all reforms and the critical nature of the implementation process. They suggest the importance of a new approach to analyzing the implementation of policy reforms.

The Strategic Management of Reform

The decision maker or manager, confronted with such an unpredictable set of outcomes, may well be reluctant to initiate any policy or institutional change. However, our cases not only suggest the wide range of possible outcomes of implementation efforts, they also indicate that it is possible to anticipate and influence the outcomes of the implementation of a reform. In order to do this, we must move from an analytic framework that helps order thinking about a particular set of relationships to an application of the framework in decision-making contexts. Thus, we begin with an analysis that emphasizes understanding the political and economic environment in which policy change takes place and how the characteristics of the particular policy will affect that environment. From this it is possible to develop a strategy for managing the implementation of reform by considering the range of factors that can potentially be altered through the activities of policy makers and managers. In the following pages, then, we attempt to go beyond the analytic framework to suggest how it can be used to guide strategic thinking about the implementation and sustainability of reform initiatives. In Chapter 8, we return to the theme of how the framework can help generate room for maneuver in the introduction and pursuit of reform measures.

Decisions to change existing practice will almost always generate opposition. In all twelve of our cases, either the consideration of a policy reform or the decision to alter existing practice produced some type of reaction.[10] Moreover, the fate of any reform depends to a critical degree on the nature and intensity of reaction to it. Reactions may vary from minor, to those that make implementation of the new policy questionable, to those that can even threaten the existence of a regime. Reactions can include overt efforts to reverse the decision as well as covert actions, in the sense that those who implement the change are not willing to alter their behavior to comply with a new initiative. Even an apparently straightforward organizational reform can run into opposition, as we saw in the case of Kenya, reviewed in Chapter 5, when a new president appointed a permanent secretary of agriculture.

If a reform measure is to succeed, reform proponents will have to overcome opposition, either passively, by having sufficient power to outlast it, or actively, by having a specific strategy to counter it. However, while decision makers often see policy reform as controversial, unpopular, and entailing risk, few of them give explicit attention to developing strategies for implementing change. Instead, the usual pattern again conforms to the linear model—policy makers decide on a reform but then divorce themselves from its implementation.[11] In our cases of macroeconomic or sectoral reforms, the decision makers frequently left the implementation of their decisions in the hands of fate or of government managers whose capabilities they often did not know. For example, in Ghana, a difficult decision was made, and then the policy makers waited to "tough out" the reaction. In other cases, the decision makers left implementation entirely in the hands of the implementing organization. This was true in Jamaica, where the remoteness of the decision makers allowed non-Jamaican consultants to alter the policy significantly. It was also true in Indonesia, where BULOG had to set its own policies and generate its own resources; although it acquired periodic political support for its actions, it was left on its own to implement the policy.

The one exception to the pattern of divorce between decision and implementation in our cases is a shift in development strategy in Costa Rica in the 1980s, where decision makers considered it important to develop a strategy for implementing reform and to involve themselves in it. The reasons for the Costa Ricans' strategy are not clear, but one can conjecture that two factors were at work. First, this was a major shift of strategy, and the policy makers were undoubtedly aware of the potential negative consequences if the change were not managed carefully. Second, Costa Rican politics have been characterized by consultation. This tradition encouraged the decision makers to select the consultative, consensual style of implementation they chose.

In general, the divorce between decision and implementation by decision makers in our cases can be ascribed to their sense that politics surrounds decision-making activities, while implementation is an administrative activity. As we indicated in Chapter 3, however, in developing countries, a considerable amount of political participation and accommodation of interests occurs during the implementation of policy (Grindle 1980). This suggests that implementation activities need to be assessed from a perspective that encourages political analysis, the examination of conflict and conflict resolution, and the development of strategic management capabilities.

To develop a strategic approach along the lines suggested here, decision makers and managers need to be able to anticipate reactions or responses to reform decisions and to understand where such they are most likely to take place, primarily in a public arena or primarily within the bureaucracy. We present two broad scenarios of reaction or response to policy change.[12] The characteristics of the policy determine which of the scenarios is likely to occur. One set of characteristics tends to generate a public reaction to reformist initiatives, where the stakes are often high for the government and incumbent elites and where the resources required to sustain the reform are considerable. A different set of characteristics leads to a response in the bureaucratic arena, where stakes are lower. In this second scenario, the resources needed to sustain the reform are also substantial, although they tend to be of a different nature than the resources needed to sustain a reform that is implemented largely in a public arena.

Scenario One: Reaction in the Public Arena

The outcome of some reforms is largely determined by societal reaction to efforts to change existing conditions among groups and interests that are most affected by the reforms. An assessment of the cases we have reviewed suggests a series of hypotheses about the characteristics of reforms that are sustained, shaped, altered, or rejected in the public arena. In large part, the characteristics of these reforms result in changes that (1) have a direct impact on broad sectors of the society or on politically important interests in society, and (2) are readily visible to the affected publics. In such cases, public reaction is likely to be strong, as it was in Ghana after the devaluation. Moreover, the stakes in pursuing such reforms can be very high and can even threaten the existence of a political regime. In such cases, reformers must be able to count on considerable political capital if the reform is to be sustained. Where this is not the case, thought needs to be given to accumulating support and managing public opposition to the anticipated reaction.

Based on evidence in our cases, we propose that reforms with the following characteristics will create a reaction that is public, will involve stakes in managing that response that are high, and will require solid political support and considerable regime stability and legitimacy if the reform is to be sustained.

Dispersion of Costs

If the costs or burden of the reform has a direct impact on the public or on politically important groups in society, opposition will emerge during implementation. The best example of such a policy is increasing the price of an important commodity such as water or food, especially as such a decision often reverses a previous policy to subsidize prices. The costs of this kind of decision are borne by a large segment of the population and are generally met with considerable protest. Economists are frequently concerned with the issue of who bears the burden of short-term costs of policy change. Dispersion of costs is a characteristic that captures much of this issue but does not make any assumption about the duration of these costs. This is sometimes confusing to economists who assume the primacy of short-term utility maximization over the distribution of longer-term benefits (Olson 1965). Instead, in this analysis our concern is to use the dispersion of costs as an indication that reactions to policy change will be in a public and overtly political arena.

Concentration of Benefits in Government

Frequently, reforms that impose broadly dispersed costs directly on a population also generate direct benefits that are not widely understood or valued by the same population. Thus, when the benefits of a reform are concentrated within government, such as those that accrue to the public budget or the efficiency of the public sector, their impact is not likely to be directly felt by the public. Using the same example of price increases, the benefits of such increases accrue to the public budget, a situation that is unlikely to create significant popular support. A similar case would be one in which a public enterprise is to be privatized. Opposition to such a change could be anticipated from managers and staff of the enterprise and a variety of groups who might have benefited from the public enterprise. In contrast, the anticipated benefits of a stronger budget or more efficient and profitable management of the enterprise would be unlikely to generate support other than among decision makers and international agencies. Concentrated benefits generally do not create a countervailing force to offset the public opposition the dispersed costs have generated.

Low Administrative or Technical Content

If a policy change does not require depth and continuity of administrative resources or highly technical skills to sustain it, it is more likely to be introduced as planned. In some cases, reforms—such as a price increase—are almost always "self-implementing." Nevertheless, sustainability will be determined by public reaction, which is often strong because of the same reform's broad and relatively undifferentiated impact. Policies such as devaluation or changes in mandated prices are relatively self-implementing in the sense that they require little in the way of technical or administrative infrastructure to carry them out. These will have broadly felt and immediate impact, and any negative reaction that is generated will be quickly forthcoming.[13]

Extensive Participation

If extensive public involvement is required to carry out the reform, it will be more visible, and public reaction is much more likely. It is difficult to mobilize large numbers of people to collaborate in a change, especially when the proposed change does not offer clear benefits to affected publics. For this reason the proposal to charge water consumers in India was not considered feasible by policy managers. However, if the populace considers the change to be in its interest, extensive participation will quickly mobilize support for the government. Changes that do not involve the public or a wide range of participants may be easier to implement, but they do not have the advantage of generating broad acceptance in society and providing a public check on governmental actions.

Short Duration

The length of time needed to implement a reform also has an important influence on the reaction generated by it. If the full impact of the change is immediately visible—again, the example of a price increase is relevant—the reaction is likely to be stronger and more public. Thus, the effect of the Ghana devaluation was easily apparent to most Ghanaians. Within days, the results were very clear in the market in terms of much higher prices and many fewer foreign goods. In Korea, in 1964 and 1965, a series of macroeconomic reforms was adopted over considerable opposition. Fortunately for the reformers, positive results of the new policies appeared quickly, and they were able to sustain the changes that led to Korea's subsequent rapid economic development.

Reforms with some or all of these five characteristics create strong reactions that are played out primarily in the public arena. They frequently bring about the mobilization of existing pressure groups or encourage the formation of new ones to oppose the reform. These groups exert pressure on political leadership and public officials to reverse or alter the decision in a variety of ways. Some of the more dramatic make international headlines, such as the protests that followed the partial removal of the subsidy on bread in Egypt or the coup that followed devaluation in Ghana.[14] More important perhaps than these dramatic reactions is that reforms with these characteristics can give impetus to longer-term organized opposition to the government. Policy reforms that generate reaction in the public arena therefore generally carry high stakes for the regime and for incumbent political elites. The legitimacy of the regime itself can be called into question, as was the case in Ghana. Less dramatically, the stability of a government and its capacity to take other needed measures may be affected by reactions to policy reform in the public arena. Certainly the sustainability of the reform is called into question if strong public reactions emerge during its implementation.

SCENARIO TWO:
RESPONSE IN THE BUREAUCRATIC ARENA

The outcome of some reforms is largely determined by how bureaucratic agencies, public officials, and administrative routines respond to the changes. In some of our cases, characteristics of the reforms meant that such agencies, officials, and routines sustained, shaped, altered, or rejected the changes. In these cases, the results (1) did not have a direct impact on large sectors of the population, and (2) were not as readily apparent to the public as they were to insiders in government. In Kenya, the decision to reorganize the Ministry of Agriculture was actively supported or resisted by public officials but went largely unnoticed by the general public. In Mali, the implementation of a new health program was stymied within the bureaucracy. During its unraveling, little protest or reaction was heard from low-income Malians, who would have been the beneficiaries of an extensive rural health system, because they had no knowledge of the proposed program or of how it would benefit them.

The Mali health project was to result in a model of rural primary health care that could be expanded to the entire population. Initially, high-level officials in the Ministry of Health were primarily interested in acquiring funds for medical inputs. USAID, on the other hand, wanted to finance a more comprehensive reform of health provisions in Mali. Discussions and negotiations about the design of the project lasted for two years. Four years after the initiation of the project, the experiment ended. In the final analysis, the Ministry of Health was not fully committed to its pursuit, and other ministries in the government blocked its progress (see Gray et al. 1990).

Based on cases such as these, we propose that the implementation of reforms with the following characteristics will be played out primarily in the bureaucratic arena, the stakes for the government will be much lower than if reaction is generated in the public arena, and the emphasis in implementing the reform will be on competence and compliance within the bureaucracy.

Concentration of Costs in Government

Where the costs of a reform are narrowly focused to affect primarily the government budget or government institutions, they are not likely to be directly or immediately felt by the public. Resistance or opposition to such change will tend to arise in the bureaucracy. The reorganization of the Ministry of Agriculture in Kenya and the establishment of planning agencies in Colombia and Argentina meant shifts in power in the bureaucracy but had little apparent impact elsewhere. The outcome in each case thus rested on the response of the administrative system.

Dispersion of Benefits

Reforms that concentrate costs in the government often have broadly dispersed benefits that become visible only in the longer term. Thus, the public may benefit over the long term from the reorganization of a ministry or the creation of a primary health care system, but the direct impact is initially borne by officials and institutions that are required to alter accustomed forms of behavior and relinquish accustomed forms of security. The public support such reforms generate may eventually be a countervailing force to opposition that may arise in the bureaucracy, but the administrators are likely to become aware of the costs long before the public appreciates the benefits. This situation is illustrated in the case of a new rural health system in Mali.

High Administrative or Technical Content

If the administrative content of a policy is high or it is technically complex, it requires the coordinated efforts of public officials and institutions to see that it is carried out. In this case of non-self-implementing reforms, the public is unlikely to be immediately affected by its implementation or to be fully aware of the costs and benefits it may impose. In this situation, implementation depends on competence and support in

139

the bureaucracy. This was the case with trade reform and the apparel industry in Jamaica, where the policy was significantly altered by technicians in the government long before the targeted beneficiaries became aware that it was harmful to their interests.

Limited Participation

When little organized participation is required to carry out the reform, or if participation is required on an individual or case-by-case basis—granting licenses, for example—response is likely to be confined to the bureaucracy. Moreover, the fewer bureaucratic actors involved, the higher the probability the reform will be carried out as intended. BULOG's effectiveness is an illustration of a single agency successfully implementing a reform. However, limited participation also eliminates the check on implementers to ensure that they are carrying out the policy as intended. In Jamaica, limited participation enabled the implementers to alter the policy in the absence of scrutiny by either the public or others with stakes in the original policy.

Long Duration

The longer the time needed to implement a reform, the more likely that potential conflict and resistance will emerge and that administrative capacity within the system will determine the implementability and sustainability of the reform. In Indonesia, BULOG responded to the government's price and supply stabilization program over a twenty-year period. Time allowed the marketing agency to solidify its bureaucratic power so it could do things in the mid-1980s that it could not have accomplished in the early 1970s.

If a reform has some or all of these five characteristics, reaction will take place largely within the bureaucratic arena, and the success of implementation will depend on the capacity and support of the bureaucracy. Opposition in the bureaucracy often comes from resistance to change or loss of power and may range from overt opposition to quiet sabotage or inaction. In Kenya, the program to decentralize development planning and implement it at the district level stagnated for three years before anything of substance happened. This occurred despite repeated statements in the national development plan that decentralization was official policy, financial support from a foreign donor, and a team of technical advisers. In some cases, alliances between factions or individuals in the bureaucracy and external interests or clienteles can result in piecemeal sabotage of the intent of the policy makers (Grindle 1980). In addition,

lack of capacity within the administrative apparatus can lead to implementation failure, however inadvertent.

When the response to a policy reform takes place in the bureaucratic
arena, the political stakes for a government are relatively low. The real
issues are whether the capacity exists to implement the reform and
whether there is support for the reform that will cause the bureaucracy
to comply with the intent of the decision. Whatever happens, the issue
is the viability of the reform and not the survival of the regime. Stakes
often tend to focus on individual or agency goals. The government and
the decision makers have a stake in the implementation of the reform or
they probably would not have undergone the risks of change. Individual
and collective credibility can be enhanced by effective government action
and weakened in its absence. Individual officials in government may have
very high personal stakes in being perceived as effective leaders, moving
upward in their careers, acquiring greater resources for their agencies,
or achieving greater efficiency in their work. Nevertheless, compared to
the high stakes of reforms played out in the public arena, these are not
ones that are likely to imply major political or economic upheaval.

It is clear that policy makers and reformers who focus on the decision
and neglect the implementation process do so at their own peril. This
review of the hazards of introducing change, whether they occur in the
public arena or within the administrative apparatus, should not discourage policy elites from making such difficult decisions but should,
rather, help them develop strategies for dealing with public reactions and
bureaucratic responses to their actions. Table 6.1 summarizes the hypotheses about policy characteristics, responses to change, and stakes
that we have proposed. It also suggests that at times, reformers may need
more resources than those immediately available in order to implement
their reform strategies. What those resources are, and how they can be
mobilized, is critical to the successful implementation of reform.

Assessing Capacity and Marshaling
Resources to Sustain Reform

We have proposed that decision makers and policy managers can analyze
their environment, in the context of a political economy framework, to
see if the conditions and capacity exist for successfully implementing a
reform. This analysis of the situation and prediction of where reactions
are likely to occur, the stakes involved, and the resources available contains the fundamental elements of a strategy. However, the environment
will be changed by the reform decision, and a dynamic dimension must

TABLE 6.1
Characteristics of Policies and Their Implications for
Implementation and Sustainability

Characteristics of Policy	Arena of Response	Stakes	Resources of Sustainability
		SCENARIO I	
Impact Dispersed cost; Concentrated benefits in government Visibility Low administrative/ technical content; Extensive participation; Short duration	Public	High: At risk is the government's viability	Government legitimacy, stability, support of elites, or relative autonomy from elites; Skills in political management
		SCENARIO II	
Impact Concentrated costs in government; Dispersed benefits Visibility High administrative/ technical content; Limited participation; Long duration	Bureaucratic	Low: At issue is the substance of the reform	Bureaucratic capacity, high-level support, hierarchical discipline, consensus, behavioral incentives

be introduced if a strategy for implementation is to be effective. An important issue, then, is how reformists can alter the situation to increase the probability of successfully implementing a reform.

Through the reflections of participants in the Ghana case, we get some idea of how steps might have been taken to manage implementation of the devaluation more effectively. If the policy makers had thought about the implementation process as well as the technical content of the decision, they might have been able to organize implementation in a way that would have reduced its negative impact. For example, a system of 180-day credits to importers allowed them that period before paying for imports. Under the devaluation, importers who had ordered goods under the old exchange rate and had sold them on the assumption of a price based on the old rate were forced to pay for the goods at the new rate, increasing their costs by over 50 percent. It would have been more equitable to authorize importers to pay for goods at the exchange rate in effect when the goods were ordered.

Another area where action might have been taken to mitigate the adverse reaction to devaluation was price controls. In 1971, Ghana maintained a series of price controls on a large number of consumer goods. Prior to the devaluation, a technical committee of the government had recommended that in the event of a devaluation, duties on these basic price-controlled goods should be lowered or removed and the benefits of the reduction passed on to consumers to buffer the impact of the devaluation. In fact, the government waited until ten days after the devaluation to take this action. By then, "the large stores had responded by taking the affected goods off their shelves, which induced correspondingly larger price increases in the small shops and in the markets, where price controls are seldom effective, thus aggravating the shock effect of devaluation" (Killick, Roemer, and Stern 1972:21–22).

Reforms call for political, financial, managerial, and technical resources. Every reform does not always call for all of these, but reformers must know which are needed and where they will be available. This requires the capacity to assess their availability and consider how they might be expanded or mobilized. A principal task of decision makers is to assess the availability of political resources for policy implementation and then to consider how they might be mobilized, as indicated in table 6.2. In the same table, we see that a principal task for public managers is to mobilize and utilize bureaucratic resources—financial, managerial, and technical. The following section reviews how these resources can be assessed, mobilized, and expanded.

POLITICAL RESOURCES

A series of questions illuminates the political resources that can be important in introducing and sustaining a reform, particularly one that generates a public reaction. First, how legitimate is the regime? If the government has strong, broad-based public support, it is not likely to be threatened by public opposition on a single issue. A tradition of political stability that makes changes of government unusual on the basis of a single issue is thus an asset.[15] A related question is whether the reform stands alone or is one of a series of unpopular actions so that it might become the straw that breaks the camel's back. If so, the question of timing becomes important, to allow the government the opportunity to assess and replenish its political bases of support. Third, how autonomous is the government? If it depends on one or two extremely powerful interests, then the issue of how the reform will affect those interests

TABLE 6.2
Assessing and Mobilizing Resources for Implementation

Decision Maker		Public Manager		
Role: Assess political resources Mobilize support, counteract opposition		Role: Mobilize and utilize relevant resources		
Resources		Resources		
Type	Time needed to mobilize	Type	Source	Time needed to mobilize
PUBLIC AND POLITICAL		BUREAUCRATIC		
Location		Financial	Budget;	Short
Concentrated	Short		Other government;	Short
Dispersed	Long		Private credit;	Short
			Foreign aid	Short
Organization		Managerial	Bureaucracy;	Short
Organized	Short		Private sector;	Medium
Unorganized	Long		Training	Long
Socioeconomic group		Technical	Technical assistance;	Medium
High	Short			
Low	Long		Private sector;	Medium
			Bureaucracy;	Medium
			Training	Long

becomes exceedingly important. Finally, is there an elite consensus in support of the reform? What is the likely response of the press, the financial community, the private sector, the military, and religious leaders? If the government can rely on these groups for overt support or can obtain some assurance that they will not be mobilized in opposition, then prospects for sustaining the policy, the administration, and the regime improve. An example of this type of elite consensus comes from the case of Costa Rica in the early 1980s, already cited, where great efforts were made to incorporate all major elite groups in the policy decision and to be sure that none bore the burden disproportionately.

In some of our cases, policy makers appear to have decided that such political resources were not sufficient to overcome the strong reaction in the public arena that they anticipated. In the case of agrarian reform in the Philippines, action was supported by some officials, some members of the elite such as the church and leaders of nongovernmental organizations, and the international community, as a way of creating greater equity in the countryside and countering the insurgent New People's Army. However, decision makers anticipated serious opposition to land reform from some powerful elites and believed that to move ahead could bring the regime into serious jeopardy. Water management reform in India is a case of implementers resisting a proposed policy reform because they believed that they could not count on sufficient political resources to impose an unpopular change. In Ghana, policy elites would have benefited from such a realistic assessment of their political resources prior to moving ahead with a major devaluation.

It is not sufficient to analyze the political resources needed to sustain a reform measure by looking only at those who support a reform and those who oppose it. Such analysis must also include an assessment of the degree to which support and opposition can be mobilized, how powerful each group is likely to be, and the sequence in which information reaches people (Lindenberg and Crosby 1981; Lindenberg 1988). The importance of potential support or opposition depends primarily on three factors: location, organization, and socioeconomic status, including literacy.

Location

If the supporters or opponents of a particular measure are concentrated in a geographic area and have easy access to political leaders and opinion makers, their power to influence the outcome of implementation efforts will be much greater than if they are dispersed geographically.[16] They can also be mobilized much more quickly than can more dispersed populations. Policy makers have long displayed a particular concern for urban residents because they get information more quickly than rural inhabitants, they can be mobilized more easily, and their actions are more visible. For example, in a wide variety of countries, basic food grain prices are held down to benefit urban consumers at the expense of rural producers, and, when such subsidies are fully or partially removed, urban riots can occur. In Ghana, cocoa producers who would have benefited from increased prices as a result of the devaluation were much less influential in determining the short-run reaction to the change in currency value than were the urban commercial and consumer groups. Similarly, if those affected by a reform are all concentrated in one region, their influence will be enhanced.

Organization

Groups that are already organized around common interests will respond more quickly to perceptions of threat to their self-interests than their less organized counterparts and will be much more effective participants in public affairs. The fact that groups have an internal communication system and an ongoing leadership structure means that the membership can be quickly mobilized to support the perceptions of threatened self-interest. Large landowners in our Philippines case, although rural and relatively few in number, were sufficiently organized that the government did not want to risk alienating them by adopting a land reform.

Socioeconomic Group and Literacy

These are attributes that determine the capacity to get information quickly, as well as the capacity to use it to wield influence. Those who have some education and can read are more likely to get information about issues that will affect their self-interest than are those who do not. In the case of Mali, the inability of rural inhabitants to get information or to organize themselves meant that they could not be easily mobilized in support of the proposed rural health care system.

These characteristics provide a basis for predicting how politically effective different categories of people may be in supporting or opposing a policy change. This type of political analysis is an essential component of a policy reform strategy in that it goes beyond political forces in place to help predict how such groups will respond once a reform decision has been taken. Beyond assessment, the policy reformer must also know how to mobilize those political forces in support of reform and how to counteract those that are likely to pose a significant threat (Ascher 1984; Cleaves 1980).

BUREAUCRATIC RESOURCES

In addition to political resources, a series of bureaucratic resources may need to be mobilized by public managers in order to encourage and sustain the implementation of policy reform. Financial, managerial, and technical resources can be instrumental to successful outcomes of many reform initiatives. These are briefly described below.

Financial Resources

Despite the apparent poverty of most governments in developing countries, acquiring the financial resources that can help sustain the implementation of a policy reform may be comparatively easy. Budgetary resources are always tight, of course, but those familiar with developing country budgets know that underspending is a recurring problem in some sectors. An effective manager can usually get some unspent resources shifted to an important program (see esp. Ames 1987). In addition, there are usually special accounts or funds that may be available to knowledgeable and influential policy elites.

Foreign aid is also frequently available to support or buffer the impact of reform measures (see esp. Nelson 1984). In fact, as already noted, it is frequently used as an incentive to encourage the adoption of reform measures. Donors are clearly interested in reform, and they have frequently gone beyond their country budgets when they have perceived themselves to be leveraging reform. In the Philippines case, for example, there were clear indications that the United States, Japan, and several European nations were ready to provide extensive support for agrarian reform if the government would take the initiative and demonstrate a strong commitment to land reform. The World Bank went even farther, issuing a confidential report making the case for a strong reform, even though, up to that point, it had not budgeted funds for this purpose. In some cases, donors' interest in being associated with a visible change may be great enough that policy makers have the opportunity to negotiate and bargain successfully among them for substantial financial responses.

In addition, policy managers can consider sources of revenues such as the sale of food grains acquired at concessional prices, a strategy pursued by BULOG. User charges for services are frequent in health care systems and other service activities, from credit systems to transport services. Productive activities such as manufacturing, processing, or even retailing also provide some opportunities to create revenues for related reformist initiatives.

Managerial Resources

The capacity to generate management inputs for implementing reforms is also extensive.[17] Control of budget, personnel appointment and promotion, and control of support services ranging from transportation to purchasing are important elements of bureaucratic power, as illustrated in the case of Mali, where there was "a vital interest in project inputs, especially medical supplies and vehicles. Malian staff were particularly interested in project perquisites; at the local level, this meant the steady paychecks that came from the project and at the regional and national level, it meant access to vehicles and medical supplies" (quoted in Grindle and Thomas 1988:27). On a more positive note, BULOG consistently increased its managerial capacity. Its managers used technical assistance to gain time to train staff and to acquire new personnel as the agency's responsibilities grew. It developed the capacity to handle a wide variety of responsibilities, ranging from agricultural promotion to international grain purchasing.

Technical Resources

The capacity for technical analysis is an important resource, and its availability can be assessed by the officials considering introducing a reform. Obviously there are many forms of technical capacity needed for evaluating a reform, such as the analytic input into policy changes in Ghana or Indonesia. The type of technical capacity needed will depend on the reform: in Indonesia, it was price analysis; in Mali, it was expertise in medical care delivery; in Colombia, it was the capacity for economic analysis and forecasting as well as data collection and analysis. In the Philippines, the absence of the capacity to plan and implement land reform was a constraint on the proponents of the reform. In the case of BULOG, the development of the capacity for technical analysis was a key ingredient in the long-term success of the agency. In the early stages, the importance of this capacity was demonstrated by a foreign adviser. Later, both analytic and managerial capacities were developed within the organization.

Of these critical resources, capacity for political analysis and maneuver may well be the most difficult to acquire. It is not something that can be obtained through technical assistance. Often it consists of policy makers' knowledge or sense of the feasible. However, good political managers can expand their room for movement. Intuitive skills may be augmented by specific analysis and strategy of the type recommended here. Political analysis must also be more explicit. In many of our cases, policy makers weighed technical arguments and evaluated financial resources but did not specifically assess the political situation and their capacity to deal with it. In addition, mobilizing essential resources is a key element in implementing policy reform. Although resources are, by definition, limited, they are not fixed. Therefore, effective managers can mobilize resources through conscious and concerted efforts.

The review of resources—political, financial, managerial, and technical—provides the decision makers or the managers with a systematic way to review the resources available to support the implementation process in the face of various forms of opposition. Implicitly, by suggesting the relevant resources, it also provides a means of assessing the opposition. Such a review is not adequate to ensure successful implementation, however. It is only a first step. From this review must come a very specific strategy of implementation tailored to the particular environment in which the reform is being implemented. The analysis of the situation and the review of resources are basic to developing such a strategy.

Conclusions

If our cases are at all indicative, a large portion of policy reform decisions lead to results that were not originally intended by decision makers. Our analyses and cases suggest that unsatisfactory outcomes result, in significant measure, from an overemphasis on the decision process, from an assumption by decision makers that fate or implementation managers will take care of carrying out the desired changes and that there is little reason for a specific strategy of implementation. In many cases, reforms have been attempted when the administrative or political resources to implement them did not exist. The result has generally been misallocated resources, wasted political capital, and frustration on the part of both those who support the reform and those who oppose it.

We have suggested an alternative approach that may increase the probabilities of implementing reforms as planned. Our framework requires looking at policy reform as a long-term process of decision making, and it focuses attention on the fact that all policy reforms will encounter antagonistic reactions. These can be overcome more easily if policy elites develop a specific strategy for implementing reforms. The starting point for such a strategy is to analyze the characteristics of a particular reform to determine whether the reaction is likely to occur in the public arena or within the bureaucracy. This information is in turn an indicator of how high the stakes for the government will be in dealing with opposition to reformist initiatives. If they are very high, the government's existence could be in question. If they are lower, the issue is usually the sustainability of the reform. This knowledge allows the government official to assess resources that are available to counter anticipated reaction. Beyond that, additional resources may be mobilized if they are needed.

While effective implementation requires good analysis and a strategy of implementation, the probabilities of success are higher if policy makers are involved in the entire process of reform rather than assuming that the decision to reform is the critical choice and that what follows is little more than a mechanical process of implementation. This means looking at policy reform as process, not as a series of phases, as the linear model would encourage us to do. Our cases make clear that decision makers frequently concern themselves only with the decision and neglect or ignore implementation. They generally have cause to regret this shortsightedness. Evidence of success, such as food grain stabilization in Indonesia or development strategy change in Costa Rica, demonstrates that it is a lengthy process and that implementation must be part of the policy makers' calculations. When policy makers leave implementation completely in the hands of others, whether in Jamaica or Mali, the probabilities of satisfactory outcomes become much lower.

In current practice, governments and donors focus extensively on the feasibility of making the reform decision. Decision makers should become more accustomed to looking beyond the decision to question whether the reform has a reasonable chance of being implemented. The reformer must also face the fact that the answer may not always be yes. In such a case, can opposition or lack of capacity be overcome? Are the obstacles to implementation insurmountable, given the political and bureaucratic resources available? If not, what resources can be mobilized to implement the reform? There will be situations in which the conditions for implementation are highly unfavorable. In these cases, decision makers may decide to forgo initiating a significant change, because reforms that fail can be worse than no reforms at all. They jeopardize future prospects for reform and unnecessarily squander resources.

CHAPTER 7

Reforming Policies
in the 1980s:
Changing Circumstances
and Shifting Parameters

with Stephen J. Reifenberg

T he policy reforms of the 1980s were different. Many of the policy
and institutional changes of previous decades had been designed to
give the state a more central role in controlling and managing the economy in order to promote development. Other changes were introduced
to increase government capacity in designing and managing programs
and projects whose purpose was to distribute goods and services among
a populace. Whether at the macroeconomic, sectoral, or organizational
level, the primary purpose of these reforms was to strengthen the role of
government as the principal agent of growth. Their consequence was to
increase the size of government and provide it with extensive capacity
to allocate resources.

In the 1980s, the focus of reform efforts shifted in important ways.
Changes in this decade were often born of harsh necessity and tended to
be less palatable to policy elites because they reduced the size and role
of the state in development and reduced or eliminated the benefits that
governments had become accustomed to allocate in prior decades. While
the process of reform remained the same in its essentials, the substance,
the principal players, and the objectives changed. This chapter explores

why and how policy reform in the 1980s was so different, and how the role of government, described in Chapter 3, changed so rapidly. It then reviews fourteen cases of reform in the 1980s and tests them against the framework and hypotheses presented in previous chapters.

The Sources of Crisis and Change

For many developing countries, the 1980s were a time of macroeconomic crisis. As the decade unfolded, most countries found themselves reaping the bitter harvest of prior decades of government expansion. These years also witnessed considerable questioning of a longstanding belief that the prospects for rapid growth were excellent and that only the limits of government efficiency and shortages of resources stood in the way. The sources of this crisis of the state were generally to be found in over-whelming debt obligations and extensive budget deficits. In response to these problems, "getting the policy framework right" was seen as the most important development task by the international aid donors and many countries.[1] Part of that framework called for substituting the market system for the state as a primary instrument of economic growth. The result was the beginning of a process, the implications of which were little recognized, that would bring about a fundamental change in the role and concept of the state.

By the early 1980s, debt had become an overwhelming burden for many developing countries, and other priorities had to give way to measures needed to accommodate these debt obligations. The World Bank's Debt Tables indicate that between 1984 and 1988, the net transfer of resources between the developing and industrialized nations was $143 billion in favor of the industrialized nations.[2] In addition, macroeconomic crisis in the form of financial shortages became a paramount reality for a large number of countries. State-owned enterprises accumulated financial losses almost everywhere, and their shortfalls had to be met from budgetary resources. Extensive subsidies, ranging from those for basic food commodities for urban consumers to subsidized interest rates on loans in most sectors to those on inputs to agriculture, placed heavy burdens on public budgets as well as producing widespread inefficiencies in the economy. The combined financial strain of debt obligations, the financial requirements of inefficient state-owned enterprises, subsidies, and poorly performing economies could not be supported in many countries.

While countries throughout the developing world staggered under these conditions, African states were doubly strained because of serious droughts in the 1970s and 1980s. Major international relief efforts helped

to deal with immediate needs, but these crises seriously depleted the resources of large numbers of African nations. In the 1970s and 1980s,
per capita food production declined, causing many countries to face substantial foreign exchange burdens for importing food. National efforts
to deal with disaster often meant that development programs were neglected or came to a halt and new investments were postponed. As a
result, the decade of the 1980s was one of little or no growth for most
African countries.

The acute economic crisis made many countries much more susceptible
to external involvement in the management of their economies and more
dependent on external assistance. Dealing with debt obligations that ex-
ceeded the capacity of most debtor countries required IMF involvement
as a prerequisite for debt renegotiation, standby loans, and increased
levels of aid. In turn, the IMF generally insisted on an established prescription for economic management based on neoclassical economics.
This prescription was not exclusive to the IMF but evolved in the 1980s
as part of an economic orthodoxy about stabilization and structural adjustment espoused and required by the major donor institutions. Pressure
to pursue stabilization tended to be associated more with the IMF, while
structural adjustment was associated primarily with the World Bank.

Stabilization tended to be the shorter-run activity. There were normally
four principal components:

– Reducing balance-of-payments deficits, primarily through correcting
  an overvalued exchange rate;
– Reducing the government's budget deficit through controlling expenditures and imposing additional taxes;
– Controlling the money supply, which in turn depended on reducing
  the budget deficit; and
– Increasing certain prices, such as interest rates, and eliminating government subsidies on goods and services.

In the 1980s, these measures affected broad sectors of the population
and inevitably had an important impact on state involvement in the economy.

The process of structural adjustment was generally a longer-term and
more complex process and had, if anything, a more profound impact on
the role of the state. The principal components of orthodox structural
adjustment programs were:

– Adjusting prices to scarcity values;
– Freeing the market to determine prices and allocate resources;
– Shifting resources from government to private decision makers;

- Rationalizing government's remaining roles in development so that some type of efficiency criteria were met; and
- Reforming institutions to bolster competition in the private sector and to carry out government's modified role.

Taken together, stabilization and structural adjustment constitute a radical reallocation of economics and political power from the public sector to the private. They mean a great reduction of state involvement in the economy and enormous loss of opportunity for political benefits, and also substantial cost to the population (an issue that is elaborated upon below). Yet country after developing country undertook these reforms in substantial measure or in their totality.

In addition to changes forced upon countries through severe economic crisis, changes were also called for by a newly popular growth strategy. A model of development pursued by four Asian countries received growing recognition as a route to successful development. The experiences of South Korea, Taiwan, Hong Kong, and Singapore in pursuing export-led growth provided a rationale for actions that forced local industry to become efficient in order to compete effectively in the world market. There were, of course, noticeable differences among these countries, and the lessons they offered to economic development strategists were not always those propounded by neoclassical economists. In particular, strong command-oriented governments were clearly present in South Korea and to some degree in Singapore. Nevertheless, the development of the East Asian countries confirmed for many that to achieve rapid growth through exports, market forces needed to be freed, national currency brought into line with its real value, and domestic enterprise made to compete internationally through the removal of tariff protection and most subsidies.

The experience of these countries provided a model reinforcing the type of reforms that developing country governments were being pushed increasingly to consider. Together, the stabilization and structural adjustment prescription for the economic crisis and the positive experience of the Asian countries pushed in the same direction of limiting government's involvement in managing the economy. Moreover, as part of the structural adjustment package, many international aid agencies promoted decentralizing the management of national development. The limited success of national governments in managing programs, especially those in the countryside—ranging from health to education to rural development—led to the advocacy of giving more power and responsibilities to local governments. The shift of funds and authority away from the national government was one more step in weakening the power and control of the state over national development.

Characteristics of Policy Reform in the 1980s

The policy reforms promoted in the 1980s had characteristics that were noticeably different from those of previous decades. First, the fact that many of the reforms grew out of financial crisis greatly enhanced the role of the IMF, the aid donor institutions, and foreign banks. To a degree not acceptable in prior decades, countries were forced to allow these institutions formal access to national development policy making. International agencies often set priorities for individual countries and effectively pushed reforms that had a profound effect on the nature and role of the state in many countries.

Second, an enhanced role for technocrats and technical analysis went along with the increased role of the international agencies. The international financial and donor institutions were, in many ways, driven by technical analysis. Although they represented a powerful political force and promoted prescriptions that had significant political implications locally, they eschewed political analysis and pursued their prescriptions for stabilization and adjustment without explicit regard for local political issues. In response to the technical orientation of these institutions, developing countries, in their own interest, sought to build increasing technical and analytic capacity into their government systems, and the power of technocrats in the developing countries often grew apace with the increasing influence of the foreign institutions.

Third, in the 1980s, policy reforms were usually pursued in packages, with several major changes instituted simultaneously or in close sequence, often with the financial backing of a major aid donor. Reform packages generally had greater impact on the economy than the single issue reforms that were more characteristic of earlier decades. Often, for example, conditions for continued lending specified as many as eight to twelve policy changes necessary to bring about the "structural adjustment" thought to be required to create a policy climate that would promote growth. In 1985 in the Gambia, for example, in response to a serious financial crisis and an austerity package prescribed by the IMF as a precondition to a standby credit from the IMF, the government took a set of related measures to reform economic policy and institutions (McPherson and Radelet 1988). Macroeconomic reforms consisted of floating the national currency and increasing interest rates. In order to increase revenues, the government undertook a major reform of the customs system. The government also froze the wages of civil servants and reduced the number of government employees by about 20 percent. Organizational reforms included establishing parastatal performance contracts, reorganizing the Ministry of Agriculture, and reforming the Gambia Commercial and Development Bank. A similar set of reforms in Indonesia started with a tax reform and involved changing trade and industrial policy (Barichello and Flatters 1988).

In some cases when these changes were undertaken, one set of reforms led to another in a cascading effect. For example, in Sri Lanka, a new export-oriented development strategy focused attention on developing skilled workers for export industries, which in turn brought about proposals for reform of primary and secondary schools (Cummings 1988). This same effect occurred in Jamaica with the expansion of the textile industry. As described in Chapter 6, expansion of the textile sector for export markets led to training programs for workers, the establishment of a system of daycare centers, and a special transportation system. The linking of reforms also generated concern about the sequences in which reforms should be carried out, in order to ensure the smoothest progression of economic change and to make the reform package politically palatable. Thus, the timing and sequence of reforms became an issue for many governments.

In response to the pressure to adopt wide-ranging changes as part of reform packages, many governments became adept at reaching agreements with donor agencies on reforms to begin the flow of aid, but then moving slowly, stalling, or carrying them out only partially, contending that the reforms originally agreed upon proved more difficult than anticipated or impossible to implement. Kenya in the early 1980s provides an example: macroeconomic policy changes were made as demanded by donors, but the donors' demands for privatization of food commodity trade was only partially carried out, and in slow increments over a period of more than five years. In response to donor demands for dismantling the National Cereals Board, steps were taken to reduce its control over trade, but neither it nor its powers were eliminated.

Finally, many of the economic policies of the 1980s forced governments to impose new hardships and burdens on their populations. The economic costs of the budget cuts imposed by austerity programs profoundly affected vulnerable groups (Cornia, Jolly, and Stewart 1987). Inevitably, the poorest and politically least powerful had to bear a disproportionate burden of reductions in services such as health care and education, which were often the first budgetary sectors to be cut. In many cases, state-owned enterprises eliminated workers and created significant new levels of unemployment. Programs to benefit the poorest were also susceptible to reduction or elimination, especially those in rural areas. This movement went almost directly against the development priorities of the 1970s, when the alleviation of poverty—and particularly rural poverty— was a major goal of much government action. This change was also more than just a shift of priorities. As we have argued, until the 1980s, the state frequently assumed the role of benefactor, providing and distributing benefits to groups and individuals in society. This role was greatly diminished in the 1980s, when state actions often imposed hardship on these same individuals and groups.

The policy changes of the 1980s also brought about shifts in the location of political power and wealth. Prior to this decade, economic power in the hands of the managers of state-owned enterprises, appointed by political leaders, was often considerable. Moreover, when the state assumed a leading role in controlling the economy, those who prospered in the private sector were those who had the influence to obtain licenses, to be allocated foreign exchange, and to obtain tariff protection. As the power to confer these privileges shifted to the market, new groups began to be benefited and gained political and economic power. While this broadening of the elite may be desirable, it also had significant political implications. The capacity of the state to apportion resources and to affect the distribution of power and influence was generally an important tool in accomplishing national political priorities in some states. For example, in states in which national integration was a priority, powerful positions were often apportioned among ethnic, linguistic, or religious groups. Thus, major elements had a share in and benefited from state power and consequently had some interest in maintaining the integrity of the state. The reforms of the 1980s undercut the opportunities to build and maintain such political bases. Whether this will lead to the reassertion of centrifugal forces that would weaken national unity in some states is an issue of serious concern to national political leaders. Similarly, in countries such as Kenya, Tanzania, Zimbabwe, the Ivory Coast, and Ghana, where non-African minorities tended to control the private sector, policy reforms that removed state bureaucracies and allowed the private sector to replace them shifted power and influence to non-Africans.

The policy reforms of the 1980s thus had a major impact on states and their role in development. They tended to be more difficult to carry out than earlier reforms because they reduced the powers and privileges of those who were expected to approve and implement them. They were undertaken in most cases because they were driven by crisis and by international institutions that offered the only apparent way out of the crisis. Thus, the reforms characteristic of the 1980s differed in significant ways from most of the cases of policy and institutional change that were considered in earlier chapters. Given these important differences in the substance of reform, is the analytic framework elaborated in this book still appropriate for capturing the process through which policy and institutional changes are introduced, pursued, and sustained?

To respond to this question, we have identified fourteen cases of reform initiatives that were introduced in the 1980s. The cases are based on papers prepared for a conference on economic systems reform held in

TABLE 7.1
Cases of Policy and Institutional Reforms from the 1980s

Policy Type	Country	Year(s)	Source(s)
Macroeconomic reform	The Gambia	1985–88	Policy advisers
Macroeconomic reform	Panama Costa Rica Guatemala	1982–87	Policy advisers; Published and unpublished papers
Custom reform	The Gambia	1985	Policy advisers
Financial system reform	Turkey	1980–88	Policy advisers
Privatization of AIDS care	Puerto Rico	1987–88	Policy advisers
Trade policy	Indonesia	1980–88	Policy advisers
Trade policy reform	Bangladesh	1980–88	Policy advisers
Industrial policy reform	Bangladesh	1980–88	Policy advisers
Decentralizing of education	Sri Lanka	1980–88	Policy advisers
Development of planning/ statistical unit	Chad	1985	Policy advisers
Restructuring of Ministry of Health	Chad	1985	Policy advisers
Reform of Commercial and Development Bank	The Gambia	1985	Policy advisers

Marrakech, Morocco, in October of 1988 (see Perkins and Roemer 1991). Table 7.1 lists the fourteen new cases and indicates their substance, country, and dates. The authors of the papers were, in each case, technical advisers to the policy elites who made important decisions and were able to observe and participate in the process of reform from inside government. In the following pages, we use these papers and subsequent structured and unstructured interviews with their authors to assess the framework and hypotheses presented in prior chapters. To what extent does our framework correctly identify the factors that shaped the dynamics and outcome of a series of macroeconomic, sectoral, and institutional changes carried out in the 1980s?

The Dynamics of Reform:
Testing the Hypotheses

Our framework allows an exploration of the important ways in which policy elites influence the process, content, and timing of reform. In the 1980s, their importance was even heightened. In the fourteen cases of reforms from the 1980s, policy elites played critical roles in determining the substance and timing of initiatives to alter existing policy and institutional arrangements. They were central in situations as diverse as structural adjustment in the Gambia, health care reform in Chad and Puerto Rico, and changes in Indonesia's trade policies. Key actors in deciding that altering an existing situation was essential, they were often prime movers in generating support for particular initiatives. In many cases, small groups of high-level officials worked in relative isolation to draft the specific content of new or revised policies. Their perceptions and preferences were central to which reforms were introduced, when they were initiated, and how they were carried out. As with the cases of reform explored previously, of course, each case is unique in that it encapsulates a complex set of interactions in a particular institutional and historical context. Nevertheless, all fourteen cases confirm that the more state-centric analysis that highlights the role of policy makers and public managers in the reform process is an appropriate one, even for the multi-faceted and difficult changes of the 1980s. More specifically, the cases indicate that the dynamics of agenda setting, decision making, and implementation conform in important ways to the framework we have developed.

AGENDA SETTING IN THE 1980s

The analytic framework hypothesizes that a critical juncture in the reform process is whether an issue is introduced and considered under circumstances of crisis or politics as usual. In Chapter 4, we suggested that under circumstances of perceived crisis, reform agenda setting is characterized by strong pressure from nongovernmental actors. In such situations, the stakes for the government in power will be high, even to the point of imperiling the continuity of the regime. High-level officials will be closely involved in making decisions, the reforms introduced will signal significant changes from existing practice (innovation), and there will be a sense of urgency about the need to act. Conversely, when a situation of politics as usual exists, reforms are likely to be chosen by the decision makers themselves, and the stakes will be relatively low. Those involved in the decision will tend to be middle- and lower-level officials, they will seek marginal or incremental changes in existing practice, and they will feel little urgency about introducing reform, however committed they are to its substance. In general, reforms of the 1980s confirmed these patterns.

Agenda Setting in Crisis-ridden Reforms

In Chapter 4, we defined a crisis as a situation in which decision makers believe one exists, there is general consensus among them that the situation of crisis is real and threatening, and they believe that failure to act will lead to even more serious economic and political realities. Based on evidence presented in the cases and additional information supplied by their authors, six of the fourteen cases can be categorized as crisis-ridden reforms. Table 7.2 presents the results of a questionnaire circulated to the authors about the circumstances surrounding the emergence of these reforms.

Consistent with our hypothesis, in five of the six cases, decision makers perceived high stakes for the future stability and viability of the regime in undertaking the reform. The reform of the Gambia's customs system is the single exception: government officials perceived a crisis, yet did not believe that failure to reform this system would imperil the regime. In all six cases of crisis-ridden reform, the highest-level policy makers were involved in the decision to undertake it. For example, in the macroeconomic stabilization and structural adjustment programs in Guatemala, Panama, and Costa Rica, the president played a decisive and visible role in the reform initiative. In the case of financial reforms in Turkey, it was the head of the state planning organization (later to become prime minister) who most significantly influenced the reform efforts (Cole and Yaser 1988). Similarly, in all six cases, there were major or innovative changes from existing policy. In Turkey, for example, there was an all-out attempt to liberalize domestic financial systems; in the Central American cases, there were large devaluations and significant attempts to liberalize markets, freeze salaries for public employees, and increase taxes. Finally, in all six cases, decision makers felt strong pressure to act immediately. For these six cases, then, the pattern of agenda setting under conditions of perceived crisis suggested in Chapter 4 generally held true.

Agenda Setting in Politics-As-Usual Reforms

Eight cases were categorized as politics-as-usual reforms because, in each case, policy elites did not believe that the failure to take action in the short term would result in severe political and economic consequences. Table 7.3 indicates that the politics-as-usual cases consistently

TABLE 7.2

Predicted Influence of Agenda-setting Variables in Crisis Situations

Cases:	The Gambia Macroeconomic Reforms	The Gambia Customs Reform	Costa Rica Macroeconomic Reforms	Guatemala Macro-economic Reforms	Panama Macroeconomic Reforms	Turkey Financial System Reforms
PREDICTED AGENDA-SETTING VARIABLES IN CRISIS SITUATIONS						
Strong pressure for reform	yes	yes	yes	yes	yes	yes
High stakes	yes	no	yes	yes	yes	yes
High-level decision makers	yes	yes	yes	yes	yes	yes
Innovative change	yes	yes	yes	yes	yes	yes
Pressure to act immediately	yes	yes	yes	yes	yes	yes

demonstrate many of the characteristics identified with such reforms. Decision makers in six of the eight cases were able to select the reform with relatively little outside pressure; that is, it was considered a "chosen reform." For example, while preparing a tax reform package in 1982, the officials in Indonesia became convinced that attempts to increase the simplicity and neutrality of the tax system would make more sense if some of the major distortions in the structure of import duties and other elements of trade policy could be removed. The government designed and initiated its trade reforms three years later.

In all eight politics-as-usual cases, decision makers believed that the stakes were low enough that the success or failure of the reform would have little impact on the stability of the regime. In six cases, the principal decision makers held middle- or lower-level positions. Interestingly, the two politics-as-usual situations involving high-level decision makers both involved major change, as well as some potential embarrassment to the government. The reorganization of the Gambia Commercial and Development Bank (GCDB) involved high-level officials because the bank was an integral part of the financial sector, and its reform was part of the comprehensive adjustment program. Moreover, the bank had accumulated large losses, some of which were attributed to extremely generous loan terms for well-connected individuals. The second politics-as-usual case involving high-level officials was the decision to reform the Indonesian customs system, which had long been a lucrative source of unofficial income for well-placed individuals. The reform included moving units of armed forces into the major customs areas to prevent disturbances at the time of the announcement of the new policies.

In five of the eight cases, reform was aimed at bringing about an incremental change from existing policy. In the three cases in which change was described as innovative (not incremental as predicted), international actors were directly involved: in the case of reform of the state-owned Gambia Commercial and Development Bank, the government brought in a group of outside consultants funded by the World Bank to review the operations of the bank and recommend fundamental changes in structure and management; in the case of trade reforms in Indonesia, dramatic change resulted when the responsibilities of the Indonesian Customs Office were assigned to a Swiss surveying company that would inspect, classify, and value shipments to and from Indonesia; and in the case of health care reforms in Chad, an international team of health workers, funded by AID, established a new planning and statistical unit. However, it is worth noting that the involvement of international teams was significantly different in these three cases. In the Gambian bank reform, foreigners advised on the decision to reform. In the Indonesia customs reform, foreigners implemented the policy, but the decision for reforming

TABLE 7.3

Predicted Influence of Agenda-setting Variables in Politics-As-Usual Situations

Cases:	Chad Restruct. Health Ministry	Chad Develop Planning/ Stat. Unit	Gambia Commercial and Develop. Bank	Bangladesh Trade Reforms*	Bangladesh Industrial Reforms*	Sri Lanka Education Reform	Puerto Rico AIDS	Indonesia Trade Reform*
PREDICTED AGENDA-SETTING VARIABLES IN CRISIS SITUATIONS								
Chosen reform	no	yes	no	yes	no	yes	yes	yes
Low stakes	yes	yes	yes	yes	yes	yes	yes	yes
Middle- or low-level decision maker	yes	yes	no	yes	yes	yes	yes	no
Incremental change	yes	no	no	yes	no	yes	yes	no
Flexible timing	no	yes	yes	yes	yes	yes	yes	yes

* Although there may have been the perception of a crisis situation, this particular reform was supplemental to the major effort to deal with the crisis.

the system was made by the Indonesians without significant foreign assistance. In the Chad health reforms, foreign consultants both advised on and implemented the reform. Finally, in all but one of the cases, reform was introduced over an extended period of time. Typical of this flexible timing was the proposed administrative reorganization of Chad's Ministry of Health, where discussions continued for over two years before the changes were approved by the Council of Ministers.

While in general these cases of politics-as-usual reform confirm predictions made in Chapter 4, they also highlight important variations. In some cases, because of potential embarrassment to the government, politics-as-usual reforms received high-level attention. In other cases, policy elites were not able to choose reforms as freely as anticipated, in large part owing to the strong presence of international actors. Finally, some cases of politics as usual, particularly when international actors played a major role, appeared to stimulate innovation rather than incremental change.

Decision Making in the 1980s

In Chapter 5, we considered the political economy of reform decision making by reviewing the concerns of policy makers in twelve cases of reform. We indicated that, with considerable consistency, they viewed reform initiatives through four sets of lenses: their understanding of the technical issues involved in the reform; the impact of their choices on bureaucratic organization and actors; the meaning of change for political stability and political support; and the impact of change on relationships with international actors. However, the salience of these four decision criteria differed by case, depending on the circumstances of agenda setting—was the reform initiative considered under conditions of crisis or politics as usual? We proposed three hypotheses:

Hypothesis 1:
In crisis-ridden reforms, decision making tends to be dominated by concern about major issues of political stability and control. Technical analysis, bureaucratic interactions, and international pressures often assume importance in these decisions but usually remain subordinate to concerns about the stability or survival of the regime in power or the longevity of its incumbent leadership.

Hypothesis 2:
When noncrisis-ridden reforms concern policy issues, decisional outcomes tend to be dominated by micropolitical and bureaucratic concerns. Technical input and international pressure are important, but not deci-

sive, in explaining policy choice under these conditions. Major issues of political survival and support building are usually not salient to decision makers.

Hypothesis 3:
When noncrisis-ridden reforms concern issues of organizational change, decision making tends to be dominated by bureaucratic concerns. International pressures often emerge as part of bureaucratic interactions in these reforms. Technical input and concern for political survival are usually not salient to reform decision makers.

To test these hypotheses, we analyzed the fourteen cases of reform in the 1980s. In addition to the papers, a questionnaire and interviews with their authors provide some insight into the salience of decisions makers' concern about four decision-making variables: technical analysis, bureaucratic interaction, political survival, and international pressure. Tables 7.4 and 7.5 indicate rankings of the criteria for each case.

Decision Making in Crisis-ridden Reforms

Hypothesis 1 predicts that in times of crisis, decision making tends to be dominated by concerns about major issues of political stability and control. According to the case study authors, in four of the six crisis-ridden reforms, decision makers considered the future viability of the political regime to be "very important" in their decision to undertake the reform (see table 7.4). Thus, in the four instances in which major macroeconomic reforms were initiated, decision makers believed that there would be serious consequences if they did not address the precarious state of their economic and political situation. Further, they were well aware that no new international resources would be available without reform. Decision makers, in these situations, appeared to have been extremely concerned about the political survival of the regime. However, in two cases of crisis-ridden reform—customs reform in the Gambia and financial reforms in Turkey—concerns about political survival were considered to have only "some relevance" in the decision to undertake the reform. Nevertheless, in both cases, these individual reforms were linked to the need for other macroeconomic reforms that had raised important concerns about the survival of the regime.

The six cases of crisis-ridden reforms also highlight the importance of the role of international actors in the decision-making process. In some contrast to hypothesis 1, the salience of international actors was rated "very important" in four of the six cases, and "important" in the other two. As indicated earlier, the important role of international actors is a

TABLE 7.4

Influence of Decision-making Variables in Crisis Situations

Cases:	The Gambia Macroeconomic Reforms	The Gambia Customs Reforms	Costa Rica Macroeconomic Reforms	Guatemala Macroeconomic Reforms	Panama Macroeconomic Reforms	Turkey Financial System Reforms	Averages
Salience of technical analysis	2	3	2	2	2	0	1.83
Salience of bureaucratic interaction	2	2	1	1	1	3	1.67
Salience of regime maintenance	3	1	3	3	3	1	2.33
Salience of international actors	3	2	3	2	3	3	2.66

0 = Unimportant; 1 = Some Relevance; 2 = Important; 3 = Very Important

TABLE 7.5

Influence of Decision-making Variables in Noncrisis Situations

Cases:	Chad Restruct. Health Ministry	Chad Develop Planning/ Stat. Unit	Gambia Commercial and Develop. Bank	Bangladesh Trade Reforms*	Bangladesh Industrial Reforms*	Sri Lanka Education Reform	Puerto Rico AIDS	Indonesia Trade Reform	Averages
Salience of technical analysis	0	2	2	2	2	2	2	3	1.88
Salience of bureaucratic interaction	3	3	3	2	2	3	3	2	2.63
Salience of regime maintenance	1	1	1	1	1	0	0	1	0.75
Salience of international actors	3	3	3	2	1	1	2	3	2.25

0 = Unimportant; 1 = Some Relevance; 2 = Important; 3 = Very Important

* Although there may have been the perception of a crisis situation, this particular reform was supplemental to the major effort to deal with the crisis.

significant aspect of reforms carried out in the 1980s. Moreover, in these reform situations, international actors often participated in roles directly tied to a regime's concern about political survival. For example, in the case of the Gambia, by the middle of 1985 the country could no longer finance its deficits: "The pressure intensified when the Managing Director of the IMF began formal proceedings to have the Gambia declared ineligible to borrow. Other donors added to this pressure when they made it clear that, unless the Government changed its economic policies, there was little that they would, or could, do to assist" (McPherson and Radelet 1988:5). In situations such as these, policy elites in the 1980s paid close attention to their relations with international actors, because the international actors were intimately linked in policy makers' minds with concerns about political survival.

However, at least three of the cases suggest that international actors were important influences at least in part because of the degree to which their involvement increased resistance to particular reforms. For example,

One of the biggest surprises to policy makers in the [Central American] region was the active resistance to devaluations [as part of a stabilization program]. . . . In perceptual terms devaluations became equated with surrendering national sovereignty to the IMF. In Honduras parity with the dollar was considered such a "sacred cow" that discussion of devaluation was barred from public forums and advocates were warned not to discuss it and were threatened with expulsion or jail sentences if they did. (Lindenberg 1988:20)

The role of technical analysis in situations of crisis was described as an "important" or a "very important" decision-making variable in all but one of the cases.[3] The importance of bureaucratic interactions in crisis situations was described in three of the six cases as having "some relevance," and only in Turkey, where financial reforms were implemented over a long period of time, was the role of bureaucratic interactions described as "very important."

Figure 7.1 presents composite scores from the last column in table 7.4 to show the relative importance of each of the four decision-making variables in situations of crisis. As predicted, in crisis-ridden reforms issues of regime maintenance had high salience, while technical analysis and bureaucratic interactions emerged as less significant. However, international actors had a much higher profile for decision makers than predicted. This is not to suggest, however, that policy elites' concern about international actors outweighed their concerns for regime maintenance. Rather, concerns about international actors consistently played significant roles in policy makers' thinking during crisis-ridden reforms, often precisely because concerns about international actors were tied to policy elites' concerns about macropolitical stability.

FIGURE 7.1
Influence of Decision Variables in
Crisis Situations

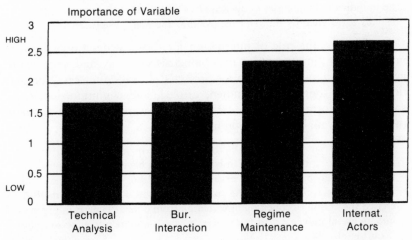

RANGE OF VARIABLES:
0 = Unimportant, 1 = Some Relevance, 2 = Important, 3 = Very Important

■ Series 1

Decision Making in Politics-As-Usual Reforms

In Chapter 5, we predicted that in noncrisis situations, concerns about the impact of the proposed reform on bureaucratic actors would be very important. Table 7.5 clearly demonstrates the importance of bureaucratic interactions: in all eight noncrisis cases examined, the impact of the reform on bureaucratic actors or organizations was considered "important" or "very important." The case of the restructuring of Chad's health ministry is typical of the descriptions of the importance of bureaucratic interactions:

> The Chadian description of this process was "creer un nouvel organigramme," that is to create a new organization chart. The intensity of the debates suggested that much more than a drawing was at stake. The major controversial issue became the number and character of each of the Ministry's major agencies, and what the responsibilities of each would be." (Foltz and Foltz 1988:19)

In some of the cases, reform strategies were specifically designed with the importance of these bureaucratic interactions in mind. In the case of industrial and trade reforms in Bangladesh:

To help break down bureaucratic barriers to reform, an effort was made to channel reform recommendations proposed by technocrats through high level inter-ministerial and interagency committees. It was hoped this strategy would reduce the risk that recommended measures could become bottled up in individual ministries or agencies by middle-level officials who felt personally threatened by the reforms. (Mallon and Stern 1988:22)

Interestingly, the role of international actors was described as "very important" or "important" in most noncrisis situations and, once again, given greater importance than we predicted. In case after case, international actors suggested, promoted, cajoled, and conditioned new resources on reform initiatives. Outside experts were also used to expand the options available to decision makers.

In the case of San Juan and AIDS, the most powerful actors, the Mayor and the Director of the Department of Health, did not have any obvious method to shift responsibility to other existing organizations or to form new alliances. They were also unwilling to relinquish power. Therefore, they exercised the option of soliciting intervention from outside experts in order to initiate useful movement of the process towards a more adequate solution. (Kouri et al. 1988:5)

Once again, however, as in crisis-ridden reforms, international actors sometimes did as much to hinder reform as to promote it. In the case of trade policy reform in Indonesia:

In 1981 the Minister of Finance prepared a new tariff schedule which involved a moderate reduction in the average level of variance of nominal rates. Unfortunately an internal World Bank study which strongly advocated such changes was completed and leaked a few days before the new Tariff Book was to have been implemented by government decree. This made it look as if the government was responding to outside pressure in determining its policies, and this pressure was sufficient to prevent the new rates from being implemented. (Barichello and Flatters 1988:15)

In none of the cases of politics as usual was the issue of regime maintenance considered "important" or "very important," and in all eight of the cases, bureaucratic interactions were rated as considerably more salient than concerns about regime maintenance. Technical analysis in cases of noncrisis ranged from unimportant to very important. In the case of restructuring the health ministry in Chad, technical analysis was considered unimportant because the issues were shaped almost entirely by the interests of the bureaucratic actors involved. However, decision makers in the case of trade reform in Indonesia were influenced significantly by technical analysis:

Previous work had classified Indonesia's trade policy regime as of the "moderate import-substitution" type. A two year study, carried out by a team of

FIGURE 7.2
Influence of Decision Variables in
Politics-As-Usual Situations

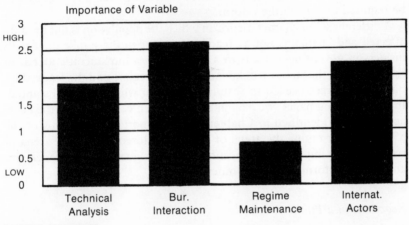

Importance of Variable

RANGE OF VARIABLES:
0 = Unimportant, 1 = Some Relevance, 2 = Important, 3 = Very Important

government and external advisors, clearly demonstrated that there was a strong import substitution bias of trade policies in the early 1980s. This information (particularly a series of detailed case material with well-documented "horror stories") were [sic] important in persuading policy makers of the need for change. (Barichello and Flatters 1988:7)

Figure 7.2 presents composite scores from the last column in table 7.5 to show the relative importance of each of the four decision-making variables in politics-as-usual reforms. As predicted, bureaucratic interaction is very important and issues of regime maintenance are relatively unimportant in politics-as-usual reforms. However, both technical analysis and the role of international actors emerged as more important than anticipated in Chapter 5.

IMPLEMENTING REFORMS IN THE 1980s

Chapter 6 explored the process through which policy and institutional reforms are implemented and sustained. We hypothesized that key characteristics of reforms—the distribution of costs, the distribution of benefits, the nature of the administrative and technical content, the duration of implementation, the extent of participation—determine the kind of conflict that will be engendered by efforts to implement changes. One set of reform characteristics, in which the population is broadly affected and change is highly visible to it, tends to generate reactions in a public arena. In such a situation, the stakes will be high for the regime and for the leadership undertaking the reform, and considerable resources will be required to sustain the reform.

A different set of characteristics, in which the population is not broadly affected and change is not as readily apparent to the public as it is to insiders in government, leads to a response in a bureaucratic arena. In this situation, the stakes will be lower for the regime and the leadership, but the resources needed to sustain the reform will also be substantial. In the following pages, we examine the fourteen cases to see if the characteristics we identified in Chapter 6 were important in reforms of the 1980s in determining the arena of response. Moreover, did the arena of response have important implications for the regime, for the leadership, and for the reform, as we hypothesized?

Reactions in a Public Arena

The authors of the case studies were asked to identify the arena of reactions or response to the reform they examined. Table 7.6 presents six cases characterized as having drawn reactions primarily in the public arena. Of the six cases, however, five also elicited responses in a bureaucratic arena. In four of the six cases that resulted in a public reaction, the costs of the reform had a direct impact on a large segment of the population. The structural adjustment packages of the Gambia, Panama, Guatemala, and Costa Rica required raising taxes, freezing salaries, and reducing subsidies. These reforms affected large numbers of people and in some cases prompted dramatic and sometimes violent public reactions. In Guatemala, for instance, President Venicio Cerezo's attempt to implement a tax reform as part of the policy package to increase revenues and cut the fiscal deficit was met with a national strike in October of 1987 and a series of demonstrations leading up to an attempted coup in 1988. In Panama, President Nicholas Ardito Barletta's administration passed a law creating new taxes and freezing salaries in response to sluggish economic growth, fiscal deficits, and increasing debt service payments. Private sector groups, labor unions, and public employees responded with a national strike. Within a month, the president was forced to rescind the law (Lindenberg 1988).

The case of the Gambia is an interesting counterexample. Although responses were generated in both the public and bureaucratic arenas, their magnitude was very small. Of particular interest is the public response, since the Gambia seems to have had all the characteristics of a reform that we suggested would result in a significant public reaction.

TABLE 7.6

Characteristics of Cases in Which Reactions Took Place Primarily in the Public Arena

Cases:	The Gambia Macroeconomic Reforms*	The Gambia Customs Reforms*	Costa Rica Macroeconomic Reforms	Panama Macro-economic Reforms*	Guatemala Macroeconomic Reforms*	Indonesia Trade Reforms*
POLICY VARIABLE CHARACTERISTICS						
Do costs have a direct impact on a large segment of population? (i.e., are costs dispersed?)	yes	no	yes	yes	yes	no
Are benefits concentrated?	no	yes	no	yes	yes	yes
Is there a relatively low technical component?	no	yes	no	no	no	no
Is there a relatively low administrative component?	no	no	no	no	no	no
Is there a relatively short length of time needed to implement the reform?	yes	yes	yes	yes	yes	yes

* There was also a response in the bureaucratic arena.

This particular case highlights the importance of mitigating factors that can significantly lessen potential public reaction. For example, the lack of organized opposition, an invasion threat posed by neighboring Senegal, and clear memories of a coup in 1981 reduced the likelihood of domestic opposition. Moreover, ample rains helped agricultural production, and major inflows of new resources were provided by international donors once the Gambia demonstrated that it was undertaking significant reforms. These factors and others counteracted the potential for reaction to the changes initiated, suggesting the importance of analyzing a series of mitigating factors in efforts to predict the nature of responses to reform initiatives.

The benefits in four of the six cases that generated public reactions were concentrated in government: most typically, they accrued as revenues in the government's attempts to balance its budget or pay off its debts. Other, more generalized benefits were often much farther down the road, such as the functioning of more effective and efficient markets. Usually the only tangible short-term benefit resulting from these cases of reform was the influx of new foreign resources. In the case of the Gambia, the large amount of concessional foreign financing (after the government undertook major reforms)

> helped The Gambia replenish its foreign reserves, reduce its arrears, meet its current foreign exchange obligations, stabilize the exchange rate, increase its food security, and reduce its bank borrowing. Perhaps most importantly, it allowed investment and consumption to be higher than they otherwise would have been during the adjustment period. The higher level of investment is critical for The Gambia to achieve sustained economic growth; the higher level of consumption helped to reduce public resistance to the ERP. (McPherson and Radelet 1988:12)

The cases indicate that reforms of the 1980s can be more complex than our framework indicated. The idea of "self-implementing reforms" with low technical and administrative components during their implementation, for instance, is overly simplistic. Many of the 1980s reforms included devaluations or removing subsidies from consumer goods, predicted to be self-implementing in our framework. Six cases of public response to implementation suggest that such reforms are rarely undertaken in isolation; it is more typical that a devaluation will be a part of a wider package of reforms. Five of the six reforms required relatively high technical components, and all six required relatively high administrative components for implementation. For example, the macroeconomic reforms in Guatemala and Costa Rica required both sophisticated administrative and technical skills to implement, even though the author maintained that the initial stabilization component (devaluation) of the package might have required a relatively lower administrative component (Lindenberg 1988). In contrast to our initial hypotheses, then, most of the reforms that resulted in public reaction in fact required relatively high technical and administrative components.

The length of time that elapsed before the impact of reform was visible emerged as a salient variable, as predicted. In all six cases of reactions in the public arena, a relatively short period of time passed before the first impact of the reform began to be visible. Whether it was new taxes in Guatemala, new taxes and frozen salaries in Panama, or the components of the Indonesian trade reforms that literally changed customs operations overnight, those directly affected realized the impact almost immediately.

In five of these cases, reactions and responses occurred in both public and bureaucratic arenas. This is also a consequence of the packaged nature of reforms in the 1980s. For example, one would expect public reactions to a stabilization program that removed subsidies from consumer goods such as bread or transportation and a bureaucratic response to a ministry reorganization. When these reforms are combined in a package, as in the cases of the Gambia, Panama, and Guatemala, there were reactions and responses of different intensity in both arenas.

We argued in Chapter 6 that public reactions tend to mobilize existing pressure groups, encourage the formation of new ones to oppose the reform, and stimulate organized opposition to the government. Thus, when the response to a policy reform takes place in the public arena, not only are the stakes high for the reform and for those directly involved in taking a leadership role in it, but often the stakes are high for the continued viability of the regime itself. Table 7.7 presents the results of authors' estimations of risk factors in the six cases with reactions in the public arena. In Guatemala, Panama, and Costa Rica, decision makers apparently believed that the stakes were high because reactions to the reform initiative could threaten the durability of the regime itself. In the Gambia and Indonesia, the stakes were not perceived to be so high. In addition to high stakes for the regime in four of the six cases, those directly involved in undertaking the reforms considered the stakes to be high for themselves because reaction to the reform could cause them to lose their jobs. Finally, in every case, decision makers believed that public reactions to the reform could cause the reform to fail. Thus, in most of the cases with reactions in the public arena, the stakes were thought to be high for the regime, for leadership, and for reform.

Response in a Bureaucratic Arena

Table 7.8 presents eight cases where, according to their authors, responses to implementation of the reform occurred primarily in the bu-

TABLE 7.7

Political Stakes in Cases in Which Reactions Took Place Primarily in the Public Arena*

Cases:	The Gambia Macro-economic Reforms*	The Gambia Customs Reforms*	Costa Rica Macro-economic Reforms	Panama Macro-economic Reforms*	Guatemala Macro-economic Reforms*	Indonesia Trade Reforms*
PREDICTED POLITICAL STAKES FOR REFORMS WITH REACTIONS IN THE PUBLIC ARENA						
Are the stakes high for the regime?	yes	no	yes	yes	yes	no
Are the stakes high for leadership directly involved in undertaking reform?	yes	no	yes	yes	yes	yes
Are the stakes high for the reform?	yes	yes	yes	yes	yes	yes

* There was also a response in the bureaucratic arena.

reaucratic arena. In all eight cases the costs were concentrated in government, often in a particular ministry or organization. For instance, in the Bangladesh trade reform, bureaucrats accustomed to managing the customs office were threatened with loss of influence, while in the health ministry reorganization in Chad, ministry officials feared loss of traditional authority and independence.

However, in only two cases were the benefits dispersed as we predicted. The concept of "dispersed benefits" is perhaps inappropriate when few reforms in the 1980s were providing, say, new direct subsidies to consumers or farmers and the benefits were only seen indirectly, if at all, in things such as the long-term, more effective functioning of markets. The important distinction, it seems, is whether the benefits are concentrated in government or not, since in relatively few cases is it possible to point to dispersed benefits that accrue in the short term to large sectors of the population. Most of the cases demonstrate that the negative impact of the costs was more significant in determining the intensity of the reaction than was the positive support gained from benefits.

Five of the eight reforms required a high technical component, and all eight required a high administrative component. In all eight cases implementation took place over a relatively long period of time, usually a number of years. The case of Chad's reorganization of the Ministry of Health is typical of the manner in which many of the reforms with responses in the bureaucratic arena were carried out; the changes were worked out over a two-year period "in the back rooms, in Ministry staff meetings and ultimately in the council of Ministers, but not until they had been remanded to lower levels several times" (Foltz and Foltz 1988:21).

In contrast to reforms that engender a public reaction, we hypothesized that when the response to a reform takes place in the bureaucratic arena, the political stakes for the leadership and for the regime are relatively low. The real issues are whether government capacity exists to implement the reform and whether there is support for the reform that will cause the bureaucracy to comply with the intention of the decision. Whatever happens, the issue is the viability of the reform and not the survival of the regime. Table 7.9 presents the eight cases that produced responses in the bureaucratic arena and indicates that in seven of the eight cases, the stakes for the regime were considered low. Turkey, once again, is the exception, because Turkey's financial reforms were closely tied to macroeconomic reforms that had created very high stakes for the government. In six of the eight cases, the stakes for the leadership directly involved in undertaking the reform were also low. In all eight cases, however, the stakes for the reform were high because decision makers believed that a negative response to reform could undermine it. Thus, in the reforms

TABLE 7.8

Characteristics of Cases in Which Reactions Took Place Primarily in the Bureaucratic Arena

Cases:	Chad Restruct. Health Ministry	Chad Develop Planning/ Stat. Unit	Gambia Commercial and Develop. Bank	Bangladesh Trade Reforms	Bangladesh Industrial Reforms	Sri Lanka Education Reforms	Puerto Rico AIDS	Turkey Financial Reforms
POLICY VARIABLE CHARACTERISTICS								
Are costs concentrated?	yes	yes	yes	yes	yes	yes	yes	yes
Are benefits dispersed?	no	no	yes	no	no	yes	no	no
Is there a high technical component?	no	no	yes	no	yes	yes	yes	yes
Is there a high administrative component?	yes	yes	yes	yes	yes	yes	yes	yes
Is there a relatively long length of time needed to implement the reform?	yes	yes	yes	yes	yes	yes	yes	yes

with responses in a bureaucratic arena, the stakes were consistently low for the regime and for leadership, while they were high for the reform.

Conclusions

This assessment of fourteen cases of policy and institutional reforms from the 1980s indicates that the analytic framework we developed in chapters 4, 5, and 6 also applies to the special instance of reforms introduced in the 1980s. First, the cases highlight a pattern of important involvement of policy elites in reform initiatives. They also demonstrate that a significantly different process results when policy elites initiate reforms under crisis conditions as compared to situations of politics as usual. Moreover, the framework correctly predicts the high salience of regime maintenance in times of crisis and the high salience of bureaucratic interactions in politics-as-usual reforms. However, the role of international actors in these fourteen cases emerged as much more important than predicted. The characteristics of particular reforms—the distribution of costs and benefits, the technical and administrative content, the length of time before their impact is visible, the extent of participation required—were often significant in predicting the arena of response. Nevertheless, the cases also suggest that the implementation scheme we developed might be simplified by asking two questions: who gets hurt? (distribution of costs), and when do they get hurt? (timing). Responses to these two questions appeared to be the most useful in determining the arena of reaction to reform initiatives.

The increasing linking and packaging of reforms characteristic of the 1980s meant that reforms often generated responses in both public and bureaucratic arenas. As responses in both arenas became more common, analysis of the types of responses increased in importance and complexity. For example, in the packaged reform typical of the 1980s, policy makers needed to anticipate public reaction to some components and bureaucratic responses to others. The types of resources needed to implement and sustain a reform were correspondingly more varied, and issues of timing and sequencing more critical. Methodologically, when more than one reform is initiated as part of a package, it will be useful to separate the different components of the reform package and analyze each independently. The analysis of the separate reforms will then need to be assessed in relation to other initiatives in the reform package to gain a clearer picture of their interactions.

Each case of policy and institutional change is surrounded by unique conditions, personalities, and institutional arrangements. Moreover, our review of the particular conditions of the 1980s indicates that the sub-

TABLE 7.9

Political Stakes in Cases in Which Reactions Took Place Primarily in the Bureaucratic Arena

Cases:	Chad Restruct. Health Ministry	Chad Develop Planning/ Stat. Unit	Gambia Commercial and Develop. Bank	Bangladesh Trade Reforms	Bangladesh Industrial Reforms	Sri Lanka Education Reforms	Puerto Rico AIDS	Turkey Financial Reforms
PREDICTED POLITICAL STAKES FOR REFORMS WITH RESPONSES IN THE BUREAUCRATIC ARENA								
Are the stakes low for the regime?	yes	yes	yes	yes	yes	yes	yes	no
Are the stakes low for leadership directly involved in reform?	no	yes	yes	yes	yes	yes	yes	no
Are the stakes high for the reform?	yes	yes	yes	yes	yes	yes	yes	yes

stance of reform tends to differ significantly from policy and institutional changes introduced in earlier eras. Nevertheless, we have argued that there are important commonalities in the process of reform that transcend the period and the specific substance of change initiatives. In Chapter 8, we return to the framework and consider its implications for reform leaders and ways in which they can assess and expand their room for maneuvering in introducing and sustaining reform measures.

CHAPTER 8

Conclusion:

Finding Room to Maneuver

Deliberate efforts to bring about changes in public policies and in the structure and function of public institutions are normal and ongoing processes of government. In this book, we have documented a series of cases of policy and organizational reform initiatives in developing countries over the past several decades. The changes sought varied from major reorientations in national development strategies to fine-tuning specific measures for achieving concrete program goals; the circumstances surrounding such efforts varied from intense crisis situations to the mundane concerns of day-to-day political and bureaucratic action; and outcomes varied from the successful achievement of goals to complete inability to address given problems.

Through the exploration of these diverse cases, we have generated a framework for understanding the emergence, discussion, implementation, and sustainability of reform initiatives. In particular, we have focused on the role of policy elites in shaping policy agendas, considering available options, and managing the political and bureaucratic challenges of implementation. Analyzing their role in the process of change has allowed us to map out conceptually the policy-relevant space within which they operate and the factors that influence the choices they make. Our cases show that public officials are almost always actively engaged in efforts to influence the scope and nature of change in their societies. Their perceptions, activities, motivations, and impact therefore deserve more systematic analytic attention than has generally been given them in discussions of the policy process in developing countries.

In focusing on decision makers and managers in government, we develop a different view of their influence and impact than what is encountered in many studies of policy and policy change. We believe that the analysis of concrete cases of reform, based on the experiences of participants in policy making and implementation, has allowed us to go beyond theoretical approaches that view policy elites as cogs in the wheels of large structures and systems which they have no capacity to influence or alter. Neither do our findings support approaches that consider policy elites to be relatively powerless referees in ongoing struggles among societal interests, or those portraying them as single-minded "rent-seekers" whose every decision is dominated by the drive to maximize power. Finally, we have presented evidence to question the view that policy elites are primarily bureaucratic infighters in multilayered games that lead to haphazard outcomes, as some approaches suggest. While at any given time the policy elites we have studied, advised, and conversed with may fit any one of these characterizations, in most cases we find they have scope for leadership, action, and maneuver within constraints set by context, circumstance, and policy. Moreover, in many situations, purposive action on the part of such policy elites can alter the extent of those constraints, enlarging or diminishing what we have called policy space for the introduction of reform initiatives. This is a central theme of the lessons we draw from our cases of policy and institutional reform.

Our framework is summarized in figure 8.1. Building on particular instances of reform in a variety of countries, we have identified a process of policy and institutional change that is determined by three critical junctures. At each juncture, the exploration of a series of questions enables us to explain the subsequent course of agenda setting, decision making, and implementation and their interrelationships. Briefly, our framework indicates that environmental context, agenda-setting circumstances, and policy characteristics influence the perceptions and concerns of policy elites and shape the nature and scope of conflict surrounding efforts to introduce change. Analysis of context, circumstance, and policy characteristics can account for a significant amount of variability in the outcome of reform initiatives, as well as variability and continuity across countries, issues, and time.

The framework begins by indicating that any particular reform initiative emerges within a preexisting situation composed of (1) the orientation of policy elites in terms of their values, expertise, experiences, and loyalties, and (2) the historical, international, political, economic, and administrative characteristics of a given country. These sets of factors form the environmental context within which decisions are made. Those involved in making authoritative decisions about policy and organizational change are constrained by such factors, which are deeply embedded

FIGURE 8.1
The Political Economy of Policy Reform

I. Environmental Context

*INDIVIDUAL CHARACTERISTICS
OF POLICY ELITES*

Ideological Predispositions
Professional Expertise and Training
Memories of Similar Policy Situations
Position and Power Resources
Political and Institutional Commitments/Loyalties
Personal Attributes and Goals

THE CONTEXT OF POLICY CHOICE

Societal Pressure
Historical Context
Economic Conditions
International Context
Administrative Capacity
Other Policies

II. Agenda-setting Circumstances

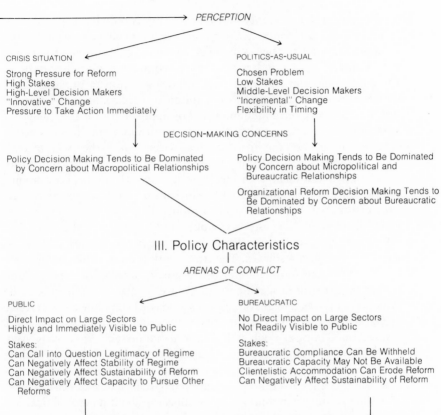

PERCEPTION

CRISIS SITUATION

Strong Pressure for Reform
High Stakes
High-Level Decision Makers
"Innovative" Change
Pressure to Take Action Immediately

POLITICS-AS-USUAL

Chosen Problem
Low Stakes
Middle-Level Decision Makers
"Incremental" Change
Flexibility in Timing

DECISION-MAKING CONCERNS

Policy Decision Making Tends to Be Dominated
by Concern about Macropolitical Relationships

Policy Decision Making Tends to Be Dominated
by Concern about Micropolitical and
Bureaucratic Relationships

Organizational Reform Decision Making Tends to
Be Dominated by Concern about Bureaucratic
Relationships

III. Policy Characteristics

ARENAS OF CONFLICT

PUBLIC

Direct Impact on Large Sectors
Highly and Immediately Visible to Public

Stakes:
Can Call into Question Legitimacy of Regime
Can Negatively Affect Stability of Regime
Can Negatively Affect Sustainability of Reform
Can Negatively Affect Capacity to Pursue Other
  Reforms

BUREAUCRATIC

No Direct Impact on Large Sectors
Not Readily Visible to Public

Stakes:
Bureaucratic Compliance Can Be Withheld
Bureaucratic Capacity May Not Be Available
Clientelistic Accommodation Can Erode Reform
Can Negatively Affect Sustainability of Reform

RESOURCES FOR IMPLEMENTATION AND SUSTAINABILITY

Legitimacy of Regime?
If strong, broad-based support, then not likely to
  be threatened
If weak support, then may be threatened

Tradition of Political Stability?
If strong tradition, then change of regime unlikely
If weak tradition, then regime is vulnerable

Individual Reform or Set of Reforms?
If individual reform, then less threat to
  government
If series of reforms, then greater threat to
  government

Autonomy of Government?
If relatively autonomous, then more capacity to
  form coalitions of support
If highly dependent on major societal interest
  groups, then more constrained

Degree of Elite Consensus?
If high consensus, then better prospects for
  reform
If low consensus, then poor prospects for reform

High Level of Political Support?
If high, then ability to counter bureaucratic
  resistance
If low, then difficulty in overcoming resistance

Organizational/Hierarchical Authority?
If high, then ability to overcome internal
  opposition
If low, then inability to overcome opposition

Consensus Building Possible?
If yes, then ability to change values
If no, then inability to change values

Existence of Behavioral Incentives?
If yes, then greater control over bureaucrats
If no, then lesser control over bureaucrats

Administrative Capacity?
If high, then ability to assume new tasks
If low, then lesser ability to assume new tasks

within perceptions of reality and very real limits on what is possible set by societal characteristics. These factors are not readily altered and often account for systematic biases in policy decisions. But these environmental factors should not be understood only as constraints on policy options. The context surrounding particular instances of reform provides scope for the influence of ideas and values, the creation of coalitions of support, and the discovery of unique moments of opportunity for the pursuit of change. If, as we argue, policy elites are important and influential actors in reform initiatives, the broad context within which they seek to craft politically and bureaucratically acceptable solutions to particular problems can provide them with ideological, personal, political, economic, and administrative resources with which to do so. Contextual characteristics thus set limits and also introduce the potential to expand or diminish the scope for purposive policy and organizational change.

Context, as described, is clearly important in our framework, but so are particular circumstances. The framework indicates that agendas for policy and organizational reform are greatly affected by the circumstances that surround specific issues. As we suggested in Chapter 4, the dynamics of issues that get on reform agendas when policy elites perceive that a crisis situation exists are distinctly different from the dynamics that surround initiatives when they believe that no such crisis exists. And, as the subsequent chapters demonstrated, the concerns of decision makers are very much influenced by these perceptions of crisis or everyday politics. We hypothesized that, given different circumstances, decision makers would be dominated primarily by concerns about macropolitical stability and legitimacy or about micropolitical and bureaucratic costs and benefits. By extension, we argue that choices among available options vary in part because policy elites apply different criteria to the decisions they make in distinct situations. The options considered and concerns voiced clearly reflect contextual factors such as ideological preferences, political organization, and historical experiences. How particular circumstances are perceived by policy elites thus serves as a bridge between the "embedded orientations" of individuals and societies and the kinds of changes considered by decision makers confronted with specific policy choices.[1]

In turn, characteristics of particular policies form a bridge between what is decided and what consequences, in terms of societal and bureaucratic conflicts, are likely to follow. Policy characteristics determine who experiences the costs and benefits of altered policies or institutions and under what conditions and timing they are likely to react to the consequences of state action. At times, costs and benefits are distributed in a way that encourages public responses such as the mobilization of societal interests to oppose or support particular measures. At other times, as we suggested in Chapter 6, bureaucratic response and resistance are most likely to emerge in the wake of proposed changes. Arenas of conflict influence the type of stakes for political regimes, policy elites, and reform outcomes in any effort to introduce change. And, given arenas of conflict and type and level of stakes, the framework indicates that different kinds of resources are needed to overcome resistance or lessen the risks of introducing change. Considering what these resources are and whether they are available to reformers pushes us to assess again the broader context of values, institutions, and experiences with which we began. The resources available to those who advocate policy and organizational change are reflections of the more embedded character-istics of a political society and its governmental culture.

The framework does not predict outcomes in terms of what choices will be made or how successfully particular reforms will resolve particular public problems. Instead, it systematizes thinking about how context influences particular situations, how circumstances shape options, how options are sorted out in terms of their political, technical, bureaucratic, and international implications, and how policy characteristics affect con-flict and the resources needed to manage it in the introduction of reform. Analytically, these are important sets of relationships to map out.

Such a mapping can also be a way of beginning to think strategically about introducing and sustaining reform. In terms of strategic concerns, it could be argued that the framework laid out in figure 8.1 merely reflects the intuitive knowledge of skilled policy makers and public managers who maneuver within complex situations to achieve particular goals. Demonstrably, however, intuition and skill are not universally sufficient to generate effective strategies to introduce and sustain reforms. It is only too clear that policy reforms often fail to be introduced and sustained, as illustrated by some of our cases, and that policy makers regularly face the risks of failing to bring about change, of losing their jobs, and of destabilizing their societies through the decisions they make. Systematic thinking about the interrelationships and consequences of context, cir-cumstance, and policy characteristics therefore provides both an analytic tool for understanding the process of reform and a first cut at developing strategies for introducing and sustaining change.

The Potential for Reform Leadership

If our framework is to be useful, it should indicate not only what the critical points are that affect outcomes and how they vary across coun-tries, circumstances, or policy issues, but also to what extent they can be altered by those promoting particular changes. Our analysis has generated a series of hypotheses, a set of if-then propositions about the process of policy and institutional reform. Admittedly, the basis for developing these hypotheses is narrow—twelve cases covering a range of policy issues and country contexts, "tested" through review of fourteen additional cases and a series of seminars and workshops with policy makers and managers from developing countries. Clearly, much work remains to be done in exploring, testing, and refining this framework.

Nevertheless, because we have tried to understand what occurs within the state and how decision makers and managers understand the problematic nature of reform, we believe we have focused long-overdue attention on the role of policy elites and how their actions can be understood as maneuvering within constraints and opportunities created by context, circumstance, and policy characteristics. We believe the framework opens up considerable scope for the analysis of leadership and principles of action that can enhance opportunities for successful policy and organizational change. Perhaps most important, it suggests that the prospects for successfully changing policy and doing so in the broader public interest are greater than those suggested by perceptions that see elites as reflections of class, interest, rent-seeking, or organizations. We can begin to use the framework, as we did in Chapter 6, as a way of providing analytic guidance to reformers within government or outside it. Reviewing figure 8.1 from a more action-oriented perspective, the possibilities for maneuvering within the variables of context, circumstance, and policy characteristics become clearer, and the extent to which these factors open up opportunities for change can be assessed.

MANEUVERING WITHIN CONTEXT

Contextual characteristics of policy elites—their ideological predispositions, professional expertise and training, memories of similar policy situations, position and power resources, political and institutional commitments and loyalties, and personal attributes and goals—are factors that exist prior to any particular instance of reform. The characteristics that policy elites bring with them to problem-solving situations are not highly variable; they tend to be relatively fixed consequences of personality factors and life experiences. To a degree, then, these characteristics set limits on what is possible. At the same time, they are or can be used by skilled reformers to enhance possibilities for bringing about change. Thus, preexisting characteristics offer them opportunities for developing support for reform initiatives based on common values, professional training, shared experiences, hierarchical power relationships, or common political commitments. Consensus building and elite coalition formation were central activities of reformers in many of our cases, and the support they pulled together often derived precisely from shared attributes among a subset of policy elites. An interesting variant of this is coalitions across organizations and national boundaries, a phenomenon that became more common in the 1980s. For example, officials of particular governments and international agencies frequently form coalitions to press for policy change in the face of opposition of other officials within their own organizations. Such coalitions may have their roots in contextual factors such as similar schools, training, or career experiences that can be more powerful than national or organizational allegiances.

Societal, historical, international, administrative, economic, and political contexts are also givens that antedate specific efforts to alter existing policy or institutional behavior. Moreover, they are not easily or quickly altered, reflecting as they do fundamental characteristics of a polity. As we have suggested, however, these factors present both constraints and opportunities. As constraints, they provide reformers with valuable insights into what is possible within a given society and thus help set feasible goals for reform initiatives. This may seem obvious, but policy and organizational changes are regularly introduced that do not reflect the very real limits of administrative capacity, international market conditions, social tolerance for change, and other such factors. Systematic awareness of contextual constraints can therefore play a valuable role in shaping feasible reform proposals. As opportunities, these same factors can provide reform leaders with the resources to mobilize societal interests, to use the realities and myths of historical experiences for generating support or tolerance for change, to seize opportune moments for launching reform initiatives, or to utilize existing human resources for developing feasible options for reform. The contextual factors that set limits on what is possible also provide grist for generating creative responses to public problems.

Maneuvering within Circumstance

In considering contextual factors related to the characteristics of policy elites and the conditions existing in particular countries, reformers can attempt to understand the boundaries of existing policy space while simultaneously seeking to enlarge it.[2] In most cases, room to maneuver is bounded, but existing boundaries are not immutable. This is also true of the circumstances that place particular issues on the agenda for public action. To some extent, reformers may have the capacity to alter the perception of circumstances surrounding particular reform initiatives. It is well recognized, for example, that those who favor the adoption of particular reforms often try to generate the perception of crisis in order to enhance the possibility that significant action will be taken. Thus, reformers may work to increase the pressure on decision makers from outside of government, to increase the sense of threat if action is not taken on an issue, to move decision making upward in government to the attention of high-level political and bureaucratic actors, to stimulate consideration of major innovative changes, and to increase the sense of urgency in addressing particular issues.[3]

While attempting to create a sense of crisis is the most common way in which reformers seek to alter agenda-setting circumstances, there may be situations in which they seek to diminish a sense of crisis. For example, where time-consuming technical analysis is considered essential to developing policy options, or where a perception of crisis is pushing in the direction of an irrational, infeasible, or inappropriate response, reform leaders may choose to try to lessen the pressure for reform, lower the stakes, remove the issue from the attention of high-level actors to that of middle-level technical analysts, suggest incremental changes, or introduce suggestions for flexible timing. Reformers may not necessarily be successful in altering perceptions about circumstances, but the fact remains that such perceptions are subject to influence, interpretation, and change over time. Circumstances can provide some room for maneuver.

Maneuvering within Available Options

Reformers within government and outside it are often heavily involved in developing policy and organizational solutions that meet the specific goals they are concerned about. Frequently, they are also concerned that the solutions they favor be politically and bureaucratically acceptable. When this is the case, it reflects a clear understanding that decision making is an eminently political process and that the principal concerns of decision makers are those of the consequences of their actions for macropolitical stability and legitimacy, micropolitical claims, and bureaucratic relationships. Indeed, our framework indicates that there is a systematic relationship between the kind of circumstances that surround the emergence of a reform issue and the kind of political and bureaucratic concerns that dominate decision making. In shaping responses to given problems, strategies for introducing reform reflect these concerns.

Reform proposals that invoke anxieties about macropolitical relationships tend to be crafted with regard to their impact on broad sectors of the population: where consultation about such initiatives takes place, it is often with peak organizations of societal interests; and where appeals for support are made, they are often in the language of national goals and symbols. In contrast, when micropolitical concerns are most salient, efforts to secure support or to craft the content of policy may emphasize resource allocations to specific interest, ethnic, regional, or ideological groups. Efforts to mobilize support for, or overcome resistance to, particular actions tend to emphasize individual leaders or representatives of such groups. When bureaucratic concerns are uppermost in decision makers' minds, reformers may be particularly concerned to develop specific mechanisms to overcome bureaucratic resistance; the language of incentives, control, and compliance may tend to dominate. In addition, when they are actively involved in developing or using technical analysis or international agency support to promote change, reformers use these resources if possible to address the primary political concerns of decision makers.

Thus, the concerns of decision makers can become the variables that reformers address in crafting solutions that they hope will be bureaucratically and politically acceptable. Again, these concerns—macropolitical, micropolitical, and bureaucratic—help define the available policy space for introducing reform initiatives. They may signal that some reform options are off-limits and that others will face particularly strong opposition. At the same time, the concerns of policy elites provide reformers with clues as to how the space for introducing reform can be expanded by directly addressing these concerns and responding with proposals that are sensitive to them. Thus, specific proposals can attempt to anticipate or reflect the principal political and bureaucratic anxieties that decision makers have.

Maneuvering within Policy Characteristics

Good policy solutions to reform issues are also crafted to anticipate the response that new initiatives will generate. With foresight, the content of the policy can be altered or the anticipated response addressed through specific provisions to moderate negative reaction and to generate support. Our framework distinguishes between policy characteristics that tend to arouse conflict in public arenas and those in which reaction takes place largely within bureaucratic environments. Both types of conflict are problematic from the perspective of reformers because both are capable of stymieing reform initiatives. Thus, as with context and circumstance, anticipated reactions also tend to define the space available for the introduction of new initiatives. In Chapter 6, we indicated the ways in which such constraints operate.

Nevertheless, policy content is not a fixed condition; thus, reactions may be moderated by carefully considering the content of policy. For any particular policy goal, there are often numerous ways that it can be pursued. Agrarian reform in the Philippines is a useful example of a variety of ways in which achieving greater equity in the countryside could have been achieved while still addressing the potential public opposition from important societal groups. As we suggested in the case of Ghana, crafting the devaluation package more carefully to anticipate public reaction might have helped a democratic regime to survive. In the 1980s, many countries proved ingenious in developing locally more acceptable "IMF packages" by anticipating public and private responses to them. The consequences of not doing so were evident in "IMF riots" in Algeria in 1987 and in Jordan in 1989. Reformers thus can consider how policy characteristics can be altered to minimize adverse public or bureaucratic reactions. They can, for example, attempt to ameliorate or compensate for policy characteristics that have a direct negative impact on large numbers of people, and they can attempt to time the introduction of new measures so that their direct impact is not immediately felt. Policy characteristics that tend to generate bureaucratic resistance can also be altered by simplifying routines, by using incentives, or by adopting mechanisms that bring obstructive behavior to attention or that mobilize nonbureaucratic actors to demand efficient and effective service delivery.

At a more general level, reformers can attempt to craft the content and specific measures of policy initiatives in such a way that they move from the category of anticipated public response to anticipated bureaucratic response or vice versa, when this promises a more supportive context for the introduction of change. While this cannot be accomplished for all reforms, it is a strategy that suggests how the boundaries of policy space can be expanded by altering the content of specific policy measures. In this way, as we suggested in Chapter 6, implementation analysis becomes a necessary part of reform analysis and decision making.

MANEUVERING WITHIN AVAILABLE RESOURCES

Strategies for ensuring the successful introduction of reform measures—or abandoning them if they appear to be infeasible—are implicit in the questions that reformers need to ask about the implementation and sustainability of their proposals. As is evident in figure 8.1, when reactions or conflict can be anticipated in public or bureaucratic settings, reformers can ask a series of questions about the resources needed to pursue the reform and can assess whether or not the resources exist or can be mobilized. As we have seen, one set of actions they can take is to address and possibly alter the content of policy. The next set of actions has to do with assessing and possibly altering the environment within which reform measures are to be implemented and sustained. In this, policy reformers are again drawn to analyze the broader and more enduring characteristics of a political, social, economic, and administrative system. They will need to ask questions about the extent of legitimacy the government enjoys, its relationships with societal interests, and the degree to which political stability and elite consensus generate a supportive environment for controversial measures. In the case of reforms that generate reactions in a bureaucratic arena, they need to understand the characteristics of the public administration and its relationship to political leaders. This set of questions can provide a useful assessment of whether an appropriate environment exists for the introduction of specific reform measures or whether the prospects for change in that environment appear very poor.

A logical extension of this form of implementation analysis is a set of questions about whether missing resources can be acquired to create a more supportive context. In some cases—obtaining high-level political support, generating consensus, or introducing behavioral incentives—such resources may be mobilizable. In other cases—creating legitimacy, stability, or autonomy for government—reformers will be relatively powerless to alter existing conditions. This set of concerns, dealing largely with contextual factors, again provides fairly clear guidance about the limits of policy space and differentiates between factors that can be altered through analysis and astute leadership, and those that cannot.

Moving from Analysis to Principles of Action

The framework we have developed is principally analytic. It is an effort to map out a process and to identify critical factors or junctures that influence the outcome of reform initiatives. Thus, we have focused on the impact of context, circumstance, and policy characteristics as determinants of process and outcome. In summarizing this framework in figure 8.1, however, we have attempted to demonstrate that it can also help generate principles of action for reform leadership. In this sense it serves as a guide to what is actionable and what is possible. It is potentially a map of the boundaries of policy space and the actions that can fruitfully be undertaken to expand the societal and bureaucratic tolerance for change. It also suggests the relationships among factors affecting the outcome of policy reforms that can also be critical ingredients in strategic thinking about introducing and sustaining initiatives for change.

Ultimately, we believe this book is addressed both to those who wish to understand the process of reform more fully and to those who wish to affect this process. It is predicated on the assumptions that change in policy and organizational environments occurs with considerable frequency, that purposive action can alter the nature and direction of these changes, and that political action is a valuable and necessary part of bringing about policy and organizational changes. We recognize that the constraints on altering existing conditions in developing countries can be overwhelming and that in many cases conditions simply do not exist that provide significant scope for the actions of reformers. In such cases, the amount of room for maneuver and the capacity to alter existing conditions may be very limited, even nonexistent.

We have been primarily concerned with going beyond an analysis of constraints to identify contexts, moments, and measures that provide some room for maneuver, and we have tried to suggest that politics, although often a constraint, is also the means through which such opportunities are identified and utilized to bring about change. We are of course concerned that our framework and analysis do not discriminate among good reforms and bad, socially responsive leaders and elitists, liberal and illiberal ends, or measures to protect vulnerable groups or harm them. Policy reform and politics more generally are means, not ends, and it must remain a primary responsibility of individual societies to define and pursue appropriate ends for national development. Governments and government officials may resist this type of analysis because those who wield power have an interest in maintaining the myths and beliefs that sustain power. Opening political decision-making processes to scrutiny is thus not entirely welcome. Yet we are persuaded that understanding processes by which reforms are or are not chosen, implemented, and sustained allows for increased discussion of competing values and options, an end that we wholeheartedly support. We strongly believe that policy definitions should emerge in democratically responsive ways and that changes should be pursued in ways that hold public leaders and managers accountable for their decisions and actions and in ways that ensure the rights and welfare of those who are seldom inside government.

Notes

Chapter 1
Introduction: Explaining Choice and Change

1. The term *policy elites* is used throughout this book to refer to political and bureaucratic officials who have decision-making responsiblities in government and whose decisions become authoritative for society. It is a term used interchangeably with *decision makers, policy makers,* and *policy planners.* Chapter 3 presents a description of the individuals and groups who typically compose the policy elite for particular types of reforms.

2. For our purposes, then, a reform initiative is any instance in which such a change is advocated; we pass no judgment on the goodness or badness of any particular change being advocated.

3. We adopt a Weberian definition of the state. That is, we define the state to be an enduring set of executive and administrative organizations whose role is to control a given territory and to make authoritative decisions for society. This definition focuses on the means of the state, not its ends (Weber 1946:78, 82). An alternative definition, which we do not adopt, comes from the Marxist tradition and considers the state to be an alliance for social control reflecting class relationships in society (Engels 1968).

4. On the role of ideas in policy formation, see especially Reich 1988; Grindle 1986a; Heclo 1974; Adler 1987.

5. We define *macroeconomic issues* as those that have a wide impact on a national economy, regardless of sector. Exchange rates, interest rates, and inflation rates are examples of macroeconomic issues. Sectoral issues refer to those that primarily affect the economic conditions or performance of a particular sector of the economy, such as agriculture or industry. *Organizational issues* refer to those that affect the performance and responsiveness of public institutions such as ministries and state-owned enterprises. For a discussion, see Cohen, Grindle, and Walker 1985.

6. A recent effort to develop a theory of state and society relationships in developing countries is Migdal 1988. In particular, he seeks to explain the preponderance of weak states in the Third World and proposes a general theory for why public policy is generally ineffective in enabling the state to control the behavior of society.

Chapter 2
Linking Theory and Practice

1. Useful discussions of society-centered and state-centered theories of political economy are found in Skocpol 1985 and Nordlinger 1987.

2. The relationship of class domination, the state, and policy is discussed in Engels 1968.

3. For a discussion, see Carnoy 1984.

4. Pluralist approaches to explaining policy choice are found in many texts on American politics. A classic statement of "interest group politics" is Truman 1951. See also Dahl 1961, 1971, and Lane 1959. More recently, Tony Killick (1976) has used a pluralist approach in explaining development policy making as a "balancing act" among competing interests, "a process of conflict-resolution in which social tranquility and the maintenance of power is a basic concern" (p. 176).

5. In explaining agricultural policies in many developing countries, for example, the lack of rural interest mobilization has been stressed. "In the developing world, and especially where imperial rule has suddenly been withdrawn, state elites frequently find themselves facing weak and disorganized societies. Their own autonomous preferences can thus play a large role—at least initially—in determining the level of protection, or taxation, imposed upon agriculture. In post-independence Africa, state elites decided to impose heavy taxes on agriculture, not only because of the societal constraints they faced, but also because of their own autonomous preference, as 'African Socialists,' to launch costly state-managed and state-financed industrial development projects, and to offer their people a sizeable menu of generous public welfare benefits" (Paarlberg 1987:20–21).

6. Analysts who have used public choice theory to explain policy in developing countries indicate that policy elites are often very concerned to maintain the support of the military and civil servants—groups located within the state (see esp. Ames 1987). In this regard, public choice considers certain state sectors to be equivalent to organized societal interests.

7. Thus, for example, Paarlberg (1987:22–23) argues: "When relatively autonomous states decide for their own reasons to intervene in the workings of the economy, they inadvertently create the basis for a more organized societal response, eventually a constraining response. Public benefits which states give to society (such as cheap food) cannot easily be taken away. Societies promptly become dependent upon the benefits and then begin organizing to defend them. Benefits become 'entitlements.' Society's defense of these entitlements can eventually mature into a genuine 'political marketplace,' strong enough to threaten the survival of political elites."

8. According to Bennett and DiLorenzo (1984:217), "The problem of reforming the rent-seeking society is widely perceived to be the adoption of an appropriate set of rules to limit the powers of government. The power of the state and its burden on the private sector have been associated with public service expenditure and employment, both of which have increased dramatically over the past decades in both the United States and the rest of the industrialized world. Thus, reform has centered on efforts, particularly in the United States, to restrict by constitutional amendment the ability of government to borrow, tax, and spend. Revenue is regarded as the lifeblood of the public sector, so that, if public sector income is limited, the instrusiveness and burden of government can be controlled, and the negative-sum game of rent-seeking contained."

9. Public choice theory thus promotes a view of politics that is both negative and cynical, perhaps in reaction to earlier assumptions among neoclassical economists that the purpose of the state was to facilitate the workings of the market and to safeguard "the public interest" (Srinivasan 1985:45).

10. Olson (1982) argues that the search for rents constricts a country's economic growth rate and eventually brings it to a stop. Only a major crisis—a war, for example—will break the stranglehold of rent-seeking groups on economic development.

11. As summarized by one analyst, much public choice theory approaches politics as "a collection of rogues competing for the favors of a larger collection of dupes" (Barry 1985:300).

12. For example, a public official from Zimbabwe explained to us in detail about how the memory of the period of independence and civil war that surrounded the withdrawal of the Belgians from the Congo had deeply influenced the perspectives of Zimbabwe's leaders about how to handle their own independence process.

13. As pointed out by Skocpol (1985:15), for example, "Autonomous state actions will regularly take forms that attempt to reinforce the authority, political longevity, and social control of the state organizations whose incumbents generated the relevant policies or policy ideas."

Chapter 3
Generalizing about Developing Country
Policy Environments

1. One unique attempt at generalizing about the planning and budgeting environment in developing countries is contained in the prologue to Caiden and Wildavsky (1974:i-iv). In this, an imaginary head of state delivers a "frank speech on planning and budgeting," which the authors use as a device to portray the environment for the planning and budgeting activities they are setting out to analyze.

2. The World Bank includes a statistical appendix to its annual *World Development Report* entitled, "World Development Indicators." In this, the Bank classifies countries by GNP per capita as low-income, lower-middle-income, upper-middle-income, and industrial market economies (see, e.g., World Bank 1988: 222–23). It also classifies four countries as high-income oil exporters and most of the eastern bloc as nonreporting nonmembers. We will exclude these two groups from our generalizations. We focus our analysis on the three categories of developing countries, with some comparisons of these to the group the bank calls industrial market economies. Most of the data reported are for 1985 or 1986.

3. Hong Kong and Singapore, both city-states, have urban populations of 93 and 100 percent respectively.

4. Perkins notes, however, that it is hard to demonstrate these observations empirically. "Given the amount of attention that has been lavished on such issues as the desirability of structural adjustment to ensure greater reliance on market

forces, the need for privatization, and the like, it is surprising how little effort has gone into collecting empirical data with which one could assess the current situation in developing countries or measure the change" (Perkins 1988:12). An interesting paradox surrounds the data on public expenditures as an indicator of state intervention in the economy in developing countries. Government spending as a percentage of GNP is lower in developing countries than in industrialized nations. The World Bank explains this phenomenon as follows: "In most developing countries the share of central government in GNP remains below that of industrialized countries. Much of the difference, though, is due to the industrialized countries' higher level of transfers for the social security and welfare. Excluding these expenditures, central government spending as a percentage of GNP is higher in low- and middle-income countries than in the industrial countries" (World Bank 1988:47).

5. For women as a subcategory of these figures, 26 percent of the appropriate age group are enrolled in secondary education in low-income countries, 51 percent in middle-income countries, and 92 percent in industrial countries (World Bank 1988:280–81).

6. The 1960s saw an outpouring of books by well-known authors on the topic of planning. See, for example, Lewis 1966; Tinbergen 1967; Waterston 1969; Meier 1965; and Chamberlain 1965.

7. The aid donor nations, remembering the planning systems that had been established during World War II, supported the trend. In fact, a significant number of those who had been in agencies like the Office of Price Administration in the United States were early officials in the foreign aid program.

8. Such systems often became distorted so that privileged groups such as the military have access to subsidized goods as well as do low-income groups.

9. Food is a critical area for virtually every developing country government. Its importance is obvious. Food shortages have brought down many governments and brought international opprobrium upon them for their neglect of their population. The African famine of 1985–86 and the focus on Ethiopia is only the most recent example. Many countries pursue food self-sufficiency as a leading goal, but in ways that may be contrary to their real economic interest, by producing food crops locally that they could import on concessionary terms, while using resources to produce food that could produce export crops that have world market value two or three times as great as the food crop. However this choice is made, it ensures that there will not be a shortage of food supplies. As in the just-cited case of East Africa, their objectives cause countries to manage their food system.

10. A dramatic indicator of the urban bias of development policies is the distribution of expenditures for health care. In the case of Kenya, for example, expenditures for health care are heavily concentrated in the urban areas. Consequently, in Nairobi there are 508 hospital beds for every hundred thousand of population, while all the rest of the provinces average 133.3 beds per hundred thousand (Republic of Kenya 1986:193). Data from countries in Asia, Latin America, and Africa reiterate this pattern. In China, per capita expenditure for health was six dollars for the rural areas and nineteen dollars for urban residents. In Senegal, urban areas have a population-to-hospital-bed ratio of 426:1, while

in the rural areas it is 7,254:1. There is a similar skewed distribution of health care expenditures and drug supplies. In Peru, according to World Bank figures, 27 percent of the population live in Lima, but 47 percent of the health budget is spent there.

11. See Hyden 1983 for a description of the semiautonomous rural populace as the "economy of affection." Alternatively, see Migdal 1988.

Chapter 4
Setting Agendas: Circumstance,
Process, and Reform

1. The case of the decision to devalue in Ghana is based primarily on Killick, Roemer, and Stern 1972, Denoon 1986, and presentations by and discussions with Joseph Stern and Michael Roemer (Roemer and Stern 1986). Tony Killick, Michael Roemer, and Joseph Stern were advisers to the Ghanaian government who worked closely with decision makers, particularly after early October 1971. David Denoon's account of the decision is based on extensive interviewing of principal decision makers and their advisers, including detailed written comments by former prime minister Busia.

2. An excellent account of the actual motivations of the military in carrying out the coup is found in Bennett 1980. She argues that "the salient factor leading to the coup d'etat appears to be the refusal of the government, in the face of the deepening economic crisis, to accede to the financial demands of the military" (p. 347).

3. Hirschman (1963:261), for example, has suggested that "it may well be that some problems simply fail in ordinary times to get attacked effectively, not for lack of knowledge, or even for lack of motivation, but simply for lack of attention. Experience also shows that crisis may make it possible to take required actions against powerful groups which are normally well-entrenched and invulnerable; finally, crisis may stimulate action and hence learning on a problem on which insight has been low and which for that very reason has not been tackled as long as it was in a quiescent state."

4. The discussion of the agrarian reform in the Philippines is based primarily on Thomas 1986, Thomas and Grindle 1988b, and internal documents and the field notes of John Thomas. John Thomas served as an adviser to the Philippines Ministry of Agrarian Reform in 1986 and 1987 and worked closely with a technical group concerned with designing an agrarian reform policy.

5. "It is suggested here that a fundamental goal of 'normal politics' in any ongoing system is to maintain the nature of the political regime, i.e., to maintain the outer boundaries of public policy debate, to maintain the norms governing the processing of political demands, and to maintain the position of those who currently hold power (or who, by extension of current recruitment norms, would hold power)" (Coleman and Quiros-Varela 1981:39).

6. The Colombian case is based primarily on Mallon 1986. Richard Mallon was an adviser to the Colombian government who was assigned to work with the planning agency.

7. The Kenya decentralization case is based primarily on Hook 1986. Richard Hook was senior adviser on Rural Development in the Ministry of Economic Planning and Development, Government of Kenya, from 1976 to 1982.

8. The Mali case is based on Cash 1987 and Gray et al. 1990 and reflects their experience in the Mali Rural Health Project in the 1970s and 1980s.

Chapter 5
Making Decisions:
The Concerns of Policy Elites

1. Some have pointed to the role of technocrats in depoliticizing policy decisions that have important distributional content (see, e.g., O'Donnell 1973). Indexing wages in highly inflationary economies is a good example of how such potentially conflictual policy choices can be made to appear neutral.

2. Ames (1987:211), for example, focuses on regime incumbents and their interest in retaining power. "Given the frequency of military coups, the dismal reelection record of incumbents, and the volatility of open economies, executives can rarely take political survival for granted. To the maximum degree possible, every program must be subjected to the executive's drive for security."

3. Stephan Haggard (1985:505–6) notes that a majority of IMF standby agreement cancellations from 1980 and Extended Fund Facility Agreement cancellations from 1978–80 were related to political and administrative concerns.

4. This case is based on Haggard and Cole 1987; Haggard, Kim, and Moon 1987; Haggard 1987; and Cheng 1986. David Cole was Chief Economics Officer in USAID in Seoul between 1964 and 1966.

5. This case is based on Doryan-Garrón 1988. This thesis includes cognitive maps of the perspectives of presidents and top-level decision makers from six administrations in Costa Rica, as well as extensive interview material from organized interest groups. Eduardo Doryan-Garrón served as Vice-Minister for Science and Technology during the administration of Oscar Arias (1986–90).

6. This case is based on Thomas and Grindle 1988a. John Thomas was a senior adviser in the Ministry of Agriculture from 1976 to 1979.

Chapter 6
Implementing Reform:
Arenas, Stakes, and Resources

This chapter is a revised version of "After the Decision: Implementing Policy Reforms in Developing Countries," *World Development* 18, no. 8 (1990):1163–81.

1. For a thorough review of the literature, see White 1987.

2. This statement does not reflect the findings of a considerable body of research on implementation. Work in the United States, often focused on the problems of implementing a variety of social programs of the 1960s, paved the way for considerable effort to understand implementation in developing countries.

On the U.S. experience, see in particular Pressman and Wildavsky 1973; Bardach 1977; Nakamura and Smallwood 1980; and Warwick 1975. See also Grindle 1980; Honadle and Van Sant 1984; Montgomery 1979; Warwick 1982; and Ingle 1979.

3. See Cohen, Grindle, and Walker 1985.

4. See Nelson 1984; Haggard 1985; and Cleaves 1980.

5. This summary is taken from a case in Grindle and Thomas 1988. It is supplemented by Timmer 1987b.

6. This case is based on Killick, Roemer, and Stern 1972 and is supplemented by Denoon 1986.

7. This case is based on Veira 1988.

8. Another example of the same phenomenon is documented in David Halberstam's *The Best and the Brightest* (1972). In chapter 11 (pp. 200–212), he describes how the military forces in Vietnam, with the advantage of distance and information, kept interpreting President Kennedy's decisions to suit their own preferences, leading to policy outcomes very different than those anticipated by the decision makers.

9. The information on which this case is based comes from Bajpai 1988.

10. The India water supply case, just cited, and the case of agrarian reform in the Philippines illustrate how even the discussion of a reform measure can induce opposition which may substantially alter the reform proposal before a decision is actually made. In the Philippines, "Adoption of an agrarian reform was considered by some leaders of the government to be central to weakening the appeal of the insurgent National People's Army. Others saw rural equity resulting from an agrarian reform as critical to agricultural growth and rural development. The fact that top leadership saw it as potentially disruptive of its support coalition meant that it was consistently given low priority in the government's policy agenda" (Grindle and Thomas 1988:21).

11. This pattern is much less apparent in instances of organizational change, as our cases of Kenya and Colombia illustrate. In the case of organizational reform, change is usually initiated by a senior manager of the organization who has a stake in the results. The decision makers are thus usually the managers of implementation efforts.

12. We use the terms *reaction* and *response* to connote different phenomena. We use reaction to describe public replies to policy change, and response to describe bureaucratic ones.

13. It should be noted that policies that are relatively self-implementing may have a high technical content during the decision-making process.

14. A dramatic case of negative reaction to reform policy took place in Algeria in October 1988. It illustrates how decision makers can miscalculate reactions to reform decisions. The *New York Times* reported riots in the major cities of Algeria: "They are protesting . . . a Government austerity program that has eliminated subsidies and prompted an increase in food prices of about 40% since January" (October 8, 1988). Two days later The *Times* reported, "Six days of rioting have left 200 Algerians dead by unofficial estimates and the Government . . . divided and under siege." The report continued, stating that the reforms were also "intended to wean inefficient state-owned industries from government

subsidies . . . but the effect has been frozen wages and shortages of consumer goods."

15. See the interesting case of the Gambia reported in Radelet 1988. See also Haggard 1985.

16. The impact of location on policy design and implementation is developed in Tendler 1982.

17. For a review of the relevant literature, see White 1987.

Chapter 7
Reforming Policies in the 1980s:
Changing Circumstances and Shifting Parameters

Data collection, initial analysis, and drafting of this chapter were done by Stephen J. Reifenberg.

1. The World Bank's report *Development Prospects for Sub-Saharan Africa* (1982) was particularly important. Commonly known as the Berg Report for its principal author, Elliot Berg, it argued forcefully that development aid and projects would be of little use until the individual countries "got their policies right." See also Timmer 1986.

2. Nelson 1990: 3; World Bank, *World Debt Tables: 1988–1989*, vol. 1, *Analysis and Summary Tables* (Washington, D.C., 1989).

3. In Turkey's financial system reforms, salience of technical analysis was described as "unimportant." However, one of the authors of the case explained that financial reform did in fact require highly technical skills, but the decision makers "did not realize it."

Chapter 8
Conclusion: Finding Room to Maneuver

1. The term *embedded orientations* is used in Bennett and Sharpe (1985) to refer to ongoing ideological and policy orientations of states.

2. *Policy space* is defined in Chapter 1 as a space determined by the ability of a regime and its political leadership to introduce and pursue a reform measure without precipitating a regime or leadership change or major upheaval and violence in the society, or without being forced to abandon the initiative.

3. It is almost as frequently pointed out, however, that reformers often fail to inculcate the sense of crisis. This was a lesson well learned by President Jimmy Carter when he called for the "moral equivalent of war" in conserving energy in 1978.

Bibliography

Abernethy, David
1988   "Bureaucratic Growth and Economic Stagnation in Sub-Saharan Africa."
        In *Africa's Development Challenges and the World Bank: Hard Ques-
        tions, Costly Choices,* edited by Stephen K. Commins. Boulder, Colo.:
        Lynn Rienner Publishers.

Adler, Emanuel
1987   *The Power of Ideology: The Quest for Technological Autonomy in Ar-
        gentina and Brazil.* Berkeley: University of California Press.

Allison, Graham
1971   *Essence of Decision: Explaining the Cuban Missile Crisis.* Boston: Little,
        Brown and Co.

Alt, James E., and K. Alec Chrystal
1983   *Political Economics.* Berkeley: University of California Press.

Ames, Barry
1987   *Political Survival: Politicians and Public Policy in Latin America.* Berke-
        ley: University of California Press.

Amin, Samir
1977   *Imperialism and Unequal Development.* New York: Monthly Review
        Press.

Anderson, Kym, Yujiro Hayami, et al.
1986   *The Political Economy of Agricultural Protection: East Asia in Inter-
        national Perspective.* Sydney: Allen and Unwin.

Ascher, William
1984   *Scheming for the Poor: The Politics of Redistribution in Latin America.*
        Cambridge: Harvard University Press.

Bacha, Edmar L., and Richard E. Feinberg
1986   "The World Bank and Structural Adjustment in Latin America." *World
        Development* 14, no. 3:333–46.

Bajpai, Shyam
1986   *Toward Renewed Economic Growth in Latin America.* Washington,
        D.C.: Institute for International Economics.
1988   "Sectoral Policy Reform: Water Supply in Indian Cities." John F. Kennedy
        School of Government, Harvard University (March). Paper.

Bardach, Eugene
1977   *The Implementation Game.* Cambridge: MIT Press.

Barichello, Richard, and Frank Flatters
1988 "Trade Policy Reform in Indonesia." Paper prepared for HIID Conference on Economic Reform in Developing Countries, Marrakech, Morocco (October).

Barry, Brian
1985 "Does Democracy Cause Inflation? Political Ideas of Some Economists." In *The Politics of Inflation and Economic Stagnation: Theoretical Approaches and International Case Studies,* edited by Leon N. Lindberg and Charles S. Maier. Washington, D.C.: Brookings Institution.

Bates, Robert H.
1981 *Markets and States in Tropical Africa: The Political Basis of Agricultural Policies.* Berkeley: University of California Press.

Bennett, Douglas C., and Kenneth E. Sharpe
1985 *Transnational Corporations versus the State: The Political Economy of the Mexican Auto Industry.* Princeton, N.J.: Princeton University Press.

Bennett, James T., and Thomas J. DiLorenzo
1984 "Political Entrepreneurship and Reform of the Rent-Seeking Society." In *Neoclassical Political Economy,* edited by David C. Colander, pp. 217–27. Cambridge: Ballinger Publishing Co.

Bennett, Valerie Plave
1980 "The Motivation for Military Intervention: The Case of Ghana." In *The Political Influence of the Military: A Comparative Reader,* edited by Amos Perlmutter and Valerie Plave Bennett, pp. 344–54. New Haven: Yale University Press.

Bhagwati, Jagdish N.
1978 *Foreign Trade Regimes and Economic Development: Anatomy and Consequences of Exchange Control Regimes.* Foreign Trade Regimes and Economic Development Series, vol. 11. Cambridge: Ballinger Publishing Co.

Bienen, Henry
1978 *Armies and Parties in Africa.* New York: Africana Publishing Co.

Bratton, Michael
1980 *The Local Politics of Rural Development: Peasant and Party-State in Zambia.* Hanover, N.H.: University Press of New England.

Braybrooke, David, and Charles E. Lindblom
1963 *A Strategy of Decision: Policy Evaluation as a Social Process.* New York: Free Press.

Brock, William A., and Stephen M. Magee
1984 "The Invisible Foot and the Waste of Nations: Redistribution and Economic Growth." In *Neoclassical Political Economy,* edited by David C. Colander, pp. 177–85. Cambridge: Ballinger Publishing Co.

Buchanan, James M.
1980 "Rent Seeking and Profit Seeking." In *Toward a Theory of the Rent-seeking Society,* edited by James M. Buchanan, Robert D. Tollison, and Gordon Tullock. College Station: Texas A & M University Press.

Bunce, Valerie
1981 *Do New Leaders Make a Difference? Executive Succession and Public Policy under Capitalism and Socialism.* Princeton, N.J.: Princeton University Press.

Caiden, Naomi, and Aaron Wildavsky
1974 *Planning and Budgeting in Poor Countries.* New York: John Wiley and Sons.

Cardoso, Fernando H., and Enzo Faletto
1979 *Dependency and Development in Latin America.* Translated by Marjory Mattingly Urquidi. Berkeley: University of California Press.

Carnoy, Martin
1984 *The State and Political Theory.* Princeton, N.J.: Princeton University Press.

Cash, Richard
1987 "Testing Alternative Health Policy Options in Mali." Harvard Institute for International Development, Workshop on Promoting Policy Reform in Developing Countries (March 17).

Cepeda Ulloa, Fernando, and Christopher Mitchell
1980 "The Trend Towards Technocracy: The World Bank and the International Labor Organization in Colombian Politics." In *Politics of Compromise: Coalition Government in Colombia,* edited by R. Albert Berry, Ronald G. Hellman, and Mauricio Solaún, pp. 237–55. New Brunswick, N.J.: Transaction Books.

Chamberlain, Neil
1965 *Private and Public Planning.* New York: McGraw-Hill.

Cheng, Tun-jen
1986 "Sequencing and Implementing Development Strategies: Korea and Taiwan." Paper.

Cleaves, Peter S.
1980 "Implementation Amidst Scarcity and Apathy: Political Power and Policy Design." In *Politics and Policy Implementation in the Third World,* edited by Merilee S. Grindle, pp. 281–303. Princeton, N.J.: Princeton University Press.

Cohen, John M., Merilee S. Grindle, and S. Tjip Walker
1985 "Foreign Aid and Conditions Precedent: Political and Bureaucratic Dimensions." *World Development* 13, no. 12:1211–30.

Colander, David C.
1984 "Introduction." In *Neoclassical Political Economy,* edited by David C. Colander, pp. 1–13. Cambridge: Ballinger Publishing Co.

Cole, David C., and Betty Slade Yaser
1988 "Reform of Financial Systems." Paper prepared for HIID Conference on Economic Reform in Developing Countries, Marrakech, Morocco (October).

Coleman, Kenneth M., and Luís Quirós-Varela
1981 "Determinants of Latin American Foreign Policies: Bureaucratic Organization and Development Strategies." In *Latin American Foreign Policies: Global and Regional Dimensions,* edited by Elizabeth G. Ferris and Jennie K. Lincoln, pp. 39–59. Boulder, Colo.: Westview Press.

Cornia, Giovanni Andrea, Richard Jolly, and Frances Stewart
1987 *Adjustment with a Human Face.* New York: Oxford University Press.

Crouch, Harold
1986 "Patrimonialism and Military Rule in Indonesia." In *The State and Development in the Third World,* edited by Atul Kohli, pp. 242–58. Princeton, N.J.: Princeton University Press.

Cummings, William
1988 "Decentralization of Education in Sri Lanka." Paper prepared for HIID Conference on Economic Reform in Developing Countries, Marrakech, Morocco (October).

Dahl, Robert A.
1961 *Who Governs? Democracy and Power in an American City.* New Haven: Yale University Press.
1971 *Polyarchy, Participation, and Opposition.* New Haven: Yale University Press.

Decalo, Samuel
1986 *Coups and Military Rule in Africa: Studies in Military Style.* New Haven: Yale University Press.

Denoon, David
1986 *Devaluation under Pressure: India, Indonesia, and Ghana.* Cambridge: MIT Press.

Doryan-Garrón, Eduardo
1988 "Explaining Development Strategy Choice by State Elites: The Costa Rican Case." Ph.D. diss., Political Economy and Government, Harvard University.

Dos Santos, Theotonio
1970 "The Structure of Dependence." *American Economic Review* 60, no. 2:231–36.

Engels, Friedrich
1968 "The Origin of the Family, Private Property, and the State." In *Selected Works of Karl Marx and Friedrich Engels.* New York: International Publishers.

Foltz, Anne-Marie, and William J. Foltz
1988   "The Politics of Health Reform in Chad." Paper prepared for HIID Conference on Economic Reform in Developing Countries, Marrakech, Morocco (October).

Frankel, Francine R.
1978   *India's Political Economy, 1947–1977: The Gradual Revolution.* Princeton, N.J.: Princeton University Press.

Frohock, Fred M.
1979   *Public Policy: Scope and Logic.* Englewood Cliffs, N.J.: Prentice-Hall.

Goldsmith, Arthur A.
1988   "Policy Dialogue, Conditionality, and Agricultural Development: Implications of India's Green Revolution." *Journal of Developing Areas* 22 (January): 179–98.

Gray, Clive, Jacques Baudouy, Kelsey Martin, Molly Bang, and Richard Cash
1990   *Primary Health Care in Africa: A Study of the Mali Rural Health Project.* Boulder, Colo.: Westview Press.

Grindle, Merilee S.
1977   *Bureaucrats, Politicians, and Peasants in Mexico: A Case Study in Public Policy.* Berkeley: University of California Press.
1980   *Politics and Policy Implementation in the Third World.* Princeton, N.J.: Princeton University Press.
1986   *State and Countryside: Development Policy and Agrarian Politics in Latin America.* Baltimore: Johns Hopkins University Press.
1987   "Civil-Military Relations and Budgetary Politics in Latin America." *Armed Forces and Society* 13, no. 2:255–75.

Grindle, Merilee S., and John W. Thomas
1988   "Policy Makers, Policy Choices, and Policy Outcomes: The Political Economy of Reform in Developing Countries." Harvard Institute for International Development. Paper. Forthcoming in a special issue of *Policy Sciences.*

Haggard, Stephan
1985   "The Politics of Adjustment: Lessons from the IMF's Extended Fund Facility." *International Organization* 39, no. 3:505–34.
1987   "Korea: From Import Substitution to Export-Led Growth." Manuscript.

Haggard, Stephan, and David Cole
1987   "Policy Reform in Korea, 1960–1966." Harvard Institute for International Development, Workshop on Promoting Policy Reform in Developing Countries (March 3).

Haggard, Stephan, Byung Kook Kim, and Chung-In Moon
1987   "The Transition to Export-Led Growth in Korea: 1954–1966." Paper prepared for Conference on the Role of the State in Economic Development, Republic of Korea. University of California, Los Angeles (August 14–16).

Halberstam, David
1972 *The Best and the Brightest.* New York: Random House.

Halperin, Morton
1974 *Bureaucratic Politics and Foreign Policy.* Washington, D.C.: Brookings Institution.

Hamilton, Alexander, James Madison, and John Jay
1961 *The Federalist Papers.* New York: New American Library.

Hampson, Fen
1986 *Forming Economic Policy: The Case of Energy in Canada and Mexico.* New York: St. Martin's Press.

Haslet, Walter C.
1976 "Characteristics and Problems of Parastatal Organizations in Zambia." Paper prepared for Management Personnel in Parastatal Organizations, Mombasa, Kenya.

Heclo, Hugh
1974 *Modern Social Politics in Britain and Sweden: From Relief to Income Maintenance.* New Haven: Yale University Press.

Hirschman, Albert O.
1963 *Journeys toward Progress: Studies of Economic Policy-Making in Latin America.* New York: Twentieth Century Fund.
1981 "Policymaking and Policy Analysis in Latin America—A Return Journey." In Albert O. Hirschman, *Essays in Trespassing: Economics to Politics and Beyond,* pp. 142–66. Cambridge: Cambridge University Press.

Honadle, George, and Jerry VanSant
1984 *Organizing and Managing Integrated Rural Development: Lessons from Field Experience.* Washington, D.C.: Development Alternatives.

Hook, Richard
1986 "The Policy Process in LDCs: Some Thoughts on Theory and Policy with Special Reference to Kenya." Harvard Institute for International Development, Workshop on Promoting Reform in Developing Countries (October 29).

Hyden, Goran
1983 *No Shortcuts to Progress: African Development Management in Perspective.* Berkeley: University of California Press.

Ingle, Marcus D.
1979 *Implementing Development Programs: A State of the Art Review, Final Report and Executive Summary.* Syracuse, N.Y.: Syracuse University Press.

Jackson, Robert H., and Carl G. Rosberg
1986 "Why Africa's Weak States Persist: The Empirical and the Juridical in

Statehood." In *The State and Development in the Third World,* edited by Atul Kohli, pp. 259–82. Princeton, N.J.: Princeton University Press.

Jervis, Robert
1968 "Hypothesis on Misperception." *World Politics* 20, no. 3:454–79.

Kasfir, Nelson
1986 "Explaining Ethnic Political Participation." In *The State and Development in the Third World,* edited by Atul Kohli, pp. 88–111. Princeton, N.J.: Princeton University Press.

Killick, Tony
1976 "The Possibilities of Development Planning." *Oxford Economic Papers* 28, no. 2:161–84.

Killick, Tony, Michael Roemer, and Joseph Stern
1972 "Devaluation and Coup d'Etat in Ghana." Harvard Institute for International Development. Paper.

Kinder, Donald R., and Janet A. Weiss
1978 "In Lieu of Rationality: Psychological Perspectives on Foreign Policy Decision Making." *Journal of Conflict Resolution* 22, no. 4:707–35.

Kouri, Yamil, John D. Balling, Steve M. Schall, and Donald S. Shepard
1988 "The Privatization of AIDS Care in San Juan, Puerto Rico." Paper prepared for HIID Conference on Economic Reform in Developing Countries, Marrakech, Morocco (October).

Krasner, Stephen
1978 *Defending the National Interest: Raw Materials Investments and U.S. Foreign Policy.* Princeton, N.J.: Princeton University Press.

Krueger, Anne O.
1974 "The Political Economy of the Rent-Seeking Society." *American Economic Review* 64, no. 3:291–303.

Lamb, Geoffrey
1987 *Managing Economic Policy Change.* World Bank Discussion Paper no. 14. Washington, D.C.: World Bank.

Lane, Robert E.
1959 *Political Life: Why People Get Involved in Politics.* Glencoe, Ill.: Free Press.

Lele, Uma J.
1975 *The Design of Rural Development: Lessons from Africa.* Baltimore: Johns Hopkins University Press.

Levine, Daniel H.
1981 *Religion and Politics in Latin America: The Catholic Church in Venezuela and Colombia.* Princeton, N.J.: Princeton University Press.

Lewis, W. Arthur
1966   *Development Planning: The Essentials of Economic Policy.* New York: Harper and Row.

Lindenberg, Marc
1988   "Managing Winners and Losers in Stabilization and Structural Adjustment: Politics and Policy Implementation." Paper prepared for HIID Conference on Economic Policy Reform in Developing Countries, Marrakech, Morocco (October).

Lindenberg, Marc, and Benjamin Crosby
1981   *Managing Development: The Political Dimension.* West Hartford, Conn.: Kumarian Press.

Lowenthal, Abraham F., and J. Samuel Fitch, eds.
1986   *Armies and Politics in Latin America.* New York: Holmes and Meier.

Lowi, Theodore J.
1969   *The End of Liberalism: Ideology, Policy, and the Crisis of Public Authority.* New York: W. W. Norton and Co.

McConnell, Grant
1966   *Private Power and American Democracy.* New York: Alfred A. Knopf.

MacDougall, John James
1976   "The Technocratic Model of Modernization: The Case of Indonesia's New Order." *Asian Survey* 16:1166–83.

McPherson, Malcolm, and Steven Radelet
1988   "Economic Reform in the Gambia: Policies, Politics, Foreign Aid, and Luck." Paper prepared for HIID Conference on Economic Reform in Developing Countries, Marrakech, Morocco (October).

Mallon, Richard
1986   "Planning Reform in Argentina and Colombia." Harvard Institute for International Development, Workshop on Promoting Policy Reform in Developing Countries (November 13).

Mallon, Richard, and Joseph Stern
1988   "The Political Economy of Trade and Industrial Policy Reform in Bangladesh." Paper prepared for HIID Conference on Economic Reform in Developing Countries, Marrakech, Morocco (October).

March, James G.
1978   "Bounded Rationality, Ambiguity, and the Engineering of Choice." *Bell Journal of Economics* 9, no. 2:587–608.

March, James G., and Herbert A. Simon
1958   *Organizations.* New York: John Wiley and Sons.

Mares, David R.
1985   "Explaining Choice of Development Strategies: Suggestions from Mexico, 1970–1982." *International Organization* 39, no. 4:667–97.

Mason, Edward S.
1958 *Economic Planning in Underdeveloped Areas: Government and Business.* New York: Fordham University Press.

Meier, Richard L.
1965 *Development Planning.* New York: McGraw-Hill.

Migdal, Joel
1987 "Strong States, Weak States: Power and Accommodation." In *Understanding Political Development,* edited by Myron Weiner and Samuel P. Huntington, pp. 391–434. Boston: Little, Brown and Co.
1988 *Strong Societies and Weak States: State-Society Relations and State Capabilities in the Third World.* Princeton, N.J.: Princeton University Press.

Milne, R. S.
1982 "Technocrats and Politics in the ASEAN Countries." *Pacific Affairs* 55:403–29.

Montgomery, John D.
1979 "Decisions, Nondecisions, and Other Phenomena: Implementation Analysis for Development Administrators." In *International Development Administration,* edited by George Honadle and Rudi Klauss, pp. 55–72. New York: Praeger Publishers.

Nakamura, Robert T., and Frank Smallwood
1980 *The Politics of Policy Implementation.* New York: St. Martin's Press.

Nelson, Joan M.
1979 *Access to Power: Politics and the Urban Poor in Developing Nations.* Princeton, N.J.: Princeton University Press.
1984 "The Political Economy of Stabilization: Commitment, Capacity, and Public Response." *World Development* 12, no. 10:983–1006.
1990 *Economic Crisis and Policy Choice.* Edited by Joan M. Nelson. Princeton, N.J.: Princeton University Press.

Nordlinger, Eric A.
1981 *On the Autonomy of the Democratic State.* Cambridge: Harvard University Press.
1987 "Taking the State Seriously." In *Understanding Political Development,* edited by Myron Weiner and Samuel P. Huntington, pp. 353–90. Boston: Little, Brown and Co.

Odell, John
1982 *U.S. International Monetary Policy: Markets, Power, and Ideas as Sources of Change.* Princeton, N.J.: Princeton University Press.

O'Donnell, Guillermo
1973 *Modernization and Bureaucratic-Authoritarianism.* Berkeley: University of California, Institute of International Studies.

Olson, Mancur, Jr.
1965 *The Logic of Collective Action: Public Goods and the Theory of Groups.* Cambridge: Harvard University Press.

1982   *The Rise and Decline of Nations: Economic Growth, Stagflation, and Social Rigidities.* New Haven: Yale University Press.

Orren, Gary R.
1988   "Beyond Self-Interest." In *The Power of Public Ideas,* edited by Robert Reich, pp. 13–29. Cambridge: Ballinger Publishing Co.

Paarlberg, Robert L.
1987   "Political Markets for Agricultural Protection: Understanding and Improving Their Function." Paper prepared for annual meeting of the International Agricultural Trade Research Consortium, Airlie Foundation, Warrenton, Va. (December 13–16).

Payer, Cheryl
1974   *The Debt Trap: The IMF and the Third World.* Harmondsworth, England: Penguin Books.

Perkins, Dwight
1988   "Economic Systems Reform in Developing Countries." Paper prepared for HIID Conference on Economic Policy Reform in Developing Countries, Marrakech, Morocco (October).

Perkins, Dwight, and Michael Roemer
1991   *The Reform of Economic Systems in Developing Countries.* Cambridge: Harvard University Press.

Poulantzas, Nicos
1973   *Political Power and Social Classes.* London: New Left Books; Sheed and Ward.

Pressman, Jeffrey, and Aaron Wildavsky
1973   *Implementation.* Berkeley: University of California Press.

Reich, Robert B., ed.
1988   *The Power of Public Ideas.* Cambridge: Ballinger Publishing Co.

Republic of Kenya
1979   *Economic Survey, 1979.* Nairobi: Government Printer.
1986   *Statistical Abstract, 1986.* Nairobi: Government Printer.

Robinson, James A., and R. Roger Majak
1967   "The Theory of Decision-Making." In *Contemporary Political Analysis,* edited by James C. Charlesworth, pp. 175–88. New York: Free Press.

Roemer, Michael, and Joseph Stern
1986   "Reform under Crisis: Devaluation in Ghana in 1971." Harvard Institute for International Development, Workshop on Promoting Policy Reform in Developing Countries (December 17).

Saasa, Oliver
1985   "Public Policy-Making in Developing Countries: The Utility of Contemporary Decision-Making Models." *Public Administration and Development 5,* no. 4:309–21.

Saulniers, Alfred H.
1988   *Public Enterprises in Peru: Public Sector Growth and Reform.* Boulder, Colo.: Westview Press.

Skocpol, Theda
1985   "Bringing the State Back In: Strategies of Analysis in Current Research." In *Bringing the State Back In,* edited by Peter B. Evans, Dietrich Rueschemeyer, and Theda Skocpol, pp. 3–37. Cambridge: Cambridge University Press.

Smith, Tony
1986   "The Underdevelopment of Development Literature: The Case of Dependency Theory." In *The State and Development in the Third World,* edited by Atul Kohli, pp. 25–26. Princeton, N.J.: Princeton University Press.

Smoke, Paul
1988   "Reforming Local Government in Developing Countries." Paper prepared for HIID Conference on Economic Policy Reform in Developing Countries, Marrakech, Morocco (October).

Srinivasan, T. N.
1985   "Neoclassical Political Economy, the State and Economic Development." *Asian Development Review* 3, no. 2:38–58.

Stallings, Barbara
1978   *Class Conflict and Economic Development in Chile, 1958–1973.* Stanford, Calif.: Stanford University Press.

Stepan, Alfred
1971   *The Military in Politics: Changing Patterns in Brazil.* New Haven: Yale University Press.
1978   *The State and Society: Peru in Comparative Perspective.* Princeton, N.J.: Princeton University Press.

Tendler, Judith
1982   *Rural Projects through Urban Eyes.* World Bank Staff Working Paper no. 532. Washington, D.C.: World Bank.

Thomas, John W.
1982   "National Decision Making and Management of Food Aid and Food Policy: Some Issues from East African Experience." In *The Developmental Effectiveness of Food Aid in Africa,* edited by Cheryl Christensen et al., pp. 113–36. New York: Agricultural Development Council.
1986   "Agrarian Reform in the Philippines." Harvard Institute for International Development, Workshop on Promoting Policy Reform in Developing Countries (October 8).

Thomas, John W., and Merilee S. Grindle
1988a   "Reorganization in the Ministry of Agriculture, Kenya." Harvard Institute for International Development. Teaching case.

1988b "Agrarian Reform in the Philippines." Harvard Institute for International Development. Teaching case.

Timmer, C. Peter
1986 *Getting Prices Right: The Scope and Limits of Agricultural Price Policy.* Ithaca, N.Y.: Cornell University Press.
1987a "Food Policy in Indonesia: Policy Change and Institutional Development." Harvard Institute for International Development, Workshop on Promoting Policy Reform in Developing Countries (April 7).
1987b "Food Price Policy in Indonesia." Development Discussion Paper no. 250. Harvard Institute for International Development (November).

Timmer, C. Peter, Walter P. Falcon, and Scott R. Pearson
1983 *Food Policy Analysis.* Baltimore: Published for the World Bank by Johns Hopkins University Press.

Tinbergen, Jan
1967 *Development Planning.* New York: McGraw-Hill.

Trebat, Thomas J.
1981 "Public Enterprise in Brazil and Mexico: A Comparison of Origins and Performance." In *Authoritarian Capitalism,* edited by Thomas C. Bruneau and Philippe Faucher, pp. 41–58. Boulder, Colo.: Westview Press.

Trimberger, Ellen
1978 *Revolution from Above: Military Bureaucrats and Development in Japan, Turkey, Egypt, and Peru.* New Brunswick, N.J.: Transaction Books.

Truman, David
1951 *The Governmental Process: Political Interests and Public Opinion.* New York: Alfred A. Knopf.

Tucker, Robert C.
1969 *The Marxian Revolutionary Idea.* New York: W. W. Norton and Co.

Veira, Valerie
1988 "The Policy Decision for the Development of the Jamaica Apparel and Sewn Products Sub-Sector." John F. Kennedy School of Government, Harvard University (March). Paper.

Warwick, Donald P.
1975 *A Theory of Public Bureaucracy: Politics, Personality, and Organization in the State Department.* Cambridge: Harvard University Press.
1982 *Bitter Pills: Population Policies and Their Implementation in Eight Developing Countries.* New York: Cambridge University Press.

Waterston, Albert
1969 *Development Planning: Lessons of Experience.* Baltimore: Johns Hopkins Press.

Weber, Max
1946 "Politics as a Vocation." In *From Max Weber: Essays in Sociology,* edited by H. H. Gerth and C. Wright Mills. New York: Oxford University Press.

Wellisz, Stanislaw, and Ronald Findlay
1984   "Protection and Rent-Seeking in Developing Countries." In *Neoclassical Political Economy,* edited by David C. Colander, pp. 141–53. Cambridge: Ballinger Publishing Co.

White, Louise G.
1987   *Creating Opportunities for Change: Approaches to Managing Development Programs.* Boulder, Colo.: Lynn Rienner Publishers.

World Bank
1983   *World Development Report.* Washington, D.C.: World Bank.
1984   *Toward Sustainable Development in Sub-Saharan Africa.* Washington, D.C.: World Bank.
1987   *Financing Health Services in Developing Countries: An Agenda for Reform* (by John S. Akin). Washington, D.C.: World Bank.
1988   *World Development Report.* New York: Published by Oxford University Press for the World Bank.
1990   *World Development Report.* New York: Published by Oxford University Press for the World Bank.

Young, Crawford
1976   *The Politics of Cultural Pluralism.* Madison: University of Wisconsin Press.
1986   "Africa's Colonial Legacy." In *Strategies for African Development,* edited by Robert J. Berg and Jennifer Seymour Whitaker, pp. 25–51. Berkeley: University of California Press.

Index

217